Social Welfare in the 21st Century

Issues, Critique & Relevance

Edited by

Jagdish

AKANSHA PUBLISHING HOUSE
NEW DELHI - 110 059 (INDIA)

AKANSHA PUBLISHING HOUSE
R-37B, Vani Vihar, Uttam Nagar
New Delhi - 110 059
E-mail: ektabooks@yahoo.com

Show Room
4649/21, Ansari Road
Daryaganj, New Delhi - 110 002

Social Welfare in the 21st Century

First Published, 2004
ISBN 81-87606-65-7
Reprint 2018

PRINTED IN INDIA

Published by M.P. Misra for Akansha Publishing House, New Delhi - 110 059 and Printed at Tarun Offset Press, Delhi.

Contents

Preface

> The rights of citizens to the benefits of the welfare state must be accompanied by reciprocal duties. The need for complementary rights and obligations is particularly great in the fields of work, law and order, education, and the social services.
>
> —William Robson

'Social welfare' is a way of thinking—society's collective image of its responsibility to its own members. Like any other aspect of societal decision making, social welfare decisions are made for the society as a whole by means of its political and economic structures. Philanthropic in essence, Social welfare is concerned with far more than needy. It is integrated into the basic structure of society in way that influence the lives of all groups—the poor and rich, minorities and those in power. Social welfare's most obvious manifest function in society is to help. People may need help in many areas of their lives. People may need rehabilitative, supportive, crisis needs and curative and preventive services.

Thus, social welfare enshrines protective and helping measures for poor and needy. Though Communist states or communism can be stated as real welfare states. The socialistic pattern was adopted in many countries, mostly the newly free third world countries. India adopted socialistic outlook in its governance. The poor and needy were given protection. Subsidy in agriculture, fuel, education, etc., was given to help the people.

Now, in the era of globalisation and WTO, the concept of 'Social Welfare is being receded to oblivion. WTO, under the influence of America and other rich countries putting ban conditions on welfare measures. Nations are being compelled to privatize public enterprises, cut subsidies etc. Under such circumstances, it is very essential to reassess the relevance of Social welfare in the 21st century.

Some pertinent issues rejuvenating the concept are given elaborate treatment. Entire information is gathered under eight chapters e.g. social welfare and welfare state, dilemma of the future of welfare state; nature and scope, free market and social welfare, social welfare models, and social division of welfare etc. The material is drawn from various secondary sources—books, journals, magazines, abstracts etc. We owe a deep sense of gratitude to all social scientists, philanthropists, their publishers, copyright holders, and editors for reproducing their works. We do not claim for originality. All credit goes to original writers, men of letters. Lastly, we thank Mr. M.P. Misra, Director, Akansha Publishing House, New Delhi for publishing this work so superbly.

—Editor

1

Social Welfare and the Welfare State: A Philosophical Analysis

A subjective term "social welfare, in a broad sense encompasses the well being and interests of large number of people, including their physical, mental, emotional, spiritual and economic need."

To quote D.R. Sachdeva,

> "Social welfare signifies the attempts made by governments and voluntary organizations to help families and individuals by maintaining income at an acceptable level, by providing medical care and public health services, by furthering adequate housing and community development, by providing services to facilitate social adjustment and by furnishing facilities for recreation. In addition, social welfare includes legislation and facilities signed to protect those who might be subject to exploitation and to core for those groups considered to be the responsibility of the community."

Basically social welfare depends on the objectives as to what type of social welfare we want to adopt; e.g. Wayne Vasey indicates that the aims of social welfare are: (*i*) to strengthen family as a basic unit in the society, and (*ii*) to strengthen individual's capacity to cope with the misery and calamity in life situation.

Apart from these there can be many more objectives according to a particular setup as it is obvious that shape and features of social welfare are different according to the societies from where they emerge. B.R. Compton says, 'Usually society and market economy should look after individual needs but when they do not function nicely social welfare services fulfil the gap. They are attending primarily to the emergency functions and "expected to withdraw when the regular social structure is again working properly."

Institutional approach is the second view of social welfare. This system takes social welfare as an accepted legitimate function of the modern industrial society. It aims of the fullest possible development of the capacities and well-being of the individual as a way of serving both the individual and the social group. According to this approach social welfare is a regular systematic or institutionalized activity for the society, it is neither temporary nor curative. It does not indicate any weakness or breakdown of the system, rather it is taken as a permanent arrangement in the society. It should work as a general development activity like providing nutrition; it should not be like providing medicine for quick relief.

We cannot say definitely that any state or society has adopted only one of these models, rather it is quite true that both of these models remain in operation in most of the developed or industrialized societies. However the welfare systems of all significant welfare states are quite different from each other. There is always a territorial or local bias. In this connection it is important to note that certain social factors influence welfare programmes. A list of these factors may be prepared which are influencing social welfare of a particular society. The following considerations may taken:

1. Political ideology and system.

2. Type of needs and level of deprivation.
3. Resources and the economy.
4. Size of the population.
5. Involvement of GOs and NGOs.
6. Nature of human resources available in the field of social welfare.
7. History of the social welfare services in the post.
8. Religious and cultural profile of the society.
9. Level of awareness among mosses.

All these factors put together create a particular type of welfare system which is adopted by the society. Let us examine the role of all these factors separately.

1. Political Ideology and System: Theocracy, secularism, socialism, liberalism and market economy all help in framing social welfare activities. In some societies welfare system adopts 'crisis intervention approach and somewhere else it may be cradle to grave coverage. It is political ideology which ultimately decides the approach.

3. Type of Needs and Level of Deprivation: It is not necessary that every society has the same or similar needs it depends on the level of deprivation. If the people are half fed then they will not need adult education or leisure time activity. They would appreciate income generation. This way level of deprivation can shape the programme of welfare.

3. Resources and the Economy: In fact resources are the most important factor in planning and shaping welfare programme. Without resources (or a little prosperity) it is difficult to have any social welfare activity. Therefore economic development is an important precondition to have a fullfledged programme of welfare in the country.

4. Size of the Population: Countries with large population always have difficulty in planning and managing welfare, firstly because of the magnitude of the population and secondly due to diversity in the nature of different sections of population and their needs. In fact more population means more requirement for social welfare activities.

5. *Involvement of GOs and NGOs:* In liberal democratic countries it is possible that voluntary agencies work along with government agencies. Voluntary agencies sometimes work as trend setters, innovative groups, pressure groups and opinion makers. Sometimes they work only as supplementary services. Voluntary agencies indicate advanced level of awareness and people's participation in welfare activities not only as beneficiaries but also as providers. This makes welfare a much more lively and vital activity.

6. *Nature of Human Resources Available in the Field of Social Welfare:* Social welfare man power or type of worker working in the field are another important dimension of the whole issue. Level of dedication and devotion on the part of human resources is definitely on asset. Their education, training and expertise make them skilful also but all this needs planning and investment. Type of human resources availed by welfare programme can not be ignored in this connection.

7. *History of Social Welfare Services in the Past:* No programme of social welfare can deviate completely from the past experiences in the field of social welfare e.g. in England some spirits of Elizabethan poor law persisted for a long time and later programmes were by and large following Beveridge's report approach. In India religion oriented charity was the nature of social welfare in the past. Even today we have the same spirits to a great extent.

8. *Religious and Cultural Profile of the Society:* Religious and cultural profile influences the welfare in many ways. Some traditional cultures and simple societies are providing

the umbrella of joint family, village and Kinship (Biradari) to support individuals at the time of old age, disease, widowhood, desertion and unemployment. But some religions take suffering and misery as a part of life and as a test from the God. This approach makes people indifferent towards welfare. According to modern thoughts social welfare system should not introduce topsy-turvy change in the society, rather it should use the existing coping mechanism e.g. instead of sending aged people to old age homes they can be rehabilitated with their children only by giving them old age pension. In other words existing religious and cultural scenario tailors the programme of social welfare in any society.

9. Level of Awareness Among Masses: Consciousness about rights and duties, general knowledge and aspiration to improve, are some other factors which colour social welfare activities of any society. In developed nations people utilise welfare services fully well. With awareness about the significance of welfare, masses are ready to pay the price for services. This situation makes social welfare activities self-help activities instead of organized charity (which some times they appear to be in poor nations).

As a result of all above mentioned influences a particular pattern of welfare emerges in most of the democratic countries. As Elizabeth Wickenden has remarked, "Social welfare includes those laws programmes benefits and services which assure or strengthen provision for meeting social needs recognized as basic to the well being of population and the better functioning of the social order."

Winfred Bill has discussed two types of welfare programmes — universal programmes and selective programmes. As a matter of fact universal programmes are also known as social services whereas selective programmes which are particularly for the needy and deprived people come in the category of social welfare. In

Indian context only the selective programme come under the category of social welfare.

Historical Development of Modern Social Welfare System

As far as ancient and medieval welfare traditions are concerned India can be proud of its contribution but in the case of modern social welfare system India can neither be considered a pioneer nor even a follower of the tradition. When we consult modern history of social welfare, India is for from being prominent in this field. One should define 'history' before he gives any historical explanation. As Paul Holmos has written quoting K. Clark. "... history is not only mode by man, it is fashioned by 'blind forces' which were not directed and controlled and which did not work according to preconceived plan. Their consequences for humanity were both good and bad."

The increase in productivity and population as those blind forces as well as industrial revolution as the third blind force are taken. While discussing the history of social welfare K. Clark has written at a particular point, "From 1850 things were getting better oil the time. Gradually the law became more effective and more humane, repressing what was savage and primitive in society and even eliminating some thing of what was absurd and brutal in operation. Gradually society learnt more of its duty to protect those who were at the mercy of economic and social forces which were too strong for them to ameliorate their environment and even to educate them."

Kilson G. Clark associates welfare with industrial revolution and he takes Great Britain as the pioneer in this field. He also feels that this was started after 1850. Here one should remember that social welfare is a response to conscious social needs and not social problems. Therefore it is different from social reform. In some countries social reform started much earlier. But Bill has written at one place, "In western industrialized nations social welfare programme came from reformers who were appalled at the personal and social cost of industrialisation and urbanisation. The subservience of man to machines, the exploitation of women and children, the disease ridden overcrowded slums, the breakdown in social controls in the wake of urbanisation all set fire to reform movement that swept over northern Europe, England and the U.S."

Reformers participated in social welfare in two ways,

(*i*) they worked for social legislation to end exploitation and

(*ii*) they helped those who were capable but could not improve their life style.

But this reform oriented welfare basically worked for 'capable' poor or slum dweller not for every one.

The natural outcome of industrial revolution was the emergence of trade unions which were working for measures like minimum wages, unemployment, old age allowance and workman compensation etc. These trade unions gave an idea that people were suffering without any fault of theirs and they deserved a better life. Therefore people thought of improving the situation. In the early twentieth century the early system of state involvement emerged beyond poor laws. Before that either individuals or church were looking after social welfare. As Paul Holmos has written at one place. "Mid-Victorian liberalisation was thus a collective ruling class response to social system in crisis". Wickenden refers to social welfare as a response of social needs not social problem. A decent income, housing, education health care, personal safety and the ability to participate in community affairs are among the most basic needs. To assure effective equitable and updated services society requires orderly planning mechanism, good social accounting prompt feed back and close coordination of economic and social policies. These are common human needs for which social welfare was evolved. During second world war new conditions and needs emerged. Lord William Beueridge's report was presented which gave the idea of covering everyone from 'Cradle to Grave.' It is still followed in some form or the other.

While studying the historical development of social welfare we see that every society has struggled in some way to achieve a particular form of social welfare with the help of trial and error method. However one thing is common that it is not so whimsical today as it was in the past. Today it is much more rational and practical. In some form state involvement has become obligatory. Therefore any discussion on social welfare aims towards the emergence of welfare states. It is quite surprising that almost all the developed and developing countries believe that they are (or becoming) welfare states. The shape and features of social welfare are now adjusting within the broader framework of welfare state, though like almost all the terms in the vocabulary of social work welfare state is also vague. As Gertrude Williams has confessed, "There is no universally accepted definition of the term... We are not even sure who first coined the term. It began to be used by a few people during the thirties and by the end of the second World war it suddenly seemed well established in ordinary conversation."[5] We may not be knowing the origin of the term but some brood and flexible definition we should find out though it wit also not be universally accepted.

Social Welfare and Welfare State

Searching a definition of welfare state Williams says- "In general way the term refers to the many methods by which the state through the host of different services tries to raise the standard of living of the population and help people to meet their various troubles through which most of us have to pass at one time or another in our lives."

Welfare state has many facts and many connotations. According to Sachdeva there are four principal approaches or models of provision and management of social welfare followed in different countries. These are:

1. The state control model.
2. The residual model.
3. The model economy model.
4. The familial model.

1. Residual Model: It is a somewhat restricted approach. It provides welfare measure only to those who are really in distress. Rest of the welfare activities are left for the private philanthropists. Here we can quote Wilensky's statement "We move towards the welfare state but we do it with ill grace carping and complaining all the way" In fact in USA and Canada many experiment in this field were done. Now it is not adopted in the typical sense of the term.

2. Mixed Economy Model: Germany has started contributory insurance plan. Non contributory benefits are only marginal. Many other countries are also adopting this model partially or wholly. It is because welfare has become a very expensive proposition specially in thickly populated countries. When the need is massive and state alone cannot sponsor oil the programmes then a partnership between state and voluntary group is required.

3. The Model of State Control: All communists and socialistic countries are following state control model because individuals do not have means to provide social welfare. In this pattern every thing is planned in advance. It takes social welfare closer to social service because it is all embracing and it does not aim towards any particular section. Sachdeva has observed while discussing the achievements of the former soviet welfare system "of these by far the most important is the success of the Soviet

Union in virtually abolishing unemployment." Of course later one could see that unemployment was abolished and jobs were created only for the jobs sake not for the sake of production and capital formation. This was borrowed light of non luminous object like moon. Perhaps all this the fall of Soviet Union.

4. The Familial Model: This is the most common and most natural system of providing support to individuals and groups. In China commune system was introduced after revolution but they have come back to family system. Former Soviet Union and Nazi Germany tried to reduce the importance of family as an institution but this effort was not successful. Japan is upholding its family tradition even today. In South East Asian countries family is still very important. In developed countries it has become weak. Therefore they can not adopt familial model of social welfare. All social welfare and social security measures have not been able to compensate for absence of the familial model.

At this point it is important to mention that the need of social welfare is growing day by day because by 2000 A.D. the population of the world would become 10 billion. Referring to this Sachdeva has mentioned. 'The developing countries where welfare services are lagging behind the standard achieved by the developed nations would be put to unbearable strain in the emerging scenario. Additional burden of social welfare services is also inevitable due to new phenomenon of terrorists and militants activities which is in evidence almost all over the world... A new dimension is added to the natural calamites by the havoc caused by dangerous gas leak in death and disabilities of thousands of people and the forced migration of people from their homes to neighbouring countries to escape persecution of their governments." The whole discussion is leading towards one finding that social welfare is broadening its boundaries but it will have its limits according to type of welfare state adopted by that country. On the basis of models mentioned above here some experiments with various philosophies of welfare state are discussed.

Welfare State in Great Britain

Generally the concept of welfare state is known to be launched by Britain. The reason is the emergence of early industrialisation in Britain. Perhaps the first step in this connection was taken in the form of social and labor legislation. It was the misery of child laborers (engaged in cotton factories due to their tender fingers) which drew the attention of social reformers and parliamentarians because overseers of the Poor who were legal escorts of orphan children sent these children in any newly opened factories. The first Factories Act 1802 was passed but remained unsuccessful in the absence of implementing infrastructure. Even then it marked a beginning. Edwin Chadwick's report on the sanitary conditions of the laboring population 1843, the first public Health Act 1848, and Housing Act 1890 were some other landmarks in this field. The real shape of social reform emerged from 1906 with Charles Booths Old Age Pension Scheme and the Royal Commission on poor law and Relief distress report, where Sidney Webb and Mrs. Beatrice Webb mode community responsible for individual's poverty. In this connection National Insurance Act of 1911 is significant. It was inspired by Mr. Lloyd George who was impressed by the compulsory sickness insurance scheme of Germany. The Act covered sickness, disablement, maternity and medical benefits. But all this was found insufficient during the period of great depression. Norman Ginsburg has written "The British welfare state has since occupied a middle ranking position amongst capitalist states. It has not been dominated by Social Democratic ideology, nor has it been dominated by voluntarism and reluctant collectivism as in the U.S... Thatcherism succeeded to some extent in moving the British welfare state away from European models and more towards the model of US."

He has further said that the political economy of welfare state in Britain is divided into two periods. First is from 1940 to mid 1970's and the second from 1975 onwards till date. In the former period welfare state was accepted at least in principle with great optimism and faith in the ideal of welfare state. After 1960 the intelligentsia became more philosophical which advocated new definition of poverty and need and planned for all sorts of unmet desires. They became politically important welfare lobby.

In the mid 1970s the welfare lobby created a political crisis as it wanted to have "the welfare state in Britain from being a direct provider of welfare to being a regulator of privately provided welfare." The free market economy was modified by social insurance and by somewhat Bismarckian social policy. On the basis of all this Keynes and Beveridge prepared the foundation of the present welfare state which was based on Liberal Collectivism. Which later on marched toward Thatcherism due to the burden of expenditure on welfare that could no longer be borne by the tax payers of Britain 'The New Rights' led by Thatcher attacked the system of state's responsibility for welfare. As a result Britain has provided another approach which can be called Liberal collectivist welfare state which is based on self help ideal to some extent.

Welfare State in the United States

American and European social systems have many programme in common but they are basically different because in USA the approach is more privatisation oriented. As it has been said by Norman Ginsberg "...the US might not be considered to be a welfare state at all, because of gaps in programme coverage and emphasis on private welfare initiative." Perspectives on American social welfare have been discussed by Winifred Bell on the following parameters: (*i*) Individual efforts in social welfare; (*ii*) Universal versus selective services, and; (*iii*) The role of the government in income maintenance.

In USA welfare was basically privately organized untill great depression of 1930s. But after that residual versus institutional social welfare developed, though residual social welfare is still on important aspect of social welfare. Residualists take poverty and deprivation as a failure of individual they take monetary incentive as a precondition of efficiency; they describe welfare as a help offered by philanthropists to the less fortunate ones but one should be careful that this help should not make them more dependent. On the contrary institutional social welfare believes ... That social welfare plays a major role equal in importance to the economic market and the family system in meeting normal every day need of average citizens as well as, helping vulnerable population."

The next important factor in US social welfare is its nature which may be divided into two categories. One is universal and the other is selective. As a matter of fact both type of services are sponsored by the state authorities. It has been noticed that universal programme have been more successful. Winifred has criticized selective programmes severely by saying "Income standards could be raised to more decent levels. But so long as Americans hold fast to their age old attitude towards the poor, selective programmes will probably be designed and administered more to deter people from applying than to help them."

The role of government in providing benefits like AFDC (Aid to families with dependent children) social security, unemployment compensation, public and private employee pension and health insurance is reflecting a welfare state pattern. But it does not ignore the role of private philanthropy, therefore it is called welfare state in the Corporate Market Economy. To explain it further Norman Ginsburg has written "The modern welfare state in US developed in two short bursts of popular pressure and social reform — the New Deal of the 1930s and the rapid expansion of social programme in the Great Society era of the 1960's. The New Deal was prompted by the deep crisis of free-market capitalism, and the political agitation of many of its victims — farmers, capitalists, unemployed people and the elderly people in particular." As a result of this approach social welfare expenditure, as a proportion of GDP, has remained below the levels of Germany, Sweden and The UK. The problems of Blacks and women's liberation have created new dimension in welfare state concept in US. No doubt constant change and experimentation in USA social welfare policy makes it more dynamic.

The concept of need based and priority based activities in social welfare has been introduced and these needs have been identified in many ways. Maslow's concept of need had also been taken as a basis which puts physiological needs the first. His order is like this: (*i*) Physiological needs; (*ii*) Belongingness and affection needs; (*iii*) Security and Safety needs; (*iv*) Self actualisation needs, and; (*v*) Self esteem self respect and autonomy needs

Besides Maslow, Alderfer also gave the concept of ERG which indicate 'Existence Relatedness and Growth' as needs. The American social security and social welfare programmes indicate that these explanations have been taken into consideration.

People's efforts are given priority in the field of social welfare. A lot of independence has been given to people in this connection. It has gone to the extent that radical social workers and Blacks have prepared their own code of ethics. Radicals' code has been discussed in the same chapter. Blacks code is given below.

"If a sense of community awareness is precondition to humanitarian acts then we as Black social workers must use our knowledge of the Black community, our commitment to self determination and our helping skills for the benefit of Black people as we marshal our expertise to improve the quality of life of Black people. Our activities will be guided

by our Black consciousness, our determination to protect the security of the Black community and to serve as advocates to relieve suffering of Black people by any means necessary.

Therefore, as Black social workers we commit ourselves, collectively, to the interest of our Black Brethren and as individuals subscribe to the following statement:-

'I regard my primary obligation the welfare of the Black individual, Black family and Black community and will engage in action for improving social conditions. I give precedence to this mission over my personal interests.

I adopt the concept of a Black extended family and embrace all Black people as my brothers and sisters making no distinction between their destiny and my own.

I hold myself responsible for the quality and extent of service I perform and the qualify and extent of service performed by the agency or organization in which I am employed as it relates to the Black community.

I accept the responsibility to protect the Black community against unethical and hypocritical practice by any individuals or organizations engaged in social welfare act Miles.

I stand ready to supplement my paid or professional advocacy with voluntary service in Black public interest.

I will consciously use my skills and my whole being as an instrument for social change with particular attention directed to the establishment of Black social institutions.

This code for Blacks shows that groupism among social worker is emerging and it is accepted by the larger community of social workers in USA.

In short we can soy that United States is the welfare state in the Corporate Market Economy but that can not be compared with other western European states because in USA most of the responsibilities in social welfare are put on the shoulders of individuals. Participation of state is somewhat indirect. State is more concerned with social services.

Welfare State in Sweden

Sweden is considered to be a good example of capitalist welfare state. As Norman Ginsburg says Sweden has achieved healthy economic growth, 'full' employment, and one of the highest standards of living in the world, combined with the largest, most expensive and possibly most egalitarian state welfare system in the west." Sweden is coiled Social Democratic Welfare State. It is due to the homogeneous society where war and civil wars have not taken place. Norman Ginsburg has written "the clearest moment of ideological shifts towards the welfare state, occurred in the 1930s when the Social Democratic Party (SAP) for the most port, abandoned both Marxist and Neo-classical or deflationary economic policies in favour of Keynesianism."

Right from the third decade of twentieth century three elements ruled the ideology of Swedish welfare state system. The first is the concept of 'people's home'. Second ideal is 'solidarity' and the third element is the commitment to Keynesian counter cyclical economic policies "particularly the use of infrastructural public employment and labor market policies to limit unemployment." The concept of flat rote benefit is also associated with the above mentioned three elements. Social policy of Sweden has also been influenced by movements like rediscovery of poverty feminism and increased social equality. In 1970 they also thought of economic democracy. They have all embracing programmes for the aged, unemployed, women, ethnic minorities and lone morhers etc.

The Swedish welfare state is financed by very high level of personal and corporate taxation minimum tax paid by a regular employee is 40% of the gross income. This quite clear to people that if they want more services they have to pay for them either directly or indirectly.

In Sweden a new centre rights government was formed in 1991. Ginsburg has said" however the likelihood is that the hegemony will adopt to new capitalist and international realities moving towards the new realism of the social market economy model in the absence of a feasible socialist model."

Welfare State in India

After discussing all these models and system of social welfare we understand that social welfare and various models of welfare state are passing through a phase of experimentation. In recent years development of any ideology of welfare state has become much more difficult because of the fall of socialist block in Eastern Europe. Earlier capitalist market economy based and Marxism based two models were existing and operating but now any type of clear-cut distinction is not possible and all the developed welfare states are experimenting new thoughts and new programmes. In Indian context the situation is somewhat different. But welfare state is deep rooted in our culture and constitution. D Palman Norman has said "The constitution of India contains many provisions designed to make India welfare state" India has a nicely made constitution. As Sachdeva has said "The preamble thus reflects all the attributes of a welfare state viz. justice liberty, equality and fraternity and the social order based on these principles. Besides these, fundamental rights and directive principles of state policy create conscience of our constitution which takes India towards welfare state. More than that, Five Year Plans, annual plans, special programmes for women, children, scheduled castes, scheduled tribes, housing rural and urban community development, adoption of human rights and establishment of various commissions, bureaux and cells for the target groups, provide a rosy picture of our approach and policy. In the field of welfare we see some outstanding programmes such as: (*i*) Economic and social development through five year plans; (*ii*) Nation wide massive programme of family planning as a ground work for social welfare; (*iii*) Grants in aid system for NGOs to promote peoples' participation in the process of forming a welfare state; (*iv*) Number of social legislations to fight against social evils and to protect vulnerable groups, and; (*v*) Integrated child development services to improve quality of life.

Though all this is quite optimistic but unfortunately all these efforts are not sufficient and poverty, ignorance, lock of aspiration, low self profile and widely prevalent social evils are putting India much lower than the standard of welfare state.

Welfare state broadly includes:

(*i*) Full employment.

(*ii*) Levelling up of the income.

(*iii*) Development of skilled labor.

(*iv*) Removal of excessive poverty, deficiency, epidemic slum condition and deprivation.

(*v*) Extension of social service.

Moreover welfare state is a concern of the government for minimum need fulfilment and for keeping the minimum standard of welfare services. It also includes economic and health security. "Welfare state was developed in the past as a response to great economic depression. In capitalist and democratic societies welfare state means need fulfilment, special provision for deprived section and encouragement to capitalist for creating jobs and bringing about more prosperity."

Due to poverty and population explosion welfare state

is only a utopia. As Sachdeva has said that during the last decade sixteen million have been added to the country's population every year. One third of world's hungry live in India. 11000 Indians die of hunger every day. Child labor constitutes one fourth of the total work force of our country in which 44 million children live in sub human conditions. Not less than 10,000 growing girls are made devdasis every year and then go to the flesh trade. These are just some glimpses of the deprivation and deprived sections. Besides these, there are many more areas of deprivation and atrocities. Keeping in mind all these issues it is very difficult for planners to visualise an ideal welfare state. It appears that some efforts have been made time to time to improve certain sections but long term welfare measures have not been discussed and planned because on the one hand need is so massive and on the other hand resources are so meagre.

Let us analyse why India is not having preconditions and prerequisites for a welfare state. As a matter of fact for adopting a welfare state we must have:

(*i*) Natural resources and prosperity.

(*ii*) Education and awareness about the rights and duties among the masses.

(*iii*) Faith in the philosophy of democracy, secularism and welfare state.

(*iv*) Efficiency, work ethos and society without corruption.

(*v*) Consensus about the policies of social welfare among planners and policy makers.

(*vi*) Political stability and national character.

Without all these pre conditions welfare state cannot be achieved. In Indian context all these prerequisites are working (if at all they are working) in a very tame manner.

Today we have cost and benefit analysis for everything. Can we have the same type of cost and benefit analysis for social welfare and welfare state? In the material sense cost of the welfare services is too much and there is hardly any immediate return of this investment from the material angle. In other words surplus money is required for welfare. In this way welfare would come after basic needs and national defence. In a poor country like India we can only have selective welfare activities. Martin Hewitt has written Finally, welfare discourse contains claims — the best researched in welfare literature — about the authenticity of individual expressions of need and offers of help; claims between, for example, client and welfare worker concerning the sincerity of each other's expression and hardship and willingness to help. It is precisely the last two types of claims about welfare provision that Marxists have dismissed as ideological in the context of capitalist society'.

It is noteworthy that according to this explanation individual scrutiny of every help seeker must be made. But Marxist approach is in favour of total coverage of all the welfare needs from cradle to grave though the priorities would be fixed according to state resources.

In Indian context it is difficult to assess whether India has adopted capitalist approach or Marxist. A combination of both has been tried under various welfare programmes. But all these programmes do not make India a perfect welfare state. It is a massive venture and due to disastrous explosion of population growth, simple services like health, nutrition education, drinking water and electricity etc. are also not provided to masses. Consequently welfare state only remains a dream.

At this point it is worth mentioning that welfare state does not depend on social welfare activities only, we must also have social services, efforts of social reform and social security in the given state, then only it can claim that it is a welfare state. Right now India is working for all these programmes but a remarkable success has not been acclaimed in any sphere. It is already mentioned that it is due to the population explosion that all our efforts are wasted. According to a conservative estimate in 1972-73, 51.5% of population was below poverty line. This percentage comes down to 25.8 in 1989-90. Now let us see it in absolute numbers. 291.5 million was the population below poverty line in 1972-73. Percentage wise if was reduced to half till 1989-90 but in absolute numbers it comes to 210.8 million.

Efforts for Providing Right to Work

Programmes like Integrated Rural Development Programme (IRDP) and the Employment Guarantee Scheme were started to fight wide spread unemployment and poverty. However, right to work has not been made fundamental right but government is trying to provide work for atleast one member of every family.

Old Age Pension Scheme

In 1991 the total expenditure on these pension schemes was not less than 270 crores but all this was just the beginning of the proposed services which should be provided to the senior citizens.

Integrated Child Development Scheme (ICDS)

According to the annual report for 1991-92 of the Deportment of Women and Child Development around 2700 ICDS projects were functioning by 31 March 1992. It has been assessed that it will help in bringing health to all by 2000 AD.

These are some important steps but still it is quite clear that a better economic and social planning (including family planning) is required for achieving a better atmosphere for social welfare.

Finally, we can say that the basic problems remain still unanswered. They are:

(*i*) Are welfare services making beneficiaries self dependent in the long run or are they developing dependence on welfare generation after generation?

(*ii*) Who should pay for social welfare services and how much should be paid?

(*iii*) Should welfare depend on the very fact that the beneficiary is a member of the society, therefore he has some right over societal resources or should he contribute something for his own welfare.

(*iv*) Is it possible for social workers to work as planner and policy maker or to participate in really broad issues such as problem of refugees, migration, disarmament and cultivation of narcotics?

(*v*) Welfare state also means interference form the side of the state. Is it possible to have welfare without interference in individual rights?

REFERENCES

Beulah R. Compton, *Introduction to Social Welfare and Social Work* (Illinois: The Dorsey Press 1980), p. 26.

D.R. Sachdeva, *Social Welfare Administration in India.* (Allahabad: Kitab Mahal, 1993), p. 2.

Wayne and Vasey, *Government and Social Welfare* New York: Renihart and Winston Inc. 1958), p. 11.

Wilensky and Lebeaux, *Industrial Society and Social Welfare,* (New York Free Press, 1965), p. 139.

Elizabeth, Wickendon, *Social Welfare in Changing World,* (U.S. Washington DC: Dept. of Health Education, and Welfare, Welfare Administration, US Govt. Printing Office 1965), p. 1.

Winifred Bill, *Contemporary Social Welfare* (New York: Mac Million Publishing Company Inc., 1983), p. 3.

Paul Holmos, *Introduction of Welfare: Concept and History* (Great Britain: The Open University Press Wallow Hall Hilton Keynes 1978), p. 106.

Rex A Skidmore, M.G. Thackeray and O. William Farley, *Introduction to Social Work* (5th Edition) New Jersey: Prentice Hall, 1991) p. 3.

Kilson G. Clark, *The Making of Victorian England* (London: Neshuen 1965), p. 270.

Paul Holmos, *Introduction to Welfare: Concept and History* p. 127.

William Beveridge, *"Social Insurance and Allied Services* (New Year) London Macmillan, 1942).

Gertrude Williams, *The Coming of the Welfare State,* London: George Allen and Unwin Ltd. 1967), p. 7.

Harold `Wilensky, *The Welfare State and Equality,* (Berkeley: University of California Press 1975), p. 32.

Armand Lauffer, *Working in Social Work* (Newsbury Park: SAGE Publication, 1987), p. 20.

Hajira Kumar, *Social Work: An Experience and Experiment in India,* New Delhi: Gitanjali Publication, 1994.

2

Dilemma of the Future of Welfare State

During the last decades of 20th century history has made cruel sport of our principal intellectual paradigms—liberalism, Marxism and social democracy. For a time it has crowned each 'king' only to dethrone him later and replace him with a rival. One lesson to be learnt from history seems to be that all three—the thesis of *laissez-faire* liberalism, the antithesis of Marxist socialism, and the synthesis of social democracy—seem to be intrinsic to the social as well as spiritual (i.e., intellectual and moral) formation of modern western society. The values of individualism and liberty, whose institutional underpinnning is the free market, private property and the rule of law, and the values of solidarity and community, whose institutional underpinning is common ownership, political democracy and collective services (social services), provide the essential tension which the social democratic. Centre has tried to relieve, rather than resolve, through attempted reconciliation and a mix of values.

The protracted crisis of the mixed economy and the apparent failure of Keynesian economics to put things right has spelled the end of the golden age of western affluence as well as of the welfare state. These changed material conditions have also spelled the breakup of the *de facto* political consensus around the mixed economy and welfare, and revived sharply the somewhat somnolent ideological conflict over the issues of welfare and economic growth. As the Centre-Left position has deteriorated materially so has its (admittedly somewhat light-weight) intellectual standing. Until the mid-1970s the Centre virtually dominated the intellectual (and political) stage. The radical Right and the radical Left represented little more than fringe ideologies which did not need to be taken very seriously since they were mere echoes of the past. The 'bad old past' of free-market capitalism with its Depression and dole queues, and its antithesis Marxism with its doctrine of class war and revolution of a managed market economy and Beveridgian social engineering.

The 1970s changed all that. The Centre began to lose ground rapidly and both neo-conservatives and neo-Marxists closed in. Humanity (or at least western humanity) was back to square one. If the 1950s and 1960s were intellectually (as well as politically) speaking the decade of the Centre-Left (the social democratic celebration of the middle path) the 1970s once again began to look outwards towards both ends of the ideological spectrum. What of the 1980s and beyond? It would be rash to venture a prediction. All of which goes to show how premature it is in the social sciences to celebrate the 'end' of anything-whether of ideology in general or of Marxism or of market liberation.

Certainly, each of these major social paradigms represent much more than simply a normative position. Each includes a 'science' component which claims to show the truth, and thus to link the normative with the positive, the ends with appropriate means. Yet, as we know from the confused intellectual odyssey of the social sciences, the search for an objective, impartial, value free basis for social knowledge has not been successful. Neverthless, since social science is ultimately a guide to action, directly or indirectly, judgements have to be made. These involve normative as well as cognitive issues. This is an important point. For an unfortunate legacy of the debate over positivism and the nature of science, and social science in particular has been the idea of a clear divide between 'facts' and 'values'. This implies that the latter involves subjectivity and choice, while the former pertains to the realm of what 'is'. The logic of this analytic distinction is not at issue. The main point to be made is that in the social sciences at any rate (whatever the position in the natural sciences) the realm of the 'positive' the 'is', is far from unambiguous and seems destined to remain so.

History, the temporal element, both provides a natural testing ground for large-scale social theories such as liberalism or Marxism, and also provides theories with a big escape clause, for we may claim that 'in the final analysis'—and only in the final analysis—would such and such happen. What happens in the interim is another matter. But when does the 'last instance' arrive? When do contradictions 'finally' 'nature'? How long does the interim last? All developmental hypotheses—and in the social sciences there are many-involve a long period of waiting during which we have to take the theory on trust. Conversely, many social scientific assertions of a universal nature (models, abstract theoretical propositions) are difficult to disprove with reference to facts. The result is that paradigms never die, they simply fade away-only to blossom again when history calls them to life.

The 1930s belonged to Marxism, and both market liberalism and social democracy were in disarray. In the 1950s the wheel of fortune turned against Marxism and, to a lesser extent, market liberalism. Neither the atomism of *laissez-faire* nor the monism of Marxist socialism but the mix of pluralistic industrialism seemed the correct path on which at last the western societies had arrived. It was to be the finest hour of social democracy, the mixed economy and the welfare state. The nature and history of these broadly comparable paradigms show that each embodies a partial truth which gives them sufficient plausibility. In the right circumstances they give their adherents the feeling that truth—the whole or at least the large part of it—it on their side. At the moment, truth seems to have deserted the Centre in favour of the extremes of the intellectual and value spectrum.

Practical Considerations

What then of the future of the welfare state which largely represents the Centre-Left position? We shall do our best to answer this question in the light of the material presented in the earlier chapters and the sceptical position sketched above. Indeed our discussion of the various perspectives, and in particular the delineation of corporatism (IWS), shows already where our normative and cognitive choices lie.

First, then, the normative position. Generally speaking, we believe that the Welfare State—which combines a managed market economy, a plural polity and a developed social welfare system—represents a social formation, however hybrid and compromised, worth preserving. Why? There are two reasons. First, consider the alternatives. Essentially they seem to be either a return to free market, or a socialist revolution.

The free-market option is currently being tried in both British and the United States. Its logic is economic and social *laissez-faire* (with pragmatic departures from this principle if, they help the business class), a return to the Social Darwinism of Spencer. The major normative issue here is that this approach would require the relatively powerless segments of the population (workers, blacks, women) to pick up the cost of change. If progress is predicated on the survival of the fittest, then the weak must by definition be allowed to go to the wall. This approach would enhance freedom (especially of the wealthy) at the cost of social justice. It attempts to put the clock back to the 1930s. However, fitfully and partially the movement for social rights (understood in the broader sense) has established a foothold in liberal market society by committing the state, the government, to certain forms of action, to taking certain measures. A return to the free market, to deregulation, amounts to a counter-revolution. It means the dis-establishment of a variety of rights which do something towards maintaining minimum standards and providing a context within which the struggle against inequities can be waged. It is above all the equity claims or entitlements that are largely inscribed in the welfare state. Take, for example, the right to work, informally recognized since the 1940s. Now in some ways it is an absurdity to claim such a right within a predominantly market economy. Indeed the guarantee of full employment itself changes the nature of the economy from a free market to a regulated one. It was the genius of Keynes to show that with only minor and indirect forms of state intervention a market economy could be made to provide full employment. And although the welfare state was more concerned with unemployment insurance, one of the assumptions of the Beveridge Report, for example, was that the government will try to maintain high levels of employment. In this sense the right to work and thereby also a fully legitimate entitlement to income has been recognized by the welfare state. The right to education, health care and a minimum level of living are other relevant examples. Attempts to create greater equity between citizens—discriminated against on sexual or ethnic grounds—through affirmative action are again measures to secure human rights.

The Neo-Conservative strategy is to discredit government and thus depoliticise, or rather desocialise, the market economy. Yet what the politicisation of the economy from below (full employment and the social services) has essentially achieved is a modicum of security which a society founded on pure market capitalism lacks and whose absence played such havoc in the 1920s and 1930s. Thus, a return to unalloyed capitalism, even if politically feasible, without repression, would be a return to insecurity and grosser forms of injustice. It would be to return to a society in which basic social rights are denied and the costs of economic change allowed to lie where they fall. We must remember too that on all accounts technological developments and industrial restructuring of advanced capitalist economies might mean continuing large-scale unemployment. What does a *laissez-faire* or market economy offer in these circumstances? Even in terms of short-term economic recovery and growth Thatcherism and Reaganomics have little to show. At a purely technical level, the monetary medicine applied by these pro-market regimes has been so strong as to endanger the patient's life itself. Inflation has been tamed and wage demands lowered at an enormously high cost in the form of unemployment and bankruptcies. In short the neo-conservative solution has little to recommend either as a value-orientation, or even as a short-term technical fix. As Thurow has pointed out, perhaps the changes that are needed for some variant of a free market to restore economic dynamic and growth (profits, investments, etc.) would be so massive as to rule itself out on grounds of equity and justice, as well as political possibility.

For the other major response to the current crisis is to move toward some varient of Marxist socialism so that the contradictions of capitalism are overcome once and for all and a social system based on the recognition of human needs at last becomes a reality. In a sense, this could be the realization of a welfare society which would take the values of welfare much further. Although attractive from this view point there are several problems with this socialist vision. Normatively speaking, socialism exalts the collective over the individual, distributive justice over liberty. Moreover, in Marxist socialism, which has so far taken a more or less elitist form, the whole question of democracy remains unresolved. At any rate 'actually existing socialism' does not inspire confidence as a model to be emulated.

Thus to end up with such a regime would be to jump out of the frying pan into the fire. Individualism, liberty and rule of law, of which we spoke earlier, constitute a valuable part of the modern western heritage and any progressive social system must incorporate these within itself. If it is conceded that collectivism and distributive egalitarianism are not the only desirable values then the socialist project must demonstrate that it can encomposs libertarian values as well and carry forward the entire complex of values and institutions to a higher level of civilisation (as Marx for example seems to have envisaged). The problem of how to organize an efficient system of production without the use of coercion and material incentives also remains unsolved (at the level of both practice and theory). Post-revolutionary societies ('actually existing socialism') show that this could be the Achilles heel of socialism.

Briefly, both at the normative and technical levels, Marxist socialism, like neo-conservatism, fails to convince as a social theory of progress for advanced western societies. This does not rule out forms of transitional or gradual socialism (e.g., Euro communism, workers' fund socialism of Sweden) which in effect promise us that we can have our cake and eat it too. But it these have to be tried within a broadly democratic framework in remains unclear (as with Eurocommunism or the 'alternative economic strategy' in Britain) how they are to realize their major objectives and how they might reconcile liberty, equality, democracy and economic growth. It may well be that historically fortunate countries (e.g. Sweden) may yet surprise us by achieving this seemingly impossible objective. But at present no one seems to have a convincing enough model of transition to democratic socialism.

By rejecting neo-conservatism and Marxist socialism, we are left with some form of Centrist position. We would like to suggest that the corporatist form of the welfare state seems to offer the possibility of overcoming some of the major defects of the post-war welfare state. Whether and to what extent corporatism might succeed is a difficult question to answer. Nonetheless a corporatist approach seems worth a try.

First, let us note that public support for state provided services remains high in capitalist democracies. The responsibility for maintaining full employment and general conditions of equity are also seen as the government's sphere. In this sense the welfare state shows no sign of having lost its popular appeal or legitimacy among the masses. Taxation may not be popular, but right-wing expectations of Proposition 13-style tax revolts spreading throughout western countries have come to nothing. There is certainly no evidence of general support for the retrenchment of government and the pricatisation of economic and social life. Admittedly, there are also some contradictory findings which suggest that conflicting tendencies may be at work. But on the whole the evidence in favour of continuing support for the basic social services and the maintenance of full employment is unmistakable. As we have argued above, the victory of the Right at the polls in several countries, notably the UK and the USA, does not by any means signify the repudiation of the objectives and values of the welfare state. Rather it suggests the search for an alternative route to roughly the same position.

Second, the recession, the fiscal crisis and other problems of the welfare state have also shown the importance of economic welfare of full employment and economic growth, for the masses in capitalist democracies. The key objectives seem to be security-economic and social—and prosperity. True, the influence of the media, manipulation by elites, and the sheer weight of dominant ideology have to be borne in mind. However, popular surveys show that the masses do not follow blindly whatever is decreed from above—by the government of the day or by the ruling class. At least in the democracies the masses are exposed to some degree of plurality of viewpoints and beliefs and it would be well not to lose sight of the fact. In any case, as we have tried to explain earlier, my own standpoint is that the market capitalist system must meet equity claims and spread the risks and costs of social change evenly. In this sense we find my own preference for the role of government to be broadly in line with those of the masses.

If the welfare state both enjoys popular support (legitimacy) and also appears to have been effective in providing a measure of security and equity, then the next problem could be stated in the form: 'But can we afford it? ' In short the problem is that of financing various services adequately and coping with the apparatently negative consequence or externalities of the welfare state. Here key economic issues such as inflation, the trade-off between the economic and social wage, full employment (or some equivalent social arrangement), profitability and investment, efficiency and productivity, budget deficits, and the like have to be addressed. It is precisely the lack of an institutional framework for addressing such problems (outside electoral competition and a free-for-all interest group politics) that has brought the welfare state into disrepute. For, as we have seen, underlying the Keynes-Beveridge model was the notion of a form of moderate collectivism that would manipulate demand to maintain employment and provide an underpinning of social security (in the wider sense) for all citizens. The assumption was that once these correctives were put in place the rest of the economy could be left, more or less, to the operation of market forces. This notion of moderate collectivism did not anticipate the possible effects of a pressure group polity on the state welfare system.

More important, the institutional separation between the 'social' (welfare) and the 'economic' (market economy) took a too static and 'social engineering' view of the social system. Social democratic reformism, typified by Richard Titmuss's approach, reinforced the idea of a sharp separation between the social (welfare and needs, etc.) and the economic (market, profits, efficiency, etc.) realms by emphasising the different values embodied in them. This emphasis had two unfortunate consequences. First, the importance of full employment and economic growth for the general welfare of the masses was obscured by the emphasis on social welfare and distribution. Second, and more important, the lack of a theoretical perspective on the social structure obscured the fact that the social and the economic were not only functionally related (inter-dependent) but both formed part of a larger reality (or values and institutions) of welfare capitalism.

The perspective of piecemeal social intervention, based on a somewhat dramatised ethic or welfare and choice (in place of a focus on society, its dominant institutions and values), also encouraged a somewhat free-floating view of social welfare isolating it from the wider social structure of which it was a part. The connection with the social structure was chiefly made at a technical-administrative level (e.g. demography, family and household composition, urbanisation) in order to formulate needs and help with social planning. The macro-level connections with the economy and the polity were on the whole missed.

The focus on the social welfare aspect of state activity has also encouraged the view in which public services, such as transport and government subsidies of various kinds to producers and consumers, were seen as lying outside the sphere of the welfare state. The upshot was that social policies were seen as unrelated not only to economic policies but to public policies as well. This may have been especially true of Britain, but a similar institutional separation in the analysis of these various sectors can be seen in other English-speaking countries.

The isolation of the social from the economic, of social welfare activities from other relevant activities of the state (e.g., subsidies, employment policy), has also inhibited the search for appropriate institutional forms through which the problem of interdependence among these spheres, especially between economic and social welfare, might be addressed. There is an important difference here between countries like Sweden with its Labour Market Board and centralised wage bargaining and Austria with its social partnership institutions on the one hand, and say Britain or Canada on the other. The corporatism of countries like Austria and Sweden, whatever its short comings, at least in principle takes the social services and social welfare out of the 'ghetto' and tends to relate them to the wider institutional and group context of society. It is due to the ability of countries like Sweden to address the problems of productivity, wage settlements, inflation and technological change through institutions which seek to arrive at a working consensus (consensus, as we saw above, has been stressed far more and quite explicity in Austria) that potentially adverse economic consequences of full employment, wage militancy and rising public expenditure have been avoided for a long period. It should also be remembered that there is a good deal of voluntarism involved in wage bargaining as well as other forms of social cooperation between employers and trade unions in these countries. Corporatism, in short, must not be equated with the extension of government.

The class relationships and interests involved in corporatist arrangements are bound to vary from one country to another. But it would be idle to pretend, as Marxists tend to do, that all such arrangements are a way of subordinating labour to capital's interests. This may be the case in countries where labour is weak organizatonally and ideologically. And that is why corporatist policies (meaning usually a one-sided imposition of wage control by the government) are normally rejected by unions in such countries in the absence of a *quid pro quo* in the form of social contract. Yet, as the example of Britain shows, free collective bargaining may be good for labour in the short run (or rather for those sections of the labour force in a strong position to drive a bargain) but in the long run the price paid for waging a class war (wage struggle) can be high in terms of mass unemployment, economic decline and inadequate social services, Britain's case also amply demonstrates that wave militancy has nothing to do with class consciousness and socialism in the Marxist sense. In the absence of socialist consciousness and an effective strategy of revolution, a free-for-all can only benefit the Right. Corporatist arrangements on the other hand have the merit of extending the notion of collective responsibility for system maintenance by involving those with most economic power in collective decision-making. In this sense corporatism (IWS) carries the logic of the welfare state (DWS) a step further. It helps realize, in some small measure, the idea of 'planning' in the context of a mixed economy and plural polity.

Undoubtedly, Corporatism involves the centralisation of the decision-making process and entails by-passing parliament to some extent, insofar as important decisions are made outside it. But it must be remembered that in the Welfare State decisions are being made outside parliament in any case (e.g., investment and pricing decisions by corporations, collective agreements between groups of workers and companies). Thus what is involved in corporatism is more the coordination and harmonisation of certain kinds of decisions rather than their removal from the parliamentary arena. Indeed corporatism adds a measure of social accountability by making certain kinds of decision-making and their underlying rationale more visible and public. It must also be remembered that what is involved primarily is a broad framework of understanding between major economic groupings regarding economic growth, wages, prices, inflation and similar economic issues. This still leaves a very large area of economic, social and political issues to be debated and decided upon through the normal political processes. True, some measure of centralisation in decision-making by major economic associations, including the state, is the essence of this approach. Given certain national objectives (economic and social) a measure of cooperation, consensus and stability seem necessary. Hence a measure of centralisation. Moreover, if the economic and social aspects of welfare are to be connected properly at the macro-level some degree of 'planning' becomes inevitable. Hence too centralisation. But general decisions about wages, prices and investment still leave plenty of room for pluralism within a broad framework of national consensus.

It is also important to remind ourselves of the limits—or rather the limitations—of the corporate welfare state (IWS). Like the welfare state (DWS) it cannot be a means to socialism, to an egalitarian society. As we have seen, the social democratic hopes of changing the nature of income distribution through a sharply progressive system of taxation and free social services have not been realized. Thirty years of welfare statism and a mountain of research into this area seem to show that such expectations were misplaced and are unlikely to be realized. The pursuit of equality (i.e., equality of rewards and outcome rather than equality of consideration) must take other forms. Other, perhaps more direct methods of intervention may have to be devised and put into practice. Social welfare as Marshall, Beveridge and other moderate collectivists have always pointed out, is primarily a means to social security and citizenship rights. No doubt, social insurance itself, as well as equity claims generally, involve greater equality of consideration and also quality of opportunity.

It will be remembered that, in the case of Austria at least, there was a tacit understanding that the respective shares of capital and labour are not a subject of bargaining and that the social consensus was based on the recognition of this point. In Sweden, on the other hand, there has been no such understanding and presumably the search for greater equality through the policy of wage solidarity and through the welfare state more generally has been active. However in Sweden too the tripartite (or bipartite) deliberations do not seem to have been concerned with a planned reduction in social (including income) inequality. Nor do data on the distribution of income and wealth show such reduction in equality. The corporatist welfare state, rather like its predecessor, is not much concerned with equality. Rather it is concerned with enhancing economic and social welfare simultaneously (what a corporatist Mao Tse Tung might have called 'walking no two legs') and ensuring that national minima are maintained and improved. This is not to say that the pursuit of equality (in its various aspects) cannot be carried on in conjunction with the structures and institutions of welfare. But it must be borne in mind that objective is extraneous to the corporatist welfare state.

.A major issue raised by the neo-conservatives, as well as Marxists like O'Connor and Offe, is the use of the state by a variety of particularistic interests which results in an unprincipled growth of the state budget and the state sector. Substantially the same question has been raised by others (e.g., Bell and Hirsch) in pointing out that the public sector has tended to become more an arena in which claims and counter-claims are made than a community with some form of social morality to underpin collective action. Can the IWS address this problem? The cooperation of major economic groups with the government in looking at the economic picture as a whole (including economic and social welfare) is helpful in moderating unprincipled government growth. In any case, because of the compartmentalisation of economic, social and public policies, the welfare state has tended to be seen narrowly in terms of social policy alone. Government's wider economic activity (e.g., aid to industry, agriculture and other sectors through subsidies, fiscal policy) is often left out of the picture. The corporatist approach would be able to take a broader view of the consequences of government action. This across-the-board view of state welfare activity may promote a more rational and principled approach to policy. At any rate, the idea of something like a public interest is more likely to be addressed through cooperation and consensus (as, for example, during the 'Social Contract' between the Labour government and the trade unions in Britain) than under the free-for-all pattern typical of the pluralist welfare state.

On the other hand, pace moderate collectivists such as Marshall and Robson, it would be more rather than less difficult under a corporatist regime to differentiate clearly something called the welfare state from the rest of the state's activities. The idea that a state welfare sector-communally oriented, based on normative consensus and with clearly defined objectives—can co-exist with competition and conflict in a plural society appears unrealistic. Indeed, one should recognize clearly that interest-group politics and government are areanas of competition, and that a variety of claims and counter-claims—both material and ideological—will continue to be made. Economic and social welfare will therefore have to be understood in a wider sense and we shall still have to ask of specific state activities as to whose welfare they are serving and in accordance with what values or principles.

It may be premature, to think of defining the nature of government activity (distributional or otherwise) in normative terms. What the IWS seems to promise is a measure of working consensus over the system of mixed economy and state-protected minimum standards. Beyond that lies the realm of pluralism, of values and of interests. Short of authoritarianism, whether of the Right of the Left, or some miracle it is difficult to see how one can have a modern society without conflict. But this need not rule out some measure of consensus and accommodation among key social groups in order to sustain better those conditions in which a wide variety of conflicts can continue without causing serious dysfunctions. It would be absurd to pretend that some form of corporatism can be a panacea for the ills of modern society in general, and welfare capitalism in particular. But it seems to offer an institutional framework, in the context of a capitalist economy and liberal polity, within which the values of the welfare state (DWS) may be better realized.

To argue in favour of corporatism is one thing: to demonstrate its political feasibility is quite another. The political question is important but too large an issue to be explored here. Moreover, the question of political action can be considered meaningfully only in relation to a particular country and its economic and political conditions. Generally speaking those political groupings and forces that lend most support to the welfare state (social democracy and the labour movement) are also the natural constituency for the IWS (remember that we have been speaking throughout of democratic forms of corporatism). The main issue seems to be to win back the ideological initiative from the Right by pointing to the model of an advanced welfare capitalism (IWS) as a realistic and evolutionary alternative. As regards the political feasibility of corporatism in a particular country, the nature of capital, working-class organization and ideology, level of union membership, political structure and traditions are among some of the more important influences. Indeed, it is best to see the IWS as *one* possible (and potentially successful) response to the current crisis among others. It may not suit all countries and diversity of national solutions and responses may not be a bad thing after all, provided it is based on popular consent.

It is likely that those of us who live under welfare capitalism of one sort or another will continue to live in similar regimes in the foreseable future. The Right is unlikely to succeed in winding down the welfare state and returning us to the pristine state of *laissez-faire* capitalism. (Right-wing authoritarianism cannot however the ruled out.) The Left is equally unlikely to usher in a really socialist regime which would spell the end of welfare capitalism. That being the case we need to understand this hybrid of democratic-welfare-capitalism as best we can. In this task of comprehension the insights of the various intellectual orientations examined in the earlier chapters can be used selectively without, as it were, having to throw in one's lot with any one of them. This is the position adopted here. And it seems to fit the normative position outlined above, which is something of the order of Centre-Left. From such a vantage point one can look at both extremes and perhaps borrow from them whatever suits one's analytical and normative purpose. Clearly, it would help a great deal if a new Marx or Keynes were to appear and so dezzle us with his (her?) brilliance that we drop our ifs and buts and follow wherever he (she?) decrees. But what happens in the meanwhile?

One thing is clear, facile sociological theories of modernisation, industrialism and convergence, piecemeal social engineering and interventionism stand discredited to a greater or lesser extend. New orientations are needed. Not, let us be clear, because some new approach will finally (!) reveal the truth to us but simply because social throught—or social science it is it preferred—is a part of our attempt to comprehend and to act on the basis of that comprehension. However unreliable a guide social thought may be we cannot do without it. Whether we like it or not, judgements have to be made and decisions arrived at. And it is better to make these in terms of ideas and beliefs that are explicit, coherent and open to public scrutiny. That, in short, is what social theory is about. But what kind of theory?

Social welfare and social expenditure institutions, on a scale on which they now exist in western countries, are a post-war phenomenon unprecedented in western history. Their relationship with the rest of the social structure, in particular the interaction between the economy, the polity and the welfare sector, needs to be understood far more adequately than is the case at present. Some form of a sociology (or, if it is preferred, political economy) of the welfare state is needed to underpin the practical, social problem focussed studies of welfare. The latter have largely served the function of handmaiden to the welfare state. More often than not this social engineering approach has been concerned with theories and concepts related to the practice of social welfare. What we also need is a structural analysis of the welfare state. Not simply forms of social analysis for the welfare state but also social analysis *of* the welfare state seen as a part of the social system. In order to do this adequately, something along these lines seems to me to be necessary.

One, it is necessary to specify the nature of western economies clearly. It is no use pretending, for example, that capitalism does not exist and what we have is an industrial or post-industrial economy. This way of conflating the economy with the level of technology so that the distinctive features of the former disappear will simply not do. Nor will it do to take capitalist market economy entirely for granted and thus assume it out of the analysis as the social administration approach has often tended to do. What is of particular importance is to recognize capitalism as a system of production (and not just distribution) with all its 'virtues' and 'vices'. For there is a strong tendency among Left Fabians and others to see capitalism, when it is so identified, as largely a system of property and class privilege—in short as a structure of distribution of life-chances. This tendency to isolate the social (i.e., distribution) from the economic (i.e., production) must be overcome if the nature of welfare capitalism is to be understood properly. Two, a systemic approach to the analysis of the welfare state must be adopted. In short, reformism and piecemeal social engineering must be situated within the context of a social system. This would allow us to explore the relationship between the institution of social welfare and the other major institutional orders (e.g., the market economy and the plural polity). The relationship between the economic and the social (e.g., wages, employment, social expenditure, subsidy) could thus be explored systematically. Institutions would be analysed both in terms of their value implications as well as functional (or dysfunctional) implications for other institutions. Above all, the 'parts' (e.g., the institutions of welfare) must be seen in relation to some conception of the social structure as a 'whole'. Three, and this is related to the previous point, the analysis of social policy needs to straddle the institutional and group perspectives. In an unrecognized, *ad hoc* way policy analysis does utilise both these perspectives. But the connection between these two aspects of social reality—between system and social integration—and its importance needs to be grasped more firmly and incorporated into analysis more explicitly. It is of course the Marxist perspective on the welfare state that recognizes the relationship between the institutional contradictions of capitalism (e.g., declining profits) and the class struggle (e.g., full employment and wage militancy) most clearly. The corporatist approach, in a sense, turns Marxism on its head in recognizing that in order to integrate the institutional level successfully (social welfare and market economy), it is necessary to harmonise group relationships (some degree of working consensus between workers and employers). Seen from another angle, to combine the institutional and group levels of analysis is to emphasise that the welfare state is both about functions (providing services, meeting needs, etc.) as well as group interests and conflicts. It has become increasingly clear that the study of social welfare institutions (e.g., the National Health Service) cannot be isolated from the study of bureaucracy and the professions as interest groups. Lastly, those of us who live in the English-speaking world need to look at the countries of Western Europe, notably Sweden and Austria, rather more closely than we have done in the past. At the close of the nineteenth century, English-speaking countries, (Britain, and to a lesser extent the United States) had turned increasingly to the Bismarckian welfare state of Germany (Lloyed George's insurance scheme was largely inpirated by the German example) to add a social dimension to *laissez-faire* capitalism. Indeed, while jealous of their national traditions and institutions western countries have also borrowed freely from each other and adapted 'foreign' elements to suit domestic circumstances. After a long interlude in which the Keynes-Beveridge model (the latter element somewhat modified) seemed adequate for welfare capitalism the time seems to have come once again for shopping around in the market place of ideas and institutions.

Post-war Britain, which used to be a positive model of the welfare state, at least for English-speaking countries, has increasingly turned into its very opposite. Britain's steady economic decline, her relative decline as a welfare spender (though the National Health Service may be providing good value for money) and her inability to solve economic and institutional problems has made the British welfare state appear increasingly unimaginative, unimovative and one the defensive. It has proved an easy target of the Right which has used it as a scapegoat for most, if not all, of Britain's ills.

spender (though the National Health Service may be providing good value for money) and her inability to solve economic and institutional problems has made the British welfare state appear increasingly unimaginative, unimovative and one the defensive. It has proved an easy target of the Right which has used it as a scapegoat for most, if not all, of Britain's ills.

Fabians reformism with its method of piecemeal social engineering (unlike the holistic approach more prevalent in Western Europe) has tended to isolate social welfare and its study from the wider structures of society. Moreover, reformist concerns have not been conductive to cross-national analysis. In the coming years therefore cross-national studies focussed on the institutions and practices (at the macro- or societal level) of relevant European as well as English-speaking countries need to be developed.

No doubt, perceptive students of British political economy have been looking at Europe for several decades now. British membership of the EEC has also encouraged cross-national studies of poverty, and the like. Nonetheless, the current impasse of welfare capitalism and the 'ascendancy' of neo-conservatism in Britain and the United States, the two major English speaking countries, makes it an urgent task to look for ways of responding to the crisis other than monetarism and orthodox laborism. For one thing is certain: Keynes is dead and we now live in the post-Keynesian era. Marx, it is true, is alive and well but it appears cannot help—at least not much. Marx and Marxism also waned gradually.

In the 21st century, an era of globalisation and WTO, 'Social Welfare' is losing conventional meaning and ground.

3

Social Welfare: Nature and Scope

Social welfare is a way of thinking. It is a society's collective image of its responsibility to its own members. This image can be very limited or very inclusive in terms of *what groups* will be helped, and *which* of *their needs* will be addressed. For example, people often see children as needing society's assistance because they are so vulnerable. Yet physically limited adults are less frequently helped in spite of their sometimes considerable vulnerability. Even children receive variable aid. Because the family has been assigned major responsibility for the care of its offspring, children raised in families with little income or little affection may be exposed to grave physical and emotional stresses.

One of the results of unemployment, a economic problem, has been the creation of an increasing tide of homeless Americans, people who have lost their jobs and homes and who crisscross the country seeking work. These people, sometimes called the "new poor" or "new homeless," are people who have generally been employed and stable, but who are now desperately searching for economic opportunities to replace those that have evaporated in their home communities due to the economic recession (Dusky, 1983; Peterson, 1982). This phenomenon is not unlike what happened in the Great Depression of the 1930s. What is very different about those forced out of work and even out of their homes and communities in 1982 compared to 1932 is the societal response to their need. Whereas the Depression resulted in the passage of the Social Security Act, this society's most comprehensive effort to provide for the needs of its citizens, the "new poor" in 1982 encountered a very different societal response.

> Phoenix does not welcome transients. At one point it closed all its public shelters and only recently, under pressure, allowed one to open. The city also passed a law making it a misdemeanor to lie down in public. It has declared garbage public property, making it illegal to pick through it, and there have been proposals to spray the dumpsters with kerosene, making the refuse inedible, to discourage foraging (Peterson, 1982).

It is these differences in a society's approach to meeting the needs of its members that defines the nature of social welfare in that society.

Societies like our own are multi-cultural and characterised by substantial socio-economic differences among various groups (called social classes). How, then, can we speak of a "collective image" about social welfare? Like any other aspect of societal decision making, social welfare decisions are made for the society as a whole by means of its political and economic structures. In a democratic society, all groups are thought to have representation in these structures through the voting process. This assumption has always represented more of an ideal than a reality. Racial and cultural minority groups and the poor have had less access to the political process, as a result of a complex interplay of many factors. These factors include exclusion from education, which makes it difficult to be aware of issues; language differences; laws that discriminated against certain groups (especially women and minorities of color) at the voting booth; economic manipulation of workers by employers, which is intended to influence voting; psychological terror tactics to intimidate voters; and the use of media to confuse and control people's votes.

As a result, decisions about social welfare do not always reflect accurately the needs of those who are most helpless. Bell (1983) is the most recent of a long line of scholars who have pointed out that social welfare can be used to help the well-to-do as well as (or instead of) the needy. The manifest function of social welfare is the one that is highly visible and intended by most people in society—to help the needy. However, there are also latent functions that are less visible and that serve the special needs of powerful groups that influence societal decision making. These functions include: substantial benefits for groups such as veterans to reward them for having done what they were told to do in spite of high risks; tax benefits to big businesses and wealthy individuals, to maintain the basic structure of capitalism; poverty-level benefits for the unemployed in order to pressure them into whatever jobs are available, even those with low and exploitative wages; and the maintenance of social welfare programmes that provide minimal income rather than full employment, which would require more planning and cooperation by the business sector.

We can see, then, that social welfare is concerned with far more than the needy. It is integrated into the basic structure of society in ways that influence the lives of all groups—the rich and the poor, minorities and those in power. This point is explored more fully in previous chapters. For now, we will return to the manifest function of social welfare— the primary focus of this book—because it allows us to describe and understand the structure of services that primarily address the needs of those who lack resources. The latent functions of social welfare are equally important, but they are best explored in courses that focus on social policy, organizational behavior, and political and economic decision making.

Social Welfare: Scope and Function

Social welfare's most obvious manifest function in society is to *help*. People may need help in many areas of their lives. Some are very obvious and dramatic—a person who has had a heart attack, someone who has been the victim of a violent crime, a person threatening to commit suicide, or a physically handicapped person who is having difficulty moving about because of obstacles like steps or unlighted areas, Sometimes people need help for problems in their lives that are less obvious to outsiders—women who live in beautiful suburban homes who have become alcoholic because of a sense of isolation and lack of importance; members of minority groups experiencing subtle discrimination, which prevents them from getting satisfying employment; or children who are made to feel worthless by their families. There are many ways in which people can be in need, and social welfare services exist to help in these situations.

Social welfare services do not exist only for specific individuals, however. Communities may also be having problems, such as deteriorated housing, the loss of jobs, inadequate roads or mass transportation, poor schools, and so on. People live in groups other than communities, too, and problems can exist in them, as well. Workers may feel exploited by their bosses, family members may experience severe tension because of problematic marital and parent-child relationships, residents of a home for the elderly may be abused by the staff, or renters in an apartment building may feel that services are inadequate. In these cases, social welfare services are also appropriate, although they are focused toward *groups* of people rather than specific individuals. Naturally, individuals ultimately benefit from group-focused services. Nevertheless, providing services to groups is often more effective and efficient than providing them individual by individual. Exhibit 2 in the "Reflections on Social Welfare" section at the end of the chapter illustrates the interplay between the individual, group, community, and even societal levels in the creation of needs for which social welfare services are helpful.

Identifying Needs

We have already seen that some needs are more obvious than others. Yet a society can only attempt to meet those needs that it knows exist and that it has decided to address, so the question of how needs become identified is an important one. Specifically, identifying needs involves at least four elements:

What Needs Exist?

Needs range from the very personal, to problems in interaction among people, to community and society needs. A commonly made distinction is between personal problems and public issues. If two people are getting a divorce, it is a personal problem, but if close to half of the marriages in society are ending in divorce, it is a public issue. In other words, the creation of a comprehensive social welfare system depends on a comprehensive definition of needs.

Who Has Needs?

Different groups usually have different needs. This fact results from different groups having had different experiences in the societal structure, resulting in different goals, different resources, and different obstacles. All groups interact in one way or another, however, so a comprehensive social welfare system depends on the needs of all groups being identified. Although the needs of the coal miners of Appalachia may seem far removed from the needs of urban San Franciscans, their mutual dependence on adequate energy and social order creates a level of interdependence.

The Frequency, Severity, and Impact of Needs

Some needs result from rare unanticipated events, such as floods or earthquakes. Others are chronic, such as some types of physical limitations. Some create minor disruptions in behavior, such as those we experience when our car breaks down and we have no transportation. Others may prevent us from functioning at all, as is the case with severe mental illness. Here again, the point is that needs occur in many different forms, affect different people differently, and have varying impacts on people and situations. Our goal is to try to identify all of them and to build a social welfare structure that offers help in all cases.

Who Defines the Needs?

Very often, persons who are actually experiencing needs are unable to interpret them to others. This may be because they lack the ability to effectively articulate their needs (children are an example), or because they are denied access to channels through which they can communicate with others. The poor, for example, are generally too powerless and fragmented to gain access to the mass media. As a result, the needs of one group are often interpreted and expressed by others— adults "know" what children need, and social researchers frequently define needs based on their research (Valle and Mendoza, 1978). Consequently, *who* defines needs is sometimes an important determinant of *what* needs are expressed and *how* they are expressed.

Given the necessity of defining needs in order to create social welfare services, how might we go about this task in an orderly way? Two major strategies have been used:

Research

One strategy is to use highly codified and systematised methods of scientific research to study behavior and identify need. Two approaches are possible: objective and subjective (Zimbalist, 1977). An *objective research approach* uses systematically collected data to identify needs and levels of need. A good example is the concept of a poverty level.

One way to try to decide whether poverty exists, and how severe the need is, is to set a base income level below which it is assumed that people will not have adequate financial resources to meet their minimal living needs. Such levels are calculated by the government on the basis of the percentage of their income that low- income people spend on food. In 1983, this official governmentally defined poverty level was $9,900 for a family of four or $4,860 for a person living alone (*Washington Social Legislation Bulletin,* 1983). One can then measure people's incomes and say that those whose income falls below the poverty line are living in poverty—regardless of whether these people actually feel poverty-stricken.

A second approach is more subjective. Instead of defining a fixed income level, one can ask people to define for themselves what they feel their needs are. Notice, however, that both approaches include the orderly, systematic collection and analysis of information. Even when asking people to evaluate their own situation and its meaning for them, this task is done systematically, and all the responses are analysed using the same methods. In general, objective research methods have tended to be more popular. It tends to be easier to collect objective data and to apply set standards to all, especially when dealing with large numbers of people. Nevertheless, we know that this method ignores many of the subtle cultural and life-style differences that exist—and which are often very important (Fitzgerald, 1983). Unfortunately, some things are not easily objectified, and no matter how convenient the objective method may be, the subjective approach remains an important and useful alternative research strategy.

Practice Feedback

Another important source of information about needs is the daily practice of social welfare professionals. In the course of their work, they are exposed to people, structures, and situations. They have the opportunity to experience firsthand the realities of the lives of a wide range of people. They see where needs are not being adequately met or are being ignored entirely, or where services are being poorly delivered. Thus it is possible for professional helping people to systematically collect information from their own practice experiences and to organize such information so that it is helpful to those with decisionmaking reponsibility. Being a helping person is not just working with people in need—it is also helping to identify needs and to influence those with decision-making responsibility to be more aware of, and sensitive to, existing needs. Unless this task is accomplished, the daily interactions with people seeking help may be frustrated by inadequate resources.

In spite of increasingly sophisticated methods for obtaining information about needs, we know that many needs continue to be ignored. There are several reasons for this:

1. *Many needs are difficult to locate because they are invisible.* Invisibility may be of many kinds. Geographical isolation characterises many rural areas, as well as many economically depressed areas in cities. As most people go about their daily affairs, they never have occasion to see the realities of urban slum life and never travel through the most economically depressed rural areas (modern high-speed expressways have increased this type of avoidance). As a result, it is easy to forget that these areas exist, often with desperate needs within them. A second kind of invisibility lies in needs that are the result of interpersonal behaviors that occur in private. This factor contributes to making child-abuse needs so difficult to identify, for example. It usually occurs in the home, where it is invisible to outsiders. Unless there are physical symptoms visible to people who see the child outside the home, it is difficult to detect. In addition, many forms of child abuse are mental

rather than physical and may be even more difficult to spot.

A third factor making needs difficult to locate is that many personal problems are either not recognised or are denied by the person who has them. Several types of physical and physically related problems are not easily identified, even by health professionals. It is common for people to have such problems and never realise it, and thus they never have occasion to make their needs known. Other problems may be recognised but may be denied because of fear or embarrassment. A woman who is abused by her husband may be afraid to report her need for help because she fears her husband will abuse her even more. A person who is losing the ability to hear may be embarrassed to admit to others that this is happening. In either case, it is difficult for outsiders to spot the problem and identify the need to the appropriate people and agencies. A final difficulty in location results from many people with needs being inarticulate and disenfranchised. Poor people are often inadequately educated and unable to read about the availability of services or to manage to get to available resources. Minority people may be so intimidated that they are reluctant to make their needs known or to participate in service structures. If these needs are not visible to helping people in other ways, these people's inability to identify their needs to others may result in these needs not being identified and therefore ignored.

2. *Some needs are difficult to identify because people find them difficult to accept.* Many needs are unpleasant, and one way to deal with them is to deny their existence. They may be messy or depressing, or they may violate societal values. The resulting response is frequently righteous indignation rather than attempts to carefully identify the need and then try to meet it. The elderly are often seen as depressing, or sometimes as scatterbrained, disheveled, and smelly. Rather than meet their needs for adequate

stimulation, physical care, and social acceptance, they may be shunted off to minimal care homes where they can be ignored. An even more dramatic example is provided in Exhibit 1 in the "Reflections on Social Welfare" section at the end of the chapter. This tragic account of the life and death of a preteenage prostitute exemplifies the way in which a desperate but morally offensive need can be ignored and hidden.

3. *Many needs are not identified* because *it is impossible to gain agreement on how to define them.* Different groups frequently have different definitions of problematic behavior, which may result from value differences that affect perceptions about what is appropriate, acceptable, or important behavior. Minority groups may define confrontation as a necessary and legitimate way to deal with oppression and discrimination; non-minority group members may define such behavior as disruptive and illegal. Women may define consciousness raising as their first priority to insure their personal integrity; men may define child rearing as a higher priority for women than their development of a personal sense of well-being.

Another source of definitional differences can result from vested interests. Groups tend to define situations in ways that maximise their own self-interests and resist definitions that will result in their own loss of power or resources. Therefore, although corporations may define assembly lines as worthwhile contributors to economic progress for everyone, workers may see them as dehumanising and demoralising. As long as groups have the ability to resist each other's definitions of situations, it is unlikely that a consensus will be reached about needs. On the other hand, sometimes precisely this dissensus helps people to realise the diversity of needs that exist.

Meeting Needs Through Social Welfare

Social welfare scholars have developed various

frameworks for understanding human needs. One of the best known is Charlotte Towle's concept of *common human needs* (1952) in which she noted that there are basic needs shared by all for food, shelter, affection, and productive activity. More recently, the Southern Regional Education Board (SREB) developed a similar but more fully described perspective (McPheeters and Ryan, 1971). Obviously the perspective on needs adopted by social welfare professionals may vary in type or degree from that used by others. Business people might have different views about the desirability of financial security versus risk, and politicians might have their own definitions of what families or communities ought to look like. These differences reflect their own interests and are based on their own experiences. The view of social welfare scholars is not necessarily "better," but it does reflect data collected from a wide range of research projects and practice experiences. As a result, it is likely to more accurately reflect the real experiences of most people than data coming only from personal experience and filtered through self-interest. Let us now look at needs and the role for social welfare in meeting them as conceptualised by SREB.

Health

Physical and mental well-being is basic to the ability of people to function effectively. Good health is in part a developmental process that results from genetic inheritance and an environment that supports the attainment of genetic potential. Genetic inheritance is itself influenced by conditions during gestation, such as ingestion of alcohol and other drugs, cigarette smoking, adequate nutrition, and stress. After birth, many environmental conditions affect health, such as pollution, nutrition, stress, and exposure to life-threatening conditions like natural disasters, wars, and accidents. Social welfare is, therefore, concerned with factors that affect the environment as well as those that more directly provide services for people with physical or mental health needs. As a result, programmes of the Environmental Protection Agency and the National Centers for Disease Control are as important as services provided by doctors, hospitals, mental hospitals, and therapists.

Financial Security

In a market economy such as our own, access to financial resources is basic to one's well-being. For most people, money is obtained by working. Social welfare programmes, therefore, are often concerned with employment and training for employment. However, they also attempt to meet the needs of those who cannot work because of parenting responsibilities, infirmity, handicaps, lack of education, and so on.

Interpersonal Integrity

An individual's sense of well-being makes it possible to relate comfortably and effectively to others. Many factors—such as prejudice and discrimination, abusive treatment, lack of opportunities to develop, and genetically determined limitations—may impede a person's sense of self, however. Social welfare programmes help individuals better understand themselves and the conditions under which they live, so that they can better use the resources available to them. Programmes also exist to change social conditions that disadvantage people and destroy their sense of self-worth. Programmes of the Civil Rights Commission are examples.

Family Integrity

The family has traditionally been the social unit of most immediate importance to individuals. Born into families, people depend on them for nurturance, physical care, and socialisation. As adults, they create new families to provide for affection, emotional support, and child rearing. Increasingly, the concept of the family has been extended to include a wide range of committed relationships in which family-like interaction occurs, even though the people involved are not married or related through blood ties. Relationships among gay men or lesbian women are often of this sort, as are such patterns as single parenthood, communal living among the elderly, and group homes for runaways, battered spouses, and those with a history of mental illness, retardation, or crime. Because stable and nurturing social relationships are so important to the well-being of humans, families and family-like ties have generally been strongly supported in the social welfare system. A wide variety of economic programmes, homemaker services, child-care arrangements, counseling resources, housing facilities, and health-care programmes exist to support the family and family-like arrangements.

Community Integrity

Communities provide geographical units within which our social relationships occur. The structure of our government and economic system relies on communities for the provision of a wide range of resources and services in order to make them more accessible to community residents. Social welfare thus focuses many services—such as schooling, recreation, police services, economic programmes, health care, and housing--in communities.

Needs and Services

Crisis Needs & Curative Services

In each of the areas just described, the level of service needed will vary by degree and type of need. Sometimes people are in crisis, a severe and often sudden period of need. Providing intensive services may resolve the crisis, after which few services are needed. A natural catastrophe, such as a flood or earthquake, or the sudden onset of an illness, are examples. Here social welfare services are curative in their focus, attempting to deal with an already-existing problem.

Rehabilitative Services

Needs may instead be chronic, whether severe or relatively minor. People living in economically depressed geographical areas, such as Appalachia or parts of the rural South, face a marginal existence every day. Social welfare services are needed on a regular basis to supplement their meager incomes and to help people cope with the debilitating effects of lack of opportunity and lack of hope. Ideally, such services attempt to be *rehabilitative* in that they seek to find long-term solutions to the problems. Community development programmes, job-training programmes, and parent-education programmes are all examples of efforts to prepare people and communities to solve long-term problems.

Supportive Services

Some problems, however, are not completely solvable. People suffering from genetic brain damage, for example, will never be able to have that damage eliminated, at least not given our present level of knowledge about human physiology. In these cases, services can only be *supportive,* helping people to achieve the best possible life within the limitations they face.

Preventive Services

Perhaps the most efficient way of providing social welfare services is *preventive.* We know enough about the functioning of individuals, groups, and social structures to know what kinds of situations will create problems. For example, we know that war and economic chaos will produce migration, yet our immigration policy has been inconsistent and inadequate to handle people seeking refuge from events in Cuba, Haiti, and Central America. We know that physical abuse leads to psychological problems, yet we have not created adequate programmes to prevent child and spouse abuse, to say nothing of the growing problems of "granny bashing," the abuse of the elderly. We also know that poverty is a physically and emotionally crippling condition for people and communities, yet we often continue to label it as a personal failing rather than a social problem. A preventive approach seeks to provide services that avoid the problems that otherwise have to be handled with either rehabilitative, curative, or supportive services (Prevention Report, 1982).

What is Social Welfare?

Now we are ready to consider a definition of social welfare. William Robson (1976) wrote:

> The rights of Citizens to the benefits of the welfare state must be accompanied by reciprocal duties. The need for complementary rights and obligations is particularly great in the fields of work, law and order, education, and the social services.

His statement expresses well the fact that society exists to meet the needs of its members as they are collectively defined and understood at any particular time, and recognising that they change over time. It also emphasises that a system of welfare services depends on the willingness of people to support it—to believe it is worthwhile, to contribute resources for it, to use its benefits in a responsible way, and to support public policy that makes a social welfare structure possible. Social welfare, therefore, seeks to balance the collective good with individual needs and desires. Finding the point at which this balance is best achieved is an ongoing activity in society since, as we have already seen, different groups have different ideas about where the balance should be.

Social welfare rests on societal definitions of the good and desirable, which in turn are embedded in societal values. These evolve over time and sometimes vary between groups in society. Keith-Lucas (1972) discusses three value bases commonly used in United States society: the capitalist-puritan, the humanist-positivist-utopian, and the Judeo-Christian. A summary of his analysis of the tenets of each and their implications for social-welfare beliefs and values is presented in Exhibit 3 in the "Reflections on Social Welfare" section at the end of the chapter. From these three value systems, a set of principles has emerged that are generally used in decision making about social welfare issues:

1. People should be free to choose (including the choice of failure).
2. Individuals matter, and their interests cannot be wholly subjected to those of the community.
3. People have neither the right nor the ability to judge others in terms of what they deserve.
4. Helping people find their own way is better than controlling them.
5. Feelings and personal relationships matter.
6. People should be treated like human beings, not as objects.

We have seen earlier, however, that various latent functions of social welfare may influence decision making in ways that violate some of these principles. For example, many social welfare programmes do control people in order to create captive populations of workers, children, or the elderly. Access to such groups may be of great benefit to businesses as well as government bureaucracies.

What, then, is social welfare? It can be defined most succinctly as *improving social functioning and minimising suffering through a system of socially approved financial and social services at all levels in the* social *structure*. This definition highlights three especially important characteristics of social welfare.

1. The phrase "improving social functioning and minimising suffering" entails problem solving as well as developmental activities. As people seek to attain their life goals, they frequently confront obstacles that can be conceptualised as problems to be solved. However, the attainment of goals also involves using resources effectively. Therefore, social welfare focuses on helping people to better use their own and societal resources and does not deal only with situations in which problems exist.

2. Saying that social welfare rests on "a system of socially approved..." means that there can be no social welfare unless the society approves of such activities. Social groups exist and function because of agreed-upon types of interaction. In that sense, any group, small or large, is constantly renegotiating or reaffirming the collective decisions that created and maintain (or change) it. This process is also true of social welfare activities. They exist because they have been considered desirable, and their form is always dependent on the wishes of the groups of people involved, ranging from societal institutions to the smallest person-to-person interaction. As these wishes change, the mandate of social welfare changes. For example, public education for everyone is considered a basic part of our current social welfare institutional structure, but this was not true in the early history of this society.

3. The phrase "services at all levels in the social structure" suggests that social welfare activities are built into the fabric of society. Where and how they exist in society is very much part of the process of group definition and negotiation. Many social welfare activities are informally provided through such structures as the family and peer groups. Others are highly formalised, existing in structures specifically created for that purpose. But whether formal or informal, all are woven into the social structure.

It is these characteristics of social welfare—purpose, social mandate, and social structure—that enable us to talk about social welfare as a social institution. This enables us to understand social welfare as we would any other social institution: the family, education, religion, the economic institution, and the political institution. The institutional perspective will also provide a framework for the rest of the book. We will systematically examine the purposes of social welfare, its value and knowledge base, the way specific services and specific helping professions are organized around the purposes of social welfare, and the way social welfare interacts with other social institutions. In previous chapters, we begin with service-delivery structures.

Summary

This chapter has introduced you to the concept of social welfare. We have seen that it is society's response to human need. Through social welfare, society attempts to respond to needs that have been acknowledged as significant and for which society has some responsibility. Society sometimes accepts responsibility because it recognises that people are suffering and need help. At other times, it responds because not to respond would risk social chaos. Whatever the reason for the response, social welfare entails a very wide range of services provided by many different helping professions. In the next chapter, we will look more closely at the way that social welfare services are organized.

REFLECTIONS ON SOCIAL WELFARE

The three exhibits in this section explore in more depth three aspects of social welfare raised in this chapter. The first addresses needs and how they get identified. The second also relates to needs, but looks at the differences in manifest and latent definitions of needs. The third exhibit goes into the value bases of social welfare in some depth.

Exhibit 1— Hurting by Helping

Exhibit 2—The Difficulty of Identifying Needs

Exhibit 3—Value Systems Underlying Social Welfare's Societal Mandate

EXHIBIT 1

HURTING BY HELPING

American society has traditionally *been protective of women in the sense of defining female roles as primarily homebound and subservient to men. The women's movement has successfully shown the latent functions of these role definitions—preserving male dominance, limiting opportunities for women, and reducing the self-esteem of many women. These are problems that crosscut many levels of behavior. Many women experience personal difficulties: relationships between family members are affected; the workplace is influenced; and the whole spectrum of women's activities in the social structure is shaken. This exhibit describes social welfare's response* to *several of these levels. It also illustrates how closely social welfare is tied to the other major institutions of society, such as the family, the political system, the economic structure, and so on.*

Many people assume that as women increasingly abandon their traditional roles, previously male domains such as burglary, larceny, and auto theft are among those infiltrated by women. Thus they connect women's rights with a rise in the number of female criminals.

In fact, the relationship of sex roles to crime is touch more complicated. For example, drug offenses account for the most precipitous rise in arrests of young women, having increased 5,375 per cent between 1960 and 1975. A study of police handling of suspected drug users showed that women who cried, blamed their boyfriends, and otherwise acted in stereotypic ways during raids frequently convinced the police not to arrest them. Those young women who displayed "male" traits of hostility and aggression, however, were often arrested and processed.

Thus, the increase in women charged with crimes may reflect increased criminal activity, or it may result from more aggressive behavior on the part of women apprehended—or both.

These ambiguities, however, do not plague the juvenile justice system. There, young women and girls come in contact with police and the courts for a variety of reasons, and, sooner or later, their sex counts against them.

Three broad categories of youths find themselves involved in the juvenile justice system. Some are judged delinquent; some are deemed to be improperly cared for at home, or have no homes; and some are charged with "status offenses"—acts that, if performed by adults, would not be considered crimes. The word substituted for "conviction" in juvenile cases is adjudication."

Between 70 and 85 per cent of adjudicated girls in detention are status offenders, compared to a detention rate for boys charged with 'children's crimes" of less than 20 per cent.

Status offenses range from school truancy and running away to refusal to do household chores, use of "vile language," and promiscuity. An informal survey of child advocates throughout the country yielded only one instance of a boy institutionalised for sexual promiscuity, while sexuality appeared to be the underlying cause of most female referrals, even where not directly cited.

Undesirable boyfriends, staying out after curfew, wanting to get married and "incorrigibility" were among the complaints parents take to the courts along with their daughters. Pregnancy, fornication, or an abortion without parental consent falls more obviously under the category of promiscuity, but "truancy and incorrigibility," according to Mary Kaaren Jolly, staff director of the Senate Subcommittee on the Constitution, hare often nothing but buffer charges for promiscuity in girls—or the court's fear of future promiscuity." At home, in school, and throughout the many stages of the juvenile justice system, female sexuality evokes patronising and/or biased treatment.

The Double Standard Revisited

Carol, 13, is now enrolled in a feminist counseling programme. She was institutionalised due to her parents' double standard rot male and female sexuality. "Boys do have it better," she says, "comparing my life to my brother's. I got sent up to an institution because I was messing around. He went out and got some girl pregnant. He was only 17 and he never got into any kind of trouble for it, She did, but he didn't."

When she has children of her own, Carol hopes they are boys:

It's *just a hassle to raise girls because you've got* to *worry if they get caught having sex, then of course it's the girl that gets arrested on an unlawful morals charge. What do they do to the guy? Nothing.*

It's just like in the family. If a man's daughter comes home and her hair's all messed up and her shirt's unbuttoned, he calls her a little slut. But if a boy comes home and tells his dad he made it with someone tonight, he says, "Oh! that's good. That's my son." *That's just how it is.*

Treatment of the crime 'of incest provides another example of the double standard. Most often, it is the girl—the victim—who is sent to a foster home while the father stays behind. And children's-rights advocate Kenneth Wooden estimates that 40 per cent of the girls and young women in city and county jails who were picked up as runaways left home after being sexually molested.

Seventeen-year-old Dominica was sexually assaulted by one of her mother's four husbands She ran away from home. Picked up by the police, she was placed on probation and returned home. Dominica left again, and was charged with violating probation. Thus she became a full-fledged delinquent.

For the young woman who engages in sexual intercourse of her own volition, school hardly' offers a more understanding environment than home, should she become pregnant. Many schools suspend pregnant students or encourage them to "voluntarily withdraw.

For the overwhelmingly male-dominated juvenile justice hierarchy, young women's sexuality is "offensive," as spelled out in the following statement made in 1975 by Hunter Hurst, Director of the Juvenile Justice Division of the National Council of Juvenile Court Judges:

The issue is that status *offenses are offenses against* our *values. Girls are seemingly overrepresented as status offenders because we have a strong heritage of being protective towards females in this country. It offends* our *sensibility and our* values *to have a 14-year-old girl engage in sexually promiscuous activity. It's not the way we like to think about females in this country.*

As long as it offends our *values, be sure that the police, or the church or vigilante groups, or somebody is going to do something about it. For me, I would rather that something occur in the court where the rights of the parties can be protected.*

"We play big daddy," confessed another judge.

Carol Zimmerman, Executive Director of the Arizona-based New Directors for Young Women, which compiled the foregoing comments, sees girls caught in a double bind: If they remain in school, they are molded along lines that limit their futures, and if they cut classes or stop going altogether, they can wind up in jail.

A great many young women Out of school drop out because school isn't meeting their needs; because they aren't getting any encouragement, because the attitude is "you don't really need to learn a career, you don't really need to go on and work, you're going to be taken care of, you're going to marry.

They find no reason to stay in school, to attend classes. They drop out—and become part of the juvenile justice system. The courts say, "You're a truant, you're a dropout, I remand you to this-and-this facility."

"Sexism," adds Shirley McKuen of the Research Center on Sex Roles in Education, "is clearly a part of the curriculum in all educational agencies and institutions.". . . .

One important factor in the disproportionate detention rate for girls is that many times their parents refuse to take them home. When it comes time for a court hearing, this parental attitude can prejudice the female youth's chances, as Chesney-Lind points out.

"Children charged with crimes have natural allies in their parents at every step in the judicial process," she writes. But, "Parents of young people charged with status offenses are, themselves, the complainants, and they not only impugn the moral character of their children but frequently refuse to take them home in an attempt to force the court official to retain jurisdiction. Since the determination of good moral character is pivotal in the determination of guilt or innocence in the juvenile justice system, this parental orientation is significant."

A parental attitude toward young female offenders and minors in general is reflected in the 1967 U.S. Supreme Court decision awarding children some rights of due process, but not the same ones from which adults benefit. In re Gault, the Court wrote that "The right of the State, as parens patriae, to deny to the child procedural rights available to his elders was elaborated by the assertions that a child, unlike an adult, has a right not to liberty but to custody."

State intervention is warranted, the Justices voted, when "parents default in effectively performing their custodial functions." When the State does inject itself in a child's life, they continued, "it does not deprive the child of any rights, because he has none."

Two years ago, adults receiving a jury trial stood a 48 per cent chance of conviction; adults facing only a judge were convicted 65 per cent of the time. In juvenile court, the "conviction" rate is a staggering 89 per cent, according to Wally Mlyniec, Director of the Juvenile Justice Clinic of the Georgetown University Law Center in Washington, D. C.

Where young women are concerned, this conviction rate, combined with the "protective" or paternal attitude, portends a high probability for confinement.

Author Kenneth Wooden asserts that female juveniles receive longer sentences than male juveniles, although the girls' crimes are usually less serious. The average term of incarceration for a young man is 9 months, Wooden says, on charges ranging from truancy to rape, while the average period of confinement for young women offenders is one year—33 per cent longer.

"The alleged justifications (for incarceration in secure facilities) may be diverse and not always apparent," Jolly offers, "but the subcommittee has discovered that the application and results are clearly discriminatory."

"The fact that . . . . sexist community norms exist," adds Chesney-Lind, "is no justification for involving agencies of the law in their enforcement, any more than community prejudices would justify judicial racism."

For Judge Lisa Richette of the Court of Common Pleas in Philadelphia, "The offense of most of the young women going before the courts was nonconformity *to* a social model of what is accepted behavior for young girls. The juvenile Courts should no longer act as a legal chastity belt placed around the waists of young women."

EXHIBIT 2

THE DIFFICULTY OF IDENTIFYING NEEDS

In the following account of the life and death of a 12-year-old prostitute, the struggle that people in and out of the social welfare system had in accepting and dealing with the needs being expressed by the young girl involved is evident. Equally evident is the girl's inability to articulate her needs and to find effective social welfare resources to meet them. In the labyrinth streets of Brooklyn and Manhattan—and many other cities—how many similar girls are hidden from view and from help?

The first time Veronica Brunson was arrested she was 11 years old. The charge was prostitution. Before another year passed, the police, unaware of her real age, arrested her 11 mote times for prostitution.

At the age of 12 Veronica was dead—killed in a mysterious plunge last July from the 10th floor of a shabby midtown hotel frequented by pimps.

Veronica's death, which is being investigated as a possible murder, is one more grim crime statistic to the police. But Veronica's life, and her encounters with the city's social service and criminal justice systems in the last year, illustrate the problems and dangers confronting thousands of runaway girls and boys who turn to prostitution to survive alone on the streets of New York.

Six public and private agencies were partly aware of Veronica's difficulties and were supposedly providing aid. But none of the agencies knew her entire history and none intervened quickly enough to rescue her.

"The Brunson case is a classic example of how a kid can float through the entire system without getting any help," said Officer Warren McGinniss of the Police Department's Youth Aid Division, a specialist in runaways. "Even a baby-faced obvious child who claims she is 18 can parade through the entire process—arrest, fingerprinting, arraignment—without anyone asking any questions."

The six agencies—the Department of Social Services, the Board of Education, the Probation Department, the Corporation Counsel's Office, the police, and the Brooklyn Center for Psychotherapy—now cite bureaucratic barriers and communication breakdowns for their failure to act more effectively.

"You can't tell me appropriate intervention couldn't have saved her life," said the Rev. Bruce Ritter, director of Covenant House, a programme assisting runaways. "The juvenile-justice and child-welfare systems in the city are chaotic. Programmes just don't exist and everyone knows it."

Prostitution by 13-, 14- and 15-year-olds posing as older persons is no longer rare, but arrest for prostitution at the age of 11 is believed by vice squad detectives to be the youngest recorded here in decades.

In the summer of 1976, Veronica Brunson was 11, living in a fatherless home with her mother, Emma, who is now 34, and her brothers, Carson, 17, Douglas, 18, and Willie, 19.

Mrs. Brunson, unable to find work in her home state of North Carolina, had moved to Brooklyn when Veronica was 2. The family lived in a neatly kept, three-bedroom apartment in the Housing Authority's Marlboro Houses in Bensonhurst. In addition to their rent, the family received $318 monthly from welfare.

No Sign of Delinquency

By 1976 each of the Brunson boys had been arrested several times and had been in the juvenile courts. In contrast, Veronica, her mother, teachers and friends agreed, was well behaved, with no sign of delinquency....

Pinched for money, Mrs. Brunson said she had made most of Veronica's clothing herself. "I tried to give her everything a little girl could want— clothing, food and some pocket money," Mrs. Brunson said in an interview. "She was a good little girl and if I told her to be home by six, she always was."

The Trouble Begins

At school, Veronica was a poor student. She had been left back once in the elementary grades, and in 1975 she was transferred to a special programme for slow learners at Public School 253 in the Brighton Beach section. Her first year in the programme went reasonably well, according to her teachers, and she was promoted to the sixth grade in June 1976.

Veronica's runaway problem suddenly began in midsummer of 1976, Mrs. Brunson said.

"One evening she came home with an older girl whose name was Diana who she met at Coney Island," Mrs. Brunson recalled. "Diana said she was 18 and wanted Veronica to spend a few days with her over the bridge (in Manhattan). I said no because I didn't think that girl Diana would be a good influence."

Several days later, Mrs. Brunson continued, Veronica

disappeared for the first time, staying away from home for three days. On her return, Veronica told her mother she had stayed with her new friend Diana in Manhattan.

That July, Veronica continued to leave home for two- or three-day periods. Mrs. Brunson said that she had failed to report her daughter to the police as a missing person because Veronica would occasionally telephone her.

When the new school year began in September of 1976, Veronica failed to appear at P.S. 253. Checking into Veronica's absence, Bernard Lew, her guidance counselor, said he was told by her mother that she had been missing for more than a month. Mr. Lew said he urged Mrs. Brunson to contact the police.

First Arrested Last Fall

Police records show that Veronica was reported missing for the first time on September 19, 1976, after the school term had begun, and that her family said she had been missing for six weeks.

One day after the missing person report was filed, Veronica was arrested on a prostitution charge. A plainclothes officer said she had solicited him on West 42nd Street. The 11 -year-old gave the police her real age and identity, and she was released in Mrs. Brunson's custody, pending action by the Family Court, which hears all criminal matters involving children up to the age of 16.

When Veronica returned to P.S. 253 in the autumn of 1976 her teachers and counselors were unaware of the arrest. Nevertheless, all of them said they noticed significant changes in her.

The year before she had dressed inconspicuously, almost shabbily. Now she used facial makeup and wore expensive looking, color-coordinated clothing, jewelry, high-heeled shoes and nylon stockings....

The teachers, who were ignorant of her arrest, were most concerned about her chronic absenteeism, which eventually reached 121 of 180 school days that year.

Mr. Lew said that numerous telephone inquiries by staff members had been made about Veronica's absences. Her mother or brothers usually replied that the girl was ill, the teachers said.

Case Kept Out of Court

In the aftermath of the first arrest, Veronica and her mother were interviewed on October 8 by a Manhattan Family Court probation department officer. At that time, the officer decided that the matter should be kept out of the court, where Veronica could have been declared a "person in need of supervision," and possibly taken from her mother.

Instead, the probation officer, after consulting with child-welfare officials in the Social Services Department, decided that the case could be "adjusted" by sending Veronica for outpatient counseling at the Brooklyn Center for Psychotherapy, a private institution.

Under a policy of "diversion," the Probation Department tries to help youngsters without exposing them to formal court hearings before a judge.

Last autumn, the department, having made no inquiries at Veronica's school, had no inkling of her increasing truancy, her unorthodox dress or conversations with teachers about being recruited by pimps. Satisfied that the girl was getting adequate attention from the Social Services Department and the private psychotherapy center, the department closed her case in December.

"She was Still a Child"

Mr. Knepper said that Veronica had made one of her infrequent visits to his classroom on her 12th birthday,

December 5, because she knew he was planning a party for her.

"She wanted that kind of attention and affection," the teacher said. "Despite all of her supposed sophistication it was obvious that she was still a child who wanted someone to help her." -

With Veronica no longer attending school, Mrs. Brunson and her son, Douglas, said that they were unable to prevent her running from home for brief periods. Mrs. Brunson acknowledged that she "sometimes" failed to report her daughter missing because she was confident of ultimately persuading her to return home and to school.

By May, Veronica was a familiar figure on the "Minnesota strip," a seedy part of Eighth Avenue from 40th to 50th Streets that is favoured by street walkers. On the strip, Veronica, now five feet, two inches tall and weighing 110 pounds was known to other prostitutes as "Shortie" and by her childhood nickname, *'Bay-Bay."*

Police and court records show that between May 7 and July 18 Veronica was arrested 11 times in the midtown area. Usually she was charged with loitering for the purpose of prostitution, the most common misdemeanor used by the police to harass and temporarily remove prostitutes from the Street.

Used Fictitious Names

Either through coaching from a pimp or older prostitutes, Veronica carried no identification and gave the police a fictitious name and address and said she was 18 when arrested. Two of her aliases were Vanessa Brown and Paula Brunscn.

She always pleaded guilty in Criminal Court and often was released after being held overnight at a police station. But for two convictions she was sentenced to a total of 12 days, which she served among adult prisoners in the Women's House of Detention.

Only once during this series of arrests did Veronica reveal her teal identity and age. Police Officer David Olenchalk, who arrested Veronica on May 12 on Eighth Avenue and 46th Street, said she wore a shoulder-length black wig and "easily passed for 18 or 19." While being booked at the Midtown North stationhouse. Veronica abruptly acknowledged her age and asked the police to call her mother.

Released in the custody of her mother, Veronica was referred for a second time to the Family Court. At an interview with a Probation Department Officer on May 20, Veronica disclosed that she had been arrested several times and had been in jail on Rikers Island.

Gerald Hecht, the city's Probation Director, said department files indicated that at the May 20 meeting, Mrs. Brunson "exhibited ambivalence about placement" of Veronica in an institution or a foster home and another interview was scheduled for a month later.

Crucial Postponement

Several hours after the May 20 interview, Veronica, once more using an alias, was arrested on a prostitution charge.

Dr. Judianne Densen-Gerber, a psychiatrist who is president of the Odyssey Institute, a group of private treatment centers for emotionally disturbed children, said that the month-long postponement by the Probation Department may have been crucial for Veronica.

"By admitting she was 12 years old, this child was clearly saying 'Help me, do something for me now.' "Dr. Densen-Gerber asserted, "Time is a critical factor for these children. They can't tolerate delay. It's like telling *a* person who's just had a heart attack to come back to the hospital in a month or."

Veronica failed to appear for her scheduled interview at the Probation Department on June 29. Yet none of the three agencies—Probation, the Corporation Counsel or the Social Services Department—would petition the Family Court to have her picked up as a "person in need of supervision."

With the Family Court proceedings in legal limbo, Veronica remained on the "Minnesota strip," occasionally getting arrested. Her last known arrest occurred on July 18 when she gave her age as 18. Pleading in Criminal Court to a charge of prostitution, she jumped bail rather than serve a 15-day sentence...

"There are two stories on the street about her death," said Lieut. James Gallagher, the commander of the prostitution squad in Manhattan South area. "One that she was thrown out by a pimp and the other that she was having a fight with her pimp and fell out the window while sitting on the ledge."

"It's not unbelievable that a pimp would throw a girl out a window," he continued. "They brutalise girls if they hold back money, get fresh or try to get away from them."

Even in death, Veronica remained forgotten. It took the police nine days to identify her. Her fingerprints, taken in her "adult" arrests, linked her to fictitious names and addresses. Since no fingerprints are taken of children under the age of 16 there was no way of identifying her through Family Court records.

Neither Veronica's family nor any of the agencies reported her missing even after she failed to appear in Family Court. Detectives traced her after learning from Times Square prostitutes that she came from a Brooklyn Housing project and that her family name might be Brunson. . . .

EXHIBIT 3

VALUE SYSTEMS UNDERLYING SOCIAL WELFARE'S SOCIETAL MANDATE

The following discussion of major value systems underlying society's approach to social welfare illustrates the complexity of societal values as well as the difficulty encountered in trying to define a coherent social welfare system based on such opposing values. Yet Keith-Lucas makes it clear that whatever the problems, values form the base upon which our social welfare institution is built. The use of he *rather than less gender-specific terminology is in the original and has not been altered in this excerpt.*

There are in our culture three.. . more or less logical [value] systems. There are variations on these, . . . but for the purposes of this discussion these three may be sufficient.

The first such system, and possibly the most powerful among people as a whole, might be called capitalist-puritan or CP for short. Its basic assumptions might be summarised as follows:

1. Man is responsible for his own success or failure.
2. Human nature is basically evil, but can be overcome by an act of will.
3. Man's primary purpose is the acquisition of material prosperity, which he achieves through hard work.
4. The primary purpose of society is the maintenance of law and order in which this acquisition is possible.
5. The unsuccessful, or deviant, person is not deserving of help, although efforts should be made, up to a point, to rehabilitate him or to spur him to greater efforts on his own behalf.
6. The primary incentives to change are to be found in economic or physical rewards and punishments.

The prevalence of these assumptions needs no emphasis at this time. . . the creed popularly thought of as "American" or even common sense, and as such is part of the heritage of most of us.

So closely have God's favour and worldly success become identified that the successful are thought of as "good" and the unsuccessful as "bad" or inferior. Man takes over what was originally God's prerogatives of judgment and chastisement and those who do not exercise sufficient ambition or will are shamed, exhorted, punished, or left to the workings of the economic system.

Where the CP system of beliefs' is associated with certain other religious values it has strong ethical content, in which success and failure to achieve certain ethical goals is thought of in almost exactly the same way as are material achievement and its opposite. The two systems meet in the matter of work, which has both a material and an ethical value, and in statements applying ethical standards to business enterprise, such as the statement, "Honesty is the best policy," or emphasis on the "service" motive in business.

Almost diametrically opposed to this system is the one that can be called humanist-positivist-utopian, or HPU for short. This is the belief of most social scientists and many liberals, but is also held to some degree by people who profess CP views and by many religious people, despite some inherent contradiction. Summarised, its basic assumptions can be presented as follows:

1. The primary purpose of society is to fulfill man's needs both material and emotional.
2. If man's needs were fulfilled, then he would attain a state that is variously described, according to the vocabulary used by the specific HPU system, as that of goodness, maturity, adjustment, or

productivity, in which most of his and society's problems would be solved.

3. What hampers him from attaining this state is external circumstance, not in general under his individual control. This, in various HPU systems, has been ascribed to lack of education, economic circumstance, his childhood relationships, and his social environment.
4. These circumstances are subject to manipulation by those possessed of sufficient technical and scientific knowledge, using, in general, what is known as "the scientific method," and consequently
5. Man, and society, are ultimately perfectible.

HPU-ism is perhaps difficult to see as a unitary theory, since many of its devotees have relied on a single specific for creating the utopia it envisages. Dewey, for instance, a strong HPU-ist, saw education as the answer, Marx, reform of the economic system; and Freud, the early Freud at least, the removal of repressions.

The sources of this system are to be found in the Enlightenment and its first prophets were Rousseau and Comte. Today. . . many of its assumptions are inherent in modem materialism, at which point it joins hands with and lives somewhat uneasily with CP thought.

Behind, and yet parallel with these two systems is a third, for which it is harder to find a name. Perhaps the best that can be devised is the familiar "Judeo-Christian" tradition. . . .

Yet the system is essentially the system of assumptions about man and the universe that are inherent in the Jewish and Christian Scriptures, and is accepted, at least officially, although not always acted upon by the mainstream religious bodies, Catholic, Protestant, and Jewish.

Summarising its basic assumptions in the same way as we have done for the CP and HPU systems, these might be presented as follows:

1. Man is a created being one of whose major problems is that he acts as if he were not and tries to be autonomous.
2. Man is fallible, but at the same time capable of acts of great courage or unselfishness.
3. The difference between men, in terms of good and bad, is insignificant compared with the standard demanded by their creator, and, as a consequence, man cannot judge his fellow in such terms.
4. Man's greatest good lies in terms of his relationship with his fellows and with his creator.
5. Man is capable of choice, in the "active and willing" sense, but may need help in making his choice.
6. Love is always the ultimate victor over force.

The position of this ethic vis-a-vis the others is a complicated one. In one sense it lies parallel to them and is a viable alternative, or a middle ground, especially in item 2, its recognition of man's simultaneous fallibility and potential. In another, it lies behind them and makes both of them possible. . . .

Probably most people are influenced to some extent by all three of these sets of assumptions. All have some value and it is not so much a matter of saying that one is good and another bad as it is of taking a position nearer or further from one or another extreme. Yet we do need to explore which set of assumptions is more likely to preserve the kind of values we see as important in helping, and which is most compatible with what we can observe in the process of helping as we know it.

Quite obviously the CP position is in general the least likely to lead to help. If man is totally responsible for his own actions, if he can better his condition by an act of will, if he can be induced to change by punishment or reward, then helping becomes a simple matter of us arranging the appropriate rewards and punishments. There is no room for relationships, or concern for another, except in a highly condescending and judgmental way.

This is the view of man that created the workhouse and the pauper's oath, which demands of children in Children's Homes or welfare clients that they work harder and behave better than other people, and which is terrified of any welfare measure that would make the receipt of relief in any way bearable or dignified. It assumes without question that welfare clients will "naturally" lie, cheat, or steal if given the chance, prefer laziness to work, and feign sickness in order to shirk working. And typically it is much more concerned to punish the few who may do such things than help the many who do not.

Yet it is not without some positive features. It does at least recognise that it is the person in trouble who must bear the final responsibility for his own betterment, and as such it has moderated some of the extreme implications of the HPU set of assumptions which, for many helping people, have appeared to supersede it.

In its initial impact on helping theory and practice HPU thought produced a tremendous outpouring of love and understanding. The helped person was freed from the total responsibility he had borne up till then for his own condition. He was no longer a second-class citizen, judged by his fellows. He was valued for his own sake. The particular social science which became the model for helping in the 1930s—analytical psychology—also stressed certain things which, if not strictly HPU—and indeed I shall argue that they are basically Judeo-Christian and not HPU at all—were at least acceptable to those who claimed to be humanists and utopians. These were in general:

1. A habit of looking at problems from the point of view of the helped person rather than from the outside, that is, treating him as subject rather than as object.
2. A sense of man's common vulnerability. There were, and this is one of Freud's greatest contributions to helping, no longer "sick" and "well" people, but people who were in greater or less difficulty with problems that trouble us all.
3. An emphasis on relationship as the principal means of help.
4. At least in the earlier stages a degree of awe in the face of new knowledge of a somewhat mysterious nature. . . .

One of the most important insights of the Judeo-Christian tradition is the nature of man himself. He is neither the evil being of capitalist-puritan belief, nor is he as good as many HPU-ists believe. But it is not so much a matter of steering between an over- and an underestimation of his nature as it is of recognising two different factors in his makeup. The first is his fallibility and the second his ability, in certain circumstances, to work out for himself something somewhat better than his fallibility would suggest. This is far from saying that he has in him a potential which needs only some triggering, or some favourable circumstance, to tap. It means rather that with help, or where he is put to it, or from the depths of despair, he can sometimes transcend his own fallibility. Moreover this ability is found in the most unlikely places. It is often demonstrated by those whom objectively one would be forced to believe are unequipped or incapable. This is the constant surprise one comes up against in helping. Not infrequently it tends to have the air of the miraculous about it.

REFERENCES

Auletta, Ken (1981). The underclass. A three-part series in the November 16, 23, and 30, 1981, issues of *The* New *Yorker* magazine.

Dusky, Lorraine (1983). Detroit's sad voices. *The* New *York Times Magazine.* June 12, 1983.

Perspectives: *The Civil Rights Quarterly.* Published quarterly by the U.S. Commission on Civil Rights, 1121 Vermont Avenue NW, Washington, D.C. 20425.

Robson, William (1976). *Welfare State and Welfare* Society. London: George Allen and Unwin.

Weinberger, Paul, ed. (1974). *Perspectives on Social Welfare.* New York: Macmillan.

4

Social Welfare in a Welfare State

The Welfare State provides the ideal form of a humanitarian and progressive society which seeks to give every individual the minimum standard of subsistence without suppressing personal enterprise; it also tries to bring about redistribution of income by a policy of progressive taxation, without pretending to establish a utopian equality among all its citizens. In a Welfare State, all are assured of adequate help in case of need, which may be due to illness, old age, physical or mental handicap or unemployment. State assistance is given as a right, not as a charity, and no stigma of pauperism attaches to those who receive it.

State participation in social welfare in India has a long and continuous history extending over hundreds of years. The right of the indigent to receive succour is recognized in societies dating back to the Vedic times. It is based on the recognition on the part of the State or community that it had a duty to help its less fortunate members. The expression 'Danam' used in the *Rigveda* originally refers to the booty captured by the victor in a tribal war. This booty belonged to the community as a whole and was usually distributed among all its members. In later years, with the growth of private property, the concept of Danam shed its social meaning and began to connote a personal duty or virtue. According to the *Bhagwad Gita*, Charity can be in the from of direct material aid (Artha) or knowledge (Vidya) or protection against fear (Abhaya); and, in practice, it should take into account the place and time and also the special circumstances of the recipient.

Kautilya's *Arthasastra* makes the king responsible for the care and protection of the helpless, the weak and the aged, and also of the families of deceased soldiers and workers There existed in those days workshops for economically handicapped women. The teachings of Buddha made rulers and laymen alike follow the path of service to their fellow beings. In Asoka's times, various forms of charitable trusts and social service institutions were founded. Social workers, called Gopas, kept records of caste, Gotra, Birth, deaths and marriages of all citizens, and also looked after people in health and illness. Superintendents of liquor and prostitutes were responsible for helping the victims of these social evils. Asoka's concern for the welfare of his subjects is evident from edicts inscribed on rocks and pillars. One of these edicts says: "I am never completely satisfied with my work or my vigilance in carrying out public affairs. I consider the promotion of the people's welfare my highest duty, and its exercise is grounded in work and constant application."

Another rock edict lays down the carious duties of the State officials in promoting human welfare. They are commissioned to work with equal zeal among the soldiers and their chiefs, the ascetics and house-holders, the poor and the aged, and to secure welfare and happiness and release from imprisonment of all those devoted to Dharma. They are also commissioned to work among prisoners, to distribute money among those who have many children, to secure the release of those who were led to crime by others, and to secure pardon for those who were old and infirm.

The impact of Muslim culture and thought on India give a new depth to the concept of charity and social service. Islam enjoins five major duties on its followers, one of which is 'Zakat', meaning charity. The Mughuls had a special governmental department to supervise the administration of charities and endowments.

No doubt, in early days charity was bound up with religion; even today it is not completely separable from it. Religious piety provided the most powerful impulse for social welfare and humanitarian work. The institutions like the joint family system had also something to do with the growth of social welfare.

Then came the British rule. Although a unified and well-knit administration prevailed for about a century and a half, the primary task of the British in India was one of maintaining law and order. Not much was done to improve the lot of the common man. Some welfare activities were, however, undertaken at the provincial or local level. These related to public health, education, industrial labour and promotion and perfection of voluntary organizations. These activities were sporadic and utterly inadequate to meet the need. Special welfare programmes were launched in times of natural calamities such as floods, famine, earthquakes, etc. The work of Christian missionaries in the various parts of the country also resulted in the establishment of welfare institutions based on the Christian ideals of service. But on the whole, the British policy of 'divide and rule' extended to the field of social welfare also. In this connection, the following extract from "Social service in India" edited by Sir Edward Blunt will be found revealing: "Since India presents so great a diversity of physical, economic and sociological features, is it possible to discuss Indian Social Welfare as if India was not manifold but one? Social Welfare is at best a relative term. Its content will differ with the nature of the society and of its environment, but whereas in most countries there will generally be only one society and one environment, in India there are many of both. In other words, is it possible to generalise satisfactorily about 353 millions of people, especially when they are broken up into many heterogeneous units?" Obviously nothing good could come out of a mentality like this.

The dawn of Independence in 1947 witnessed the beginning of an era of intensive developmental activity in the country. The aim was to improve the economic and social conditions of the masses, a majority of whom were leading a sub-standard life under the alien rule. Political freedom is incomplete without freedom from economic and social wants. These wants are many and diverse: some have been always with us; others are the product of the modern age. Illiteracy, dirt, disease, squalor, superstition, ill-health and ill-housing—all these have to be removed from our midst as speedily as our resources and talents permit. With this aim in view, our Constitution enjoins upon the Government to secure a social and economic order based upon the values of freedom and democracy in which "justice, social, economic and political shall inform all the institutions of the national life". The idea of a Welfare State is more fully defined in Article 41 of the Constitution which runs as follows:

"The State shall, within the limits of its economic capacity and development, make effective provision for securing the right to work, to education, and public assistance in case of unemployment, old age, sickness, disablement and other cases of undeserved want."

A little further, Article 46 lays down that "the State shall promote with special care, educational and economic interests of the weaker sections of the people and shall protect them from social injustice and all forms of exploitation". The nation thus is firmly and fully committed to the ideal of a Welfare State.

If it is the duty of the State to secure welfare of the community, what can be the role of Voluntary organizations working in the social welfare field? In this context, it must be pointed out that even in a welfare State, There will be sections of people—victims of various physical, mental, economic or social disabilities—requiring special attention and special programmes to enable them to overcome these disabilities and stand on par with the rest of the community. A blind child, for instance, can benefit only from specialised instruction not generally available in ordinary schools; similarly, a physically handicapped person has to be specially trained to secure gainful employment for himself. The case of deserted women also falls in this category. This is the field for voluntary social welfare organizations to concentrate upon. This can provide services which will enable the weaker and handicapped sections of the community to reach a point where they can draw upon the social service available to the community as a whole.

As pointed out earlier, our social problems are many and varied. Being an underdeveloped country, India would be able to tackle them all only over a period of time. The gap that exists between actual needs of the country and available resources is very wide, and that makes a system of priorities inevitable. This explains the higher priorities that have been assigned to industry and agriculture in our development plans. If the provision allotted for social services or social welfare in the plans is not as much as one would wish it to be, it is not due to the fact that these services are considered of lesser importance. The country's resources are limited, and great care has to be exercised in the utilisation of these resources for the maximum good of the community.

In the First, Second and the Third Five Year Plans, the provision made for social services was Rs. 531 crores (about 14% of the outlay), Rs. 850 crores (18% of the outlay) and Rs. 1,300 cores (about 19% of the outlay) respectively. Similarly, the provision made for social welfare in the three Five Year Plans was Rs. 5 crores (1% of outlay for social services), Rs. 19 crores (2.2%) and Rs. 31 crores

(2.3%) respectively. This, however, does not include the provision made by the State Governments outside the Plans for development of social welfare activities in their respective regions. The programmes included in social welfare for which specific funds have been allotted in the Plans include schemes for the advancement of women, child welfare, youth welfare, rehabilitation of the handicapped, removal of juvenile delinquency, eradication of beggary and vagrancy, propagation of social and moral hygiene, after-care services, welfare of prisoners, research and surveys, and training of welfare personnel.

The task involved in carrying out all these programmes is stupendous and cannot be completed without the help from voluntary organizations. They have done much valuable and pioneering work in this field, and their closest possible collaboration with the Government is absolutely essential. We quote here what the Report on Charitable Trusts published by the British Government in December 1952, says regarding the relation between State and voluntary action in the field of social welfare. "State action and voluntary action" the Report points out, "were not the antithesis of each other, rather they sprang from the same roots, were designed to meet the same needs and had the same motivating force behind them. Indeed, historically, the State action is voluntary action crystallised and made universal. An analysis of public welfare action at any time would reveal mixed motives, some genuinely humanitarian, some inspired by cupidity or self-aggrandizement. But neither in the historical record not in an examination of their motives would there be discovered the making of a fundamental distinction between State action for public welfare and voluntary action for the same purpose." The Report then goes on to say: "We have endeavoured in this brief historical survey to underline our conviction that the same essential desire to improve the lot of one's fellows lies behind both voluntary and State social action." Lord

Beveridge's book on the subject expresses similar ideas, and tells us how co-operation between public and voluntary social welfare organizations has been a feature of British public life.

That the pattern of development in India has been more or less the same could be seen from the First Plan statement that the voluntary agencies must continue to shoulder the major responsibility for organizing social welfare services for some time to come. The Central Social Welfare Board was set up, in August 1953, primarily to coordinate welfare activities in the voluntary sector.

The importance of voluntary agencies is fully recognized. They have a considerable background of experience in the organization and conduct of welfare programmes and can react more quickly to changing social needs than can be expected of official machinery. Also, they are more capable of bringing to their work the 'human touch' that follows from a less formal but equally effective approach. For this reason, they are at a great advantage in securing popular support for their cause and public participation in their programmes.

Therefore, it is realized, voluntary agencies can no longer be associated on a merely advisory basis but must be accepted as joint partners on an equal footing in the framing and implementation of the national plans for social welfare. While it is neither possible nor desirable to demarcate the respective roles of voluntary organizations and the State in the field of social welfare, particularly as their functions are mutually complementary, yet, broadly the official agencies should be required to deal with problems that exist on a very extensive scale and that require resources beyond the reach of voluntary agencies. The State should also be responsible for sponsoring social legislation and for meeting statutory responsibilities that flow from such legislation. Voluntary agencies should be entrusted with the actual execution of programmes in the field and for securing community support and public participation in these programmes. Voluntary organizations should be provided with special assistance by the State for undertaking welfare services in neglected areas, for conducting experimental pilot projects and for organizing research and training programmes. At the same time, the importance of healthy co-operation and coordination between the official and non-official organizations and among voluntary agencies themselves, cannot too well be emphasised in the interest of better development of social welfare programmes in the country.

The results so far achieved may not appear not appear striking and spectacular. There can be no yardstick for measuring the pace of development and success in this sector as it deals with the most complex entity, that is, the human being. Yet, it must be conceded that a good deal of spade work has been done. Today more social welfare programmes are tax-supported than at any one time in the pat. The Welfare State is not built in a day. It is built through hard and honest labour, and there is no short cut to it. In the United Kingdom, it took a full century of intense economic and social activity before a Welfare State could be established. The social security programme of the United States of America and the Scandinavian countries also took time to fully mature. India has just started her march towards the goal of a Welfare State. We have a long way to go, but we are on the right path.

This book sums up the progress so far made in India in the field of social welfare. An attempt has also been made to indicate the position at the beginning of the First Plan period in respect of various schemes in this field. As far as possible, a complete picture of the stage of development attained in these fields under the two Five Year Plans has been presented. Proposals for the Third Plan, both scheme-wise and State-wise, are also included. While reviewing the progress of all social welfare activities undertaken by the Central and State Governments, local bodies and non-official organizations wherever possible, problems peculiar to each field have also been heighlighted and suggestions for overcoming these difficulties given.

It is now generally accepted that social welfare programmes play a vital role in the over-all development of a country. The term "social welfare services" denotes services intended to cater for the special needs of persons and groups who, by reason of some handicap, social, economic, physical or mental, are unable to avail themselves of, or are traditionally denied, the amenities and services provided by the community. In this sense, welfare services are meant to benefit the weaker, dependent or under-privileged sections of the population, like children or the handicapped for example. The beneficiaries of these services may be physically handicapped persons, such as the blind, the deaf or the crippled, socially dependent individuals, like the orphan, the widow or the destitute, mentally retarded persons, economically under-privileged groups such as those living in slum areas and women handicapped by restrictive social traditions or practices. Social welfare services also embrace those special amenities which do not from part of the normal cervices in the spheres of public health, education and medical relief. Examples of such special services are provided by the programmes for the welfare of youth or children. The purpose of these social welfare schemes is to promote the happiness and well-being of such sections of the population as are a special charge on the State under the various provisions of the constitution and under the Directive Principles of State Policy embodied in it. They are intended to pave the way for the establishment of a Welfare State.

From what has been said in the following Chapters, it will be evident that our welfare services have improved vastly since the Constitution came into force, and more especially since the First Five Year Plan was launched. These vast improvements may be attributed to the special organization, namely, the Central Social Welfare Board which was set up during August 1953 to assist in the improvement and development of social activities in the country. The Board, from its inception, by pursuing a dynamic and progressive policy of social welfare, has been mainly responsible for giving a fillip to social welfare programmes in the country, especially in the voluntary sector. Since then the State has, in various ways, strengthened the hands of voluntary organizations doing pioneering work in the field of social welfare. This has led, naturally, to a considerable increase in the tempo of welfare activities. In this advance one notices certain important and significant trends which are portent of a more hopeful future for the needy and the under-privileged.

State's Increasing Role

One of the most significant trends in social welfare during the past ten years has been the increasing responsibility the State has assumed in promoting the well-being of the weaker sections of the community. Under the First and Second Five Year Plans, expenditure on social welfare programmes has been Rs. 3 crores and Rs. 20 crores (including Rs. 1 crore and Rs. 5 crores for youth welfare and other welfare schemes under the Ministry of Education), respectively. In the Third Plan Rs. 31 crores has been provided for social welfare programmes—Rs. 28 crores in the social welfare sector and Rs. 3 crores in the education sector. Again, Rs. 30 crores and Rs. 79 crores were spent during the First and Second Plan periods, respectively, on the welfare of the scheduled castes, scheduled tribes and other backward classes, including the former criminal tribes. Against this, a provision of Rs. 114 crores has been made in the Third Plan. These figures do not include the provision made by State Governments outside the Plans for development of welfare activities. Specific items under the head "Social Welfare" for which specific funds were allotted under both Plan include the promotion of the welfare of women and children, youth welfare, the welfare of the scheduled castes, scheduled tribes and other backward classes. Rehabilitation of the handicapped, elimination of juvenile delinquency, beggary and prostitution.

While the Central Government set up a Central Social Welfare Board fairly early during this period, most state governments established social welfare departments or directorates as also Social Welfare Advisory Boards, and entrusted to them increasing functions. It is true that the picture of the administrative set-up in the first stages was somewhat confusing; but improvements were effected in the light of the invaluable experience gained over the years. Side by side, the State evolved a substantial programme of grants-in-aid to voluntary organiztions. The Central Government execute it through the agency of the Central Social Welfare Board. The programme, which has brought into the fold nearly 6,000 institutions, has been a useful instrument for the promotion of social welfare activities by voluntary organizations on a systematic basis. State Governments have not yet been able to adopt such extensive aid programme, but they too have gone far beyond what they ever attempted before.

Another significant development is the recognition of the role of voluntary organizations and voluntary workers and the encouragement afforded them. In the early days, most of the work in the field of social welfare was carried out by voluntary agencies without help in the shape of regular Government grants. The results obtained were, therefore, uneven. Each organization went its own way. Very few of them either pursued systematic methods or were inspired by long-terms objectives. The measures adopted during 1951-61, however, brought them all together in an effective partnership in schemes which formed part of the national Plan. Many of these organizations were sustained and reinforced by regular grants. They were further encouraged to look upon themselves as equal partners in the combined effort to bring about a Welfare State. By the end of the Second Plan period many of them had attained full maturity and were capable of shouldering executive responsibility; no longer were they content merely with being advisory bodies or with conducting their own modest experiments in a small way. This is perhaps one of the most auspicious developments during this period.

Yet another feature was the planned development of welfare service in rural areas which released a great deal of potential energy and created a feeling of hopeful participation. It was evident at the very start that much of the work had to be concentrated in rural areas which had been grossly neglected in the past. Thus, when Government initiated and sponsored welfare schemes in the villages, the weaker sections of the community soon became active participants and adopted them as their very own. Such popular identification has led to a genuine rural revival. It has demonstrated how villagers can be persuaded to operate programmes of self-help with just a little initial State assistance and a sympathetic understanding of their needs. The vitalising influence of self-confidence is evident in the way land and other contributions have been willingly offered to the many centres of welfare extension projects, which the villagers have come to regard as their own.

Social Welfare Legislation

With social welfare programmes coming increasingly within the purview of the State, the Central Government have facilitated their successful implementation by enacting appropriate legislation. The Suppression of Immoral Traffic in Women and Girls Act of 1956, the Probation of Offenders Act of 1958, the Orphanages and other Charitable Institutions (Supervision and Control) Act of 1960 and the Children Act of 1960 are some of the measures thus passed into law. These Act not only aim at tackling some of the existing social evils and problems, but are also designed to ensure uniformity in the various remedial measures. At the same time, in view of the fact that conditions differ from State of State, rule-making powers under these Acts have been vested in the State Governments. The Central legislation on social welfare services to ensure uniformity in services are programmes. A number of State Governments did in the past adopt such legislation, but the laws often remained unenforced. There is now growing emphasis on their effective implementation, and care is taken to provide adequate administrative machinery for the purpose.

This extension of the area of partnership between the State and the voluntary organizations in the sphere of social welfare has led to certain very good results. The first is that the State has been able to secure a better understanding of problems and to ensure that more effective methods are adopted. There is thus an appreciable trend away from the belief that welfare services can be rendered only in residential institutions. The concept of community service, taking the family as a unit, is gaining ground. At the same time, increasing stress is being laid on the preventive rather than the curative or treatment aspects of the war against social evils like beggary, prostitution, and juvenile delinquency. And, thanks to the efforts of the voluntary workers and experts, several salutary reforms have been introduced. For example, first offenders are not sent to penal or correctional institutions, and jail rules and jail discipline have been made more humane. Besides, the special needs of the physically handicapped and the mentally retarded are accorded special attention with a view to their eventual assimilation in normal society as self-respecting wage earners.

An equally noteworthy feature is the recognition that welfare work consists in measures of real long-term rehabilitation and not merely in those of temporary relief.

This awareness has been accelerated by the State's assumption of long-term responsibility in the sphere of social welfare. Voluntary organizations with their know-how are now in a position to work out long-term schemes with reasonable guarantee of continuous financial assistance.

A necessary corollary to this is the realization of the importance of the quality of service rendered and of the need for laying dawn minimum standards of service. It has to be admitted that this realization came only towards the end of the ten-year period. The years immediately preceding were occupied in urgent work in long neglected fields or in operations with limited objectives. The evolution of standards is necessarily a gradual process.

Another trend that deserves notice is the importance that is coming to be attached to investigations, surveys and research in social welfare problems. Such surveys or research are now considered an essential preliminary to the formulation of schemes for the eradication of social evils or for the amelioration of the conditions of under-privileged groups. The Advisory Board on Social Welfare set up by the Ministry of Education and the Research Programme Committee of the Planning Commission provide grants to voluntary organizations or individual research scholars for the purpose of conducting surveys for undertaking research on selected social subjects. The State Social Welfare Departments of Bombay, Madhya Pradesh, Bihar and Rajasthan have set up research units to conduct studies on current social problems. Apart from these, State Governments have taken up several pilot schemes in the field of social welfare which may serve as models to other non-official and official organizations.

Training Schemes

When social welfare programmes were first taken up as an integral part of the Five Year Plans, the various State Governments and Union Territories faced a serious paucity of trained personnel to organize and man these services. Trained hands were needed not only for the efficient running of the existing services, but also for their expansion and for the operation of new schemes. To meet this shortage of personnel, particularly in respect of field-level workers, certain Central Ministries such as the Ministry of Food and Agriculture and the Ministry of Community Development, Panchayati Raj and Co-operation have started training programmes of their own. The Central Social Welfare Board, which is exclusively incharge of welfare services for women and children and the handicapped, has experienced a woeful lack of trained personnel for operations in the rural areas. It has therefore taken advantage of the facilities offered by the Kasturba Gandhi National Memorial Trust for training women village level workers or *gram sevikas*. A few State Governments also have initiated training programmes of their own. In this field there has been a growing awareness among both governmental and non-governmental agencies of the importance of standardising and grading the training programmes for similar categories of personnel. In the absence of such standardisation it is difficult to obtain the right type of person with the right type of training for a given job. On the administrative side, there has been a rapid change, with more and more emphasis on the employment of trained personnel with a knowledge of the necessary skills and techniques.

Evaluation

Every scheme of systematic operations should make provision for periodical evaluation, both internal and external, and every organization charged with carrying out a programme should have its own method of self-evaluation. This is particularly necessary in the field of social welfare, where the programmes have not yet crystallised in any set pattern and where large numbers of voluntary workers and experts with habits of independent thinking are actively engaged. A fairly comprehensive evaluation was carried out recently by the Study Team on Social Welfare, and a little earlier, from a slightly different view-point, by the Estimates Committee of Parliament. The Study Team has recommended a fairly continuous process of evaluation, which is well worth a trial.

Social Assistance and Social Security

Another trend worthy of notice is the emergence of social assistance and social security programmes on the horizon of social welfare activity. An old age pension scheme has been introduced by the State Governments of Uttar Pradesh, Andhra Pradesh, Kerala and Madras, while legal aid to the poor is ensured under a scheme formulated by the Kerala Government. A scheme for providing legal aid to the poor is also engaging the active attention of the Central Government. Various Central Ministries have their own social assistance schemes, to which references have been made in relevant parts of this volume. Broadly speaking, the nationalisation of life insurance and the establishment of Live Insurance Corporation may be regarded as part of a social insurance programme. The Janata pilot project formulated by the Life Insurance Corporation covers both industrial and agricultural workers. Maternity benefits and industrial injury benefits, which now form an integral part of the laws relating to labour and are applicable to large sections of workers, are likely to be extended to other groups as well. The Contributory Health Service Scheme for Central Government employees which has been in force for the past seven years, may well serve as the foundation for a national health service. A Study Group on Social Security had recommended the integration of the existing social security schemes and the conversion of the various Provident Fund schemes into a statutory scheme for old age, invalidating and survivorship pension-*cum*-gratuity. The various aspects of the question of integration, when given proper consideration, will give a new shape to the entire scheme. In addition to these social assistance programmes, there is need for an insurance-*cum*-assistance programme which will ensure freedom from want.

This analysis of some of the more important developments during the past ten years of multifarious effort should serve to show how vast is the scope of these services and how difficult are the problems involved. At the same time it should infuse courage and hope for the future. In a vast country like ours the problems are naturally magnified. They have been accentuated, too, by long years of neglect by our alien rulers and by a prolonged spell of economic emasculation. With an enormous leeway to make up in almost every field, it was only natural that first priority should have been accorded to economic rehabilitation through increased agricultural and industrial production. But no national development plan can afford to neglect the social services, and more particularly social welfare. The goal of economic development is the betterment of the individual human being; in order to enable the individual to benefit from such development it is necessary to help the growth of his or her personality through social services. Formally important is special care for the weaker and more vulnerable sections of the population through specialised social welfare services. Only this will enable them, first, to absorb the benefits of the general social services, and later share, in common with all others, the blessings of economic development.

Adequate social welfare services are essential for the prosperity and well-being of the country. Integrated programmes operating on a nation-wide scale must help bridge the void the long decades of neglect have left in our social and economic life. These programmes must be imbued with a sense of purpose; they must keep in view clearly defined objectives. It is imperative, too, that certain minimum standards should be maintained, and work conducted on well-regulated lines. During the past ten years there have been countless agencies operating in this field. What they have accomplished so far may not, indeed, be spectacular. But they have served to enlarge our understanding of the problems and to give us a better appreciation of the techniques of welfare work. That is a substantial gain. In the years ahead our activities in this particular sphere of national development will be all the more meaningful for the sound foundations laid during the past decade.

The subject of Labour Welfare is a very wide one and covers a very broad field. Its concept varies from country to country, depending on the character of the social system and the stage of economic development. Even within the same country, the significance attached to the terms varies from industry to industry and from unit to individual unit of the same industry. A universally acceptable definition of the term not being possible, the ILO Conference in 1947 adopted a resolution which enumerated the following, viz., "such services, facilities and amenities as adequate canteens, rest and recreation facilities, sanitary and medical facilities, arrangement for travel to and from work and for the accommodation of workers employed at a distance from their homes and such other services, amenities and facilities as contribute to improve the conditions under which workers are employed," as generally falling within the framework of welfare facilities for workers.

In the earlier stages, the provision of such welfare facilities was looked upon with varying degrees of suspicion or doubt, even hostility. Only in recent years has there been a change of attitude on the part of employers, employees and government; and there is appreciation of the fact that the provision of such facilities either by themselves or in collaboration with others is genuine need, whether looked at from the social angle or the economic. Much of this change in attitude is attributable to the significant work done by the ILO in focussing attention on labour and social problems. Nowadays, some of these facilities are ensured to the workers by legislation, while others are left for voluntary action by employers or by the community.

Origin of Labour Welfare in India

In the case of India most of the important legislation in the labour welfare field can be traced back to the last 20 years. Being in the Concurrent List of the Constitution, such legislation has been enacted by both the State and Central Governments. In the content of planned economic development and the concept of a welfare State within a socialistic pattern of society, labour welfare has come to assume added significance. In the First and Second Five Year Plans, in the labour and labour welfare field emphasis was placed on training of craftsmen and the organization of a comprehensive employment service. In recognition of the importance of suitable facilities, a number of steps to ensure better working conditions, safety at work place, etc., have been taken by enlarging the scope of the existing laws and effectively implementing them. A Central Labour Institute has been set up to study systematically the problem of production in relation to the health and safety of the workers. A number of welfare centres have been set up during the two Plans with the cooperation of employers, employees and government and some progress, though not very striking, has also been made in the field of industrial housing. A massive programme of Workers' Education has also been launched. The impact of all these programmes is already being felt. It is now proposed to examine in detail in the subsequent paragraphs the advances made in recent years in providing suitable working conditions inside and outside undertakings, in the field of social security, workers' Education, etc., under various schemes like the Coal and Mica Mine Labour Welfare Funds, the Employees' Provident Fund, the State Insurance Schemes, etc.

Coal Mines Labour Welfare Fund

The Coal Mines Labour Welfare Fund was set up in

1944, and it is by far the largest statutory fund in the country devoted to the promotion of the welfare of colliery workers. It is based on a cess which was raised from 37.5 nP. per ton to 50 nP. per ton with effect from January 1, 1961, levied on despatches of coal and coke from all collieries. The Fund is administered by the Government of India in consultation with a tripartite body consisting of employers, employees and Government. An indication of the size of the Fund and the extent of its activities can be had from the fact that, during 1960-61, a sum of nearly Rs. 0.98 crore was collected by way of cess and an expenditure of roughly Rs. 1.64 crores (Rs. 0.90 crore on General Welfare and Rs. 0.74 crore on housing) was incurred. The balance to the credit of the Fund at the end of the year was about Rs. 8 crores.

The activities of the Fund in the welfare field include provision of medical facilities, public health and sanitation, anti-malaria operations, water supply, education and recreation, co-operative credit societies, holiday homes, dependents' benefits, etc.

In the field of medical facilities, the Fund runs at present a network of two central hospitals, one each at Dhanbad and Asansol with a bed strength of 200, and seven regional hospitals each with a bed strength of 30. To each regional hospital is attached a Maternity and Child Welfare, Centre. The Rehabilitation Centre attached to the Central hospitals treated over 17,000 patients in 1960-61. The facilities provided by these hospitals include, *inter alia,* a blood bank at Asansol, provision of deep X-ray therapy and treatment of cancer, leprosy, etc. In regard to maternity and child welfare, apart from the seven regional centres, the Fund runs six more centres in the Madhya Pradesh, Andhra and Orissa coal-fields, in addition to subsidising over 50 centres run by colliery owners. Grants-in-aid to the tune of Rs. 5 lakhs was given in 1960-61 by the Fund to colliery owners for maintaining dispensary services. The Fund, in addition, maintains two allopathic dispensaries, two mobile medical, units and 13 Ayurvedic dispensaries.

In regard to TB, which is a special problem in mining areas, the number of beds maintained by the Fund at present is 148. Two hundred more beds are expected to be added shortly. In addition, domiciliary treatment is extended to over 1,000 patients. A special feature of the Fund's work in this connection is the provision of subsistence allowance to dependents of TB patients. In connection with malaria eradication, the Fund has been doing very good work since its inception. The activities of the Fund also include family planning, family counselling, etc.

The Fund provides recreational, social and educational facilities through the organization of multi-purpose welfare institutes. In 1960-61, sixty women-*cum*-children's centres were run in multi-purpose institutes and in accommodation offered by colliery owners. Sixty-one full-fledged adult education centres were also functioning during the year. To strengthen this programme about 113 feeder centres have been opened. The list of activities includes free education, milk, tiffin, etc., to children of miners up to class II, adult education, sewing, indoor and outdoor games study tours, giving of grants-in-aid to primary schools and educational scholarships to deserving wards of colliery workers, etc. The Fund has also made considerable progress in enforcing rules regarding the provision of pit-head baths and provision of creches for children of women workers. By the end of 1960-61, 225 pit-head baths and 392 creches were in existence and 80 baths and 61 creches under construction.

A substantial part of the Fund's expenditure in recent years has been on housing schemes. Under the schemes of experimental townships, the organization constructed in all 1,566 houses at Bhuli, 48 homes at Bijoy Nagar, 219 homes at Bokaro, 180 homes at Kargali, 50 at Girdih, 50 at Bhurkunda and 40 at Kursasia. The Fund also provides loans as well as subsidies to colliery owners for the construction of homes. The number of homes constructed under these schemes was about 3,698 at the end of March 31, 1961, and 103 more were under construction. Under the New Housing Scheme of the Fund, which provides for the construction of 30,000 homes by the Fund, itself at a cost of more than Rs. 10 crores, at the end of 1960-61, 13,525 homes were in different stages of construction at 296 collieries.

Mica Mines Welfare Fund Organization

In 1946, legislation was enacted for setting up the Mica Mines Labour Welfare Fund. The resources are secured through the levy of a customs duty, not exceeding 64 per cent *ad valorem* on mica exports. (The present rate is 2½ per cent *ad valorem.*) There tripartite advisory committees have been set up in the States of Bihar, Andhra Pradesh and Rajasthan to administer the scheme.

The objectives and activities of the Mica Mines Organization are identical with those of its counterpart working for the welfare of coal miners. The medical facilities provided for mica miners include a 70-bed Central Hospital at Karma (Bihar), a 15-bed hospital at Tisri and a 14-bed hospital at Kalichedu. A 30-bed hospital at Rajasthan is almost complete. The construction of a 50-bed TB hospital as annexe to the Central Hospital is in progress.

In the field of education, the Fund has set up six multi-purpose institutes each with an adult education centre and a women's welfare centre, where training in handicrafts like sewing, knitting, etc., is given. A Community Centre in Andhra Pradesh provides training in carpentry to male workers. Educational facilities to miners' children are provided in six primary schools and two community centres in Bihar, two primary schools and one middle school in

Rajasthan, and six primary school and one high school in Andhra pradesh. Primary educations also imparted in 11 more welfare sub-centres. In most of the schools, children are provided with free midday meals, milk, slates, etc. Scholarships to deserving students for higher studies are also provided by the Fund. Other important facilities provided by the Fund include recreation and drinking water facilities and financial assistance to widows and children of miners.

The original subsidised housing scheme for mica miners (June 1953) was replaced in 1955 by a subsidy-*cum*-loan scheme (subsidy of 25 per cent and loan of 37½ per cent of cost of construction, subject to certain ceilings). As not a single house was constructed under he revised scheme, it has been decided to introduced a new subsidised housing scheme, under which the subsidy is 50 per cent of the cost of construction, subject to certain ceilings. The Estimates Committee of Parliament have agreed that it is necessary to make it obligatory for the mica mine owners to provide their workers with houses, as has been done in the case of plantation labour.

Health Insurance Scheme

The earliest steps in the field of social insurance of workers include the Workmen's Compensation Act of 1923, which provides for the payment of cash benefits in case of employment injury and the Maternity Benefit Acts that provide for the payment of cash benefits before and after confinement to women working in factories, plantations and mines. In these enactments, however, the liability is placed directly on the shoulders of the individual employer and does not require any contribution from the worker, and as such cannot be strictly classified under the head "social insurance."

The first real step towards the securing of a comprehensive programme of health insurance for industrial workers on a contributory basis was taken in 1948 with the passing of the employees' State Insurance Act. The Act provides for cash and medical benefits in the event of sickness, maternity and employment injury. The medical benefits provided under the scheme include:

(a) hospitalisation, specialist care, drugs and dressings pathological and X-ray examinations, anti-natal, confinement and post-natal care for women;

(b) domiciliary visits; and

(c) out-door treatment through static and mobile dispensaries, etc.

Medical care, except hospitalisation, is also being provided to the families of insured workers. The Employees' State Insurance Corporation, which administers the Act, has also got a plan for the construction of hospitals and dispensaries at a capital cost of Rs. 15 crores. Some of these are under construction and the entire programme is expected to be completed by the end of Third Plan.

The cash benefits include:

(a) Sickness benefits payable during periods of certified sickness amounting to about half average daily wage for a total period of 56 days. (Insured workers who suffer from prolonged disease, e.g., tuberculosis, leprosy, cancer, mental illness, etc., are entitled to extended cash benefits at a reduced rate for an additional period of 309 days).

(b) Maternity benefits payable to insured women workers at 75 nP. per day or twice the rate of sickness benefit for a period of 12 weeks.

(c) Disablement benefits payable to an insured person affected by employment injury (temporary disablement benefit is payable at the rate of half average daily wage for the duration of disablement and permanent disablement benefit is payable in the form of a life pension on the basis of a decision by a Medical Board as to the extent of disablement whether partial or total).

(d) Dependents' benefits payable to the widow/children or parents/dependents of an insured worker who dies as the result of an employment injury. The widow receives this benefit for life or until she re-marries and the children receive the benefit up to the age of 15 years or, if they are being educated, up to 18 years.

The Act covers industrial workers in perennial factories employing 20 or more persons and using power. All persons who remuneration in the aggregate does not exceed Rs. 400 p.m. are covered. The scheme had been extended by the end of the year 1960-61 to 121 centres with a total coverage of 16.74 lakh employees and medical care was extended to about 5.73 lakhs family units, *i.e.,* about 18 to 19 lakh additional beneficiaries. With the decision to extend medical benefits (except hospitalisation) to the families of insured workers, it is expected that a major obstacle to progress will be removed, and the scheme will also cover the major industrial cities of Calcutta and Ahmedabad.

Provident Fund Schemes

Provision for the future of an industrial worker after he retires or for his dependents in case of his early death is made by the Coal Mines Provident Fund and Bonus Scheme Act of 1948 and the Employees' Provident Fund Act of 1952. There is also a separate scheme for the tea garden workers in Assam.

The Coal Mines Provident Fund Scheme is administered by a Central Board of Trustees and is at present applicable to all coal mines in India. All employees drawing less than Rs. 300 as basic monthly wage are required to become members of the Fund as soon as they qualify for a bonus under the Coal Mines Bonus Scheme. In July 1956, the qualifying wage ceiling of Rs. 300 per month was removed, so as to include managerial and supervisory staff within the benefits of the scheme. The total number of collieries covered at the end of September 1961 was 801 and the amount invested came to Rs. 29.62 crores at the end of February 1962.

The Employees' Provident Funds Act, 1952, extended the benefit of such a scheme to workers in 47 industries by the end of 1960-61. In these industries, the act covers all establishments which (a) employ 20 or more persons, and (b) have been in operation for over three years. Exemption is granted only to those establishments which already have a similar provident fund scheme with comparable benefits. The total number of establishments covered under the Act at the end of December 1960 was 8,131 units with a membership of 33.03 lakhs subscribers. The employer contributes 6-¼ per cent of the basic wage and dearness allowance (including the cash value of any food concessions that may exist) and the employee contributes an equal amount with the proviso that he can contribute up to 8-$^1/_3$ per cent, if he so desires. The feasibility of increasing the employers' contribution to 8-$^1/_3$ per cent in certain industries is also under consideration. The amount of contributions in the Fund at the end of August 1961 was Rs. 292.84 crores, of which Rs. 212.59 crores stood to the credit of members, the balance having been refunded to outgoing members or made available in the form of loans.

For the last three years, interest at the rate of 3-$^1/_3$ per cent has been paid to the members on accumulations. Full accumulations with interest are refunded to members in the event of death, permanent disability, retirement, retrenchment and resignation after completing 15 years of service. In other cases, the member gets back his contribution with interest along with a portion of the employers' contribution on a graduated scale, subject to a minimum of 25 per cent. Advance are also granted to member for paying life insurance premia or expenses incurred on account of serious illness, and it has also been agreed to make available advances for house-building.

Integrated Social Security Scheme

A Study Group on Social Security examined the feasibility of integrating the existing social security schemes with a view to reducing overhead costs, improving administrative efficiency and increasing the benefits to the worker. In addition to the existing benefits, the Group also recommended an old age, invalidity and survivorship pension-*cum*-gratuity scheme. The implementation of this scheme is under consideration.

Housing of Industrial Workers

The problem of housing industrial workers must be viewed not only as a measure necessary for securing industrial efficiency, but also as part of the more complex problem of urban housing. In 1949, a scheme for the housing of industrial workers was drawn up, under which the Central Government agreed to provide interest-free loans to State Governments and private employers to cover two-thirds of the cost of construction. This scheme made little progress and was replaced in 1952 by the subsidised Industrial Housing Scheme under the First Five Year Plan. In addition to long-term loans at low interest rates, the scheme provided for a capital subsidy up to 50 per cent. The benefits of the scheme were also extended to cover statutory housing boards, municipal bodies and co-operative housing societies. As a result, it has been estimated that 1 lakh housing units were constructed by the end of the Second Plan and about 40,000 were under construction. The housing situation will be further eased with the extension of the programme of slum clearance and the efforts of public sector industrial employers, such as the steel plants, the railways, the port trusts, etc., to provide adequate housing facilities for their workers. Substantial provision is also made in the Third Plan for housing. Certain modifications have also been introduced to bring down the cost and extend the benefits to a wider range of workers. There are also other schemes like the Low-Income Group Housing Scheme, the Middle-Income Group Housing Scheme, etc., which will benefit industrial workers. There is a scheme for providing housing accommodation to plantation labour also.

Labour Welfare in the States

As stated earlier, the State Governments made provision in the Second Five Year Plan for running labour welfare centres. Out of a total provision of Rs. 14.10 crores for "Labour and Labour Welfare" in the State Plans, Rs. 2.5 crores was earmarked for labour welfare centres. The State-wise allocation is detailed on page 308.

It may be mentioned that in certain States like Kerala and Madras, the programme for labour welfare centres has not been brought within the plan and that the State Governments have provided for this scheme from the normal expenditure. These welfare centres have proved popular and successful, and have been set up not only in States like Maharashtra, Gujarat, West Bengal and Uttar Pradesh with major industrial concentrations, but also in smaller territorial units like Delhi, Tripura and Pondicherry. Most of these centres are simple structures which provide the worker and his family with opportunity for relaxation in clean and restful surroundings and the services of a reading-room, a library, a radio and the opportunity to participate in healthy in-door and out-door games. The more ambitious centres have been set up in permanent buildings and provide a comprehensive programme tailored to meet the special needs of men, women and children. Typical items include sewing and embroidery classes, discussion groups, amateur dramatics, excursions, social education classes and sports meets. Most of these centres are run by the Labour Departments of the State Governments through paid staff appointed for the purpose. The programme is generally supervised by tripartite committees which draw upon the services of employers, workers and experienced social workers. The number of such centres run by the various State Governments at present is about 250. In 1953, the Government of Bombay introduced a variation of this theme by setting up an autonomous Labour Welfare Board, to which the existing welfare centres and staff were handed over the sufficient funds for continuing the activities were made available. The Board has been conducting 55 Labour Welfare Centres located in various industrial towns in the State. In the Third Plan a provision of Rs. 27.3 crores has been made by the State Governments/ Administrations for labour and labour welfare programmes. It is estimated that about Rs. 4.45 crores would be spent on labour welfare centres.

Welfare Activities of Employers

In examining the welfare facilities provided by the employer, it is necessary to draw a distinction between the facilities that are required under law and those provided by the good sense and goodwill of the employer. Although a number of welfare items are now covered by labour legislation, there still are many progressive measures that are provided by employers on the basis of enlightened self-interest. Such a gesture helps to improve the climate of industrial relations and to boost employee morale and, in the process, productive efficiency. These efforts should be encouraged, specially because, while labour legislation can ensure that all employers provide the minimum welfare facilities, this minimum tends to stabilise itself as the standard, with very little scope for reaching the optimum.

The Factories Act, 1948, deals in great detail with working conditions in factories. The main provisions relate to: (a) health, safety and welfare (b) hours of work; (c) employment of young persons and women; and (d) annual leave with wages.

The section that deals with welfare touches upon items such as washing facilities, facilities for storing and drying clothes, facilities for seating, rest-shelters, first-aid appliances, canteens in factories that employ over 150 workers, creches in factories employing more than 50 women workers and appointment of labour welfare officer in factories employing more than 500 workers.

The Plantations Labour Act of 1951 is another item of protective legislation designed to regulate the working conditions of labour in tea, coffee, rubber and Cinchona Plantations. The main provisions of the Act deal with: (a) hours of work, rest-interval, etc.; (b) health and welfare; (c) leave with wages and (d) employment of children and young persons.

Under the section "Health and Welfare," the employer is required to provide housing for worker and his family according to standards prescribed by the respective State Governments. They also prescribe the standards of medical aid, sickness allowance and maternity allowance provided for the worker. In respect of welfare, the employer must provide facilities such as drinking water, separate latrine and urinals for men and women, a school in estates where there are more than 25 children between the age 6 and 12 years, canteen in estates employing more than 150 workers, creches in estates employing more than 50 women workers and appointment of labour welfare officer in estates employing 300 or more workers.

The Mines Act, 1932, regulates working conditions in mines The main provisions of the Act deal with (a) hours of work, rest-interval, weekly off, etc., (b) leave with wages; (c) health, safety and welfare; and (d) employment of women and young persons.

The section on "Health, Safety and Welfare" deals with the provisions of such items as drinking water, separate latrines and urinals for men and women, first-aid appliances, ambulance and stretchers, creches, locker rooms and pit-head baths, rest shelters, canteens and appointment of labour welfare officers.

Similar protective clauses are to be found in the Indian Merchant Shipping Act, 1923, the Dock Workers (Regulation of Employment) Act, 1948, and the Shops and Commercial Establishments Act of the various State Governments.

A number of employers' association and individual employers have taken the initiative in anticipating statutory labour welfare programmes. As part of a progressive employee-employer relations policy, they have provided their workers with welfare centres, gymnasia, sports clubs, hospitals, dispensaries, schools for children and adult education classes. The Indian Jute Mills Association provides for welfare facilities for workers in its affiliated units. Educational facilities for workers and their children and recreational facilities form important activities of the welfare centres run by the Association. Similar facilities are also provided by all the members of the Mill-owners' Association, Bombay. Some of the Cotton textile mills in Bombay and Ahmedabad even give medical facilities.

Welfare Activities of Trade Unions

Trade Unions have yet to come to the fore in organizing welfare facilities for their members on a significant scale. The reason for this can be traced back to the meagre funds available with them for financing such programmes. There are, however, certain pioneering unions that have shown what can be done with energy and imagination. The Textile Labour Association, Ahmedabad, has organized a chain of reading rooms, libraries, social and cultural centres, gymnasia and schools and has even extended its activities to running its own allopathic and Ayurvedic dispensaries and a 24-bed maternity home. It is expected that, as the trade union movement gathers strength, it will be able to raise its own funs for welfare activities and branch out more vigorously into the fields of co-operative organization, housing etc. There is a considerable body of experience built up by trade unions in countries where unions are better organized and financed, and we could profitably draw upon this experience in extending the activities of Indian trade unions.

Workers' Education

To ensure that the worker enjoys his rightful place as a partner in industry and also that the programmes of national development are put through according to schedule an without industrial strife, it is necessary to prepare him for this responsible role. Then again, if responsible leadership is to be built up from within the ranks, it is necessary to organize an effective programme of workers' Education. The experiment with workers' participation in the management of industry makes it all the more important that such a programme of workers' education should succeed. The emphasis in this programme cannot be focussed merely on adult literacy, but will necessarily have to extend also to training in trade union philosophy and methods.

In September, 1958, a semi-autonomous Central Board for Workers' Education was set up to administer the scheme. It was intended to train a cadre of teacher-administrators who would, in turn, train a group of worker-teachers, who, on their own return to the industrial units from which they were drawn, would organize classes for the rank-and-file of workers. Forty-three teacher-administrators were put through a six-month training course, and the second training course for teacher-administrators was started in November, 1959, and completed in April, 1960, and with a batch of 53 trainees, including some nominees of the trade unions themselves. A third batch of teacher-administrators is now under training. Worker-teachers are at present being trained in 13 regional centres, the duration of the training course being three months. Workers' Education classes at the factory level have also been undertaken. It is intended to extend the programme of Worker' Education further during the Third Plan.

Assessment of Outlook

It may be useful to examine at this stage the prospects for labour welfare in this country in the coming years. The assessment made in the foregiong paragraphs shows clearly that in the field of working conditions inside the factory, healthy and sanitary arrangements, rest-shelters, arrangements for eating, etc., the provisions under the law are adequate and compare favourably with similar provisions in the laws of more advanced countries; or where such laws do not exist, with the agreements between employers and workers which are more or less observed as strictly as any such social legislation. There is scope, however, for improving the quality of services provided at present and also for the extension of these services to new units. Considerable attention has of late been paid by the Labour Ministers at their periodical conferences to the strengthening of inspectorates set up under the law. The Plan reports have all along emphasised, however, that apart from the inspectorates provided by the Government, it is useful to have tripartite agreements on the standards to be maintained and frequent reviews of maintenance. Workers employed in small and medium scale industries do not get the benefit of the facilities, mainly because of the small scale on which they operate. The possibility of extending bare welfare facilities on a co-operative basis for such units should received urgent attention. In the field of social security, the average of existing schemes requires to be extended. An aspect of labour welfare on which nothing has been done so far is unemployment insurance. While a large-scale scheme of this kind cannot be accommodated within the resources of the country, a beginning in this regard is expected to be made in the Third Plan in the interests of employment by arranging financial assistance to units which are well managed but have run into temporary difficulties, and also to individual workers who have become unemployed because of closure of industrial units.

The Ministry of Labour appointed a study Team to examine all aspects of Labour welfare before a policy in that regard could be laid down in the Third Five-Year Plan. The Team, after a review of the existing facilities, came to certain conclusions which found acceptance at the informal meeting of the Labour Ministers in October 1961. Some of the important conclusions have already been referred to earlier. But in view of the need for augmenting labour welfare facilities for workers, the State Governments have agreed to consider the feasibility of setting up welfare funds for workers. Essentially, these funds will be formed out of money belonging to workers but accumulating with the employers; fines collected from workers, unclaimed wages, and contributions from Government for workers' welfare.

Finally, it does seem necessary to conclude by drawing attention to a controversial issue that arise in all labour welfare programmes, namely, is the burden of welfare too high? The opinion has been expressed that if this burden continues to increase, it will raise labour costs to such a point that it will affect the costs of production and our competitive position in international markets. The contrary view is that the so-called 'burden' of labour welfare is no burden at all, that it is not intended to retain our competitive strength on the basis of sweated labour and that urgent steps are necessary to deal with discriminatory measures adopted by certain unprogressive employers in attempting to evade their liability under existing labour legislation. It does seem, however, that a compromise will have to be reached, whereby labour does not make any unrealistic demands for welfare facilities beyond the paying capacity of the employer and, in turn, the employer realizes that a contended labour force is the best foundation for raising efficiency and maximising production.

A brief survey of social legislation in force in the country at the commencement of the Constitution which synchronises with the opening of an era of planning was undertaken in the monumental work entitled "Social Welfare in India," published by the Planning Commission in 1955. A revised and abridged edition, bringing the law up to date, was issued in April 1961. A more detailed study and exposition of the several Laws enacted in the field of social legislation with particular reference to their motivation, content and application is to be found in "Social Legislation, Its Role in Social Welfare," also published by the Planning Commission in October 1956. It is not proposed to cover the same ground in full here. Where more detailed information is sought, reference may be made to these works.

What this chapter sets out to do is to give a summary of the position of social legislation at the commencement of the Constitution on January 26, 1950, a description of the legislation undertaken during the decade covered by the first two Five Year Plans, and an assessment of the present position and the prospects for the future. It will also indicate briefly the programmes for maintaining certain services under the laws initiated in this period, and their projection into the period of the Third Plan.

The basic fact to be borne in mind is that our Constitution declares India to be sovereign democratic Republic resting on the four pillars of: Justice—Social, economic and political; Liberty—of thought, expression, belief, faith and worship; Equality—of status as well as of opportunity; and

Fraternity—assuring the dignity of the individual and the unity of the nation.

The Fundamental Rights embodied in a chapter of our Constitution proclaim the equality of all citizens before the law, more particularly the equality of the sexes. This is significant in view of the subordinate position to which women were relegated under the personal laws that were in force even after the Constitution by virtue of Article 372. The rights and status of women had been left in a position of subordination. This constituted a gross anachronism. Next, the Directive Principles of State Policy, which all flow from concern for the human problems of its citizens, impose on the Government the obligation to establish social justice. This means much more than what it appears on the surface. Every assumption and principle underlying our laws and their enforcement is questioned and viewed in an entirely new light. This applies even to the punitive treatment meted out, under the sanction of law, to juvenile delinquents, beggars, prostitutes, lunatics and even criminals.

All legislation, it is now held, should be inspired by a consciousness of our collective duty to help them to an adequate life. They are no longer looked upon as undesirables outside the pale of society, against whom society has to be protected.

The new outlook calls for a fundamental re-appraisal of problems. Those entrusted with the application or enforcement of laws have to be trained and oriented to the true social purpose.

One other significant factor is the role of the State in providing relief for the physically, mentally or socially handicapped persons. In the past the task had been left to be performed, however inadequately, by their kinsmen, and where they failed, by voluntary philanthropy. Indeed valuable service was rendered both by private and public charities in a period in which it was unthinkable that public funds should be diverted to social welfare. But when the satisfaction of social needs has become one of the primary duties of the modern State, it behoves it to anchor the existing services in the voluntary field in the State-maintained services and secure the well-being of the community.

The decade that has just passed has witnessed growing appreciation of the new social philosophy in Government quarters as well. Evidence of this is to be found in the setting up of the Central Social Welfare Board, with considerable devolution of powers and functions. During the period the Government has implemented in some degree certain recommendations of the advisory committees set up by the Central Social Welfare Board—the After-Care Advisory Committee, the Social and Moral Hygiene Advisory Committee and the Grants-in-Aid Committee. In formulating and enacting social legislation, the Government has not only consulted the Central Social Welfare Board but has also been guided by its advice. This is particularly noticeable in the Suppression of Immoral Traffic Act of 1956, and the Women's and Children's Institutions (Licensing) Act of 1956. These are small beginnings, but it is hoped that pattern has been set for the future.

For the present purpose social legislation may be defined as the body of laws calculated to bring the existing laws into conformity with the Constitution and help establish the social order envisaged by the Directive Principles of State Policy. Notwithstanding the fact that these Directives are non-justiciable, the Constitution declares that these principles are to be treated as fundamental in the governance of the country, enjoining on the State to apply them in making laws.

Position of Women in Law

The first Governor-General of India, Warren Hastings,

decreed that as regards inheritance, marriage, caste and other religious usages and institutions, the laws of the Koran were to be administered for the Mohammedans and the laws of the Shastras for the Hindus. Express recognition was given to this decree in the Act of Settlement of 1781. Judicial interpretation extended to those communities the benefit of their own laws and customs in all family and religious maters. Attempts at codification, at the instance of Macaulay, were given up by the Second Law Commission, which held that both Hindu and Mohammedan Laws derived their authority from religion, and that the British legislature was no more entitled to make Hindu or Mohammedan Laws than it was to make Hindu or Mohammedan religion. Later came the declaration of Queen Victoria, which laid down that in framing and administering the law due regard should be paid to the ancient rites, usages, and customs of Hindus. Successive Government of India Acts have preserved these laws, and Article 372 of our present Constitution maintains this position until it is altered or amended.

The personal laws which thus came to be maintained as a matter of deliberate decision by the British Government, whether based on the code of Manu or the Koran, were supposed to be linked up with religion. The laws thus administered excluded women from all rights of inheritance. Where a woman, falling within a narrow list of admitted heirs, inherited the divided property of a deceased male Hindu, she took only a limited interest. A woman could not be a coparcener. Barren daughters and mothers of daughters only or wife or other female heir forfeited such right if she was unchaste. A woman was not herself legally competent to adopt and her consent was not required to an adoption by the husband. A widow would adopt only within the authority circumscribed by the directions of the deceased husband.

The right of a mother, though recognized, next to father, as guardian of her minor children, could be defeated by any testamentary appointment made by her husband. The ancient Hindu rule gave the father the right to the custody of children, both legitimate and illegitimate. A mother could not appoint a guardian by will; the preferential claims of the father received statutory recognition in the Guardians and Wards Act. The mother could not *validly* give away her daughter in marriage, through she might be her legal guardian, and she was subordinated not only to the father but to all the paternal relations of the girl in this respect. A Hindu woman, once married, remained wedded to the husband in a tie not dissolved even by the death of her husband, a disability from which the husband was free even during the life-time of the wife. Even *stridhana,* where the women is supposed to have absolute power of disposition, was subject to the husband's restraint during coverture. The woman's earnings through her own exertions during coverture did not fall within the definition of *Stridhana.* The illegitimate daughter had no claim against the putative father even to maintenance, whereas an illegitimate son among the Sudras was admitted to share in the putative father's property.

These disparities have now been removed by four Acts passed in 1955 and 1956. It is not necessary here to refer to earlier legislative attempts to remedy certain hardships that women suffered in law, as they have all been superseded by these four Acts:

The Hindu Marriage Act, 1955: This Act came into force on May 18, 1955. It codifies the law relating to marriage among Hindus (which term includes, Buddhists, Sikhs and Jains also for purposes of all the for Acts). It makes monogamy he rule for men as well as for women. The age of marriage is fixed at 15 for the bride and 18 for the bride-groom. An idiot or a lunatic cannot marry. No particular form of solemnisation is prescribed, the parties being free to solemnise a marriage according to customary rites and ceremonies. It provides for the registration of marriages, without rendering the marriage itself invalid for failure to register.

The ground on which a marriage may be annulled by court and the grounds on which either spouse may seek judicial separation or divorce are carefully defined, and they may be availed by either spouse. A petition for dissolution of marriage may not be entertained until three years have expired from the date of marriage, except on the grounds of exceptional hardship to the petitioner or exceptional depravity on the part of the respondent. Children conceived or born during the subsistence of a voidable marriage are deemed to be legitimate, and their right to inherit the property of either parent protected. The court may award maintenance and costs to either spouse against the other and make all such interim and final orders as may be deemed necessary for the maintenance and welfare of the children of the marriage.

The Hindu Succession Act, 1956: This Act came into force on June 17, 1956. It repealed the Hindu Law of Inheritance (Amendment) Act (II of 1929) and the Hindu Women's Rights to Property Act of 1937. This is a bold attempt to bring under a single Act the law of succession among the Hindu, Buddhist, Sikh and Jain and the several communities following the matiarchal system in the South. The provisions are not identical and recognize certain differences, but they resolve the whole law of intestate succession, now largely customary, into a few well defined rules. The Act purports to determine the heir on secular test of consanguinity and affinity without any discrimination on the ground of sex. The traditional limitations on the capacity of Hindu women to hold, dispose of and transmit property have been done away with. It vests a Hindu woman with full ownership in all property however acquired. The daughter, the widow and the mother now inherit property along with the son, and take an equal share with him.

The Hindu Minority and Guardianship Act, 1956: This Act came into force on August 25, 1956. It recognizes the mother, after the father, as the natural guardian of her children. The natural guardian of a boy or unmarried girl is the father and, after him, the mother; the natural guardian of illegitimate children is the mother and, after her, the father. The natural guardian of a married girl is the husband. The mother shall ordinarily be entitled to the custody of children under five years of age. The words 'father' and 'mother' do not include a 'step-father' for this purpose, but include an adoptive father and adoptive mother. The natural guardian has also the power to deal with the minor's property within certain limits, and may also deal with the minor's property with the permission of the court in all cases of necessity or of evident advantage to the minor. The father may appoint a guardian for his minor children by will, but any such appointment will be held in abeyance during the life-time of the mother if she survives the father. The appointment takes effect on the death of the mother, unless she has appointed a guardian by her own will. The Hindu widow and the Hindu mother, acting as natural guardians, have the same power to appoint guardians for their minor children by will. A Hindu mother can act as the natural guardian of her minor children, if the father ceases to be a Hindu, or renounces the world and becomes a hermit.

The Hindu Adoptions and Maintenance Act, 1956: This Act came into force on December 21, 1956. "Maintenance" under this Act is defined to include food, clothing, residence, education, medical attendance and treatment. In the case of an unmarried daughter, it includes the expenses incidental to her marriage.

Maintenance: The wife is entitled to maintenance for life. She may live separately from her husband without forfeiting her right to maintenance on certain grounds. She forfeits her rights if she ceases to be Hindu or is unchaste. Children, both legitimate and illegitimate, are entitled to be maintained by their parents. The duty extends to aged and infirm parents, including a childless step-mother, and unmarried daughters. The factors to be taken into account in determining the quantum of maintenance are laid down in detail. In addition, the right of certain dependents to maintenance is declared, and the right is enforceable against those who inherit the estate of the deceased.

Adoption: Any male Hindu of sound mind and not being a minor may adopt a son or daughter with the consent of the wife, unless the wife has renounced the world, ceased to be a Hindu, or is declared to be of unsound mind by a competent court.

Any female Hindu of sound mind and not a minor, if unmarried, may adopt a son or daughter. A married woman may not take in adoption unless her husband is dead, or the marriage is dissolved, or the husband has renounced the world, or ceased to be a Hindu, or has been declared by a competent court to be of unsound mind.

A child may be given in adoption only by the father, mother, or guardian. The father may not give a child away except with the consent of the mother. The mother may do so only if the father is dead, and guardian only with the permission of the court. An adoptive father and adoptive mother cannot give the adopted child away in adoption as no child may be adopted twice.

The child to be taken in adoption must be a Hindu; should not have been already adopted once; and must be under 15 years of age and unmarried unless the custom or usage applicable to the parties permits it. A person may not take a son in adoption if there is a 'son' (son's son or son's son) in existence; and may not take a daughter in adoption if a daughter or son's daughter is in existence.

Ceremony is not essential, but there should be proof of intention to transfer the child from the family of birth to the family of adoption.

The Special Marriage act, 1955: There is also the *Special Marriage Act,* which came into force on January 1, 1955, which succeeded an earlier Act of 1872 providing for a form of marriage for persons who do not profess the Christian, Jewish, Hindu, Mohammedan, Parsi, Sikh or Jain religion. The Act of 1872 was amended in 1929 to permit inter-marriage among Hindus, Buddhists, Jains and Sikhs. Under its present form any two persons of the opposite sex may marry each other irrespective of the religion professed by either of them.

The conditions for a marriage under this Act are that neither party has a husband or wife living; neither party is an idiot or lunatic; the bridegroom must have completed the age of 21 years and the bride 18 years, and the parties are not within the prohibited degrees of relationship.

A marriage under this Act effects the severance of the person from any undivided Hindu family to which he may belong. But the Caste Disabilities Removal Act protects him from forfeiture of property or other rights. Secession to property is governed by the Indian Succession Act of 1925.

The grounds on which either party to the marriage may obtain judicial separation or dissolution of marriage are laid don in this Act and recourse to the Divorce Act is not necessary. The Act also provides for divorce by mutual consent if the parties have lived separately for one year, and provided three years have elapsed since the date of marriage, Persons married under other forms may also obtain registration of their marriage under this Act, and upon such registration the rights of parties are governed by this Act.

Position of Child in Law

The Indian Majority Act declares a person who has not completed the age of 18 years to be minor, but this Act does not affect matters of marriage, dower, divorce and adoption. Under Hindu Law minority terminates on the completion of 15 years in Bengal and 16 years in other parts of India.

Personal law recognizes are undefined personal obligation on the part of the father to maintain his minor sons and unmarried daughters. But this is often left to the good sense and natural affection of the parent. No limits have been set to parental control and discipline, nor has any standard of parental duty been prescribed, for law appears to have regarded the parent-child relationship more or less as a sacred trust. The right of the father to the custody, control, services and earnings of the child, which have long been recognized and universally acknowledged to be indisputable, are not derived from any positive rule of Hindu Law; they arose out of necessity and were sanctioned by practice. Law, however, recognized guardianship as a right of the parent and provided for its protection from interference.

The Constitution prohibits the employment of children below the age of 14 years in any factory, mine or other hazardous vocation. It permits legislation making special provision for the benefit of women and children, and protects all such legislation from any attack on the ground that it offends against the principle of equality or on the ground that it is discriminatory. The Directive Principles enjoin the State to take measures for the prevention of abuse of the tender age of children, and for the protection of childhood and youth from exploitation and moral and material abandonment. It also requires the State to endeavour to provide free and compulsory education for all children under 14 years of age within 10 years of the commencement of the Constitution.

The law, recognizing that a child is unable to act for itself in the matter of contract or in any proceeding in court, declares it incompetent to enter into any contract and provides a guardian to look after any legal proceedings in which it may be involved.

No child under seven years of age may be convicted of any offence under the Indian Penal Code, neither a child under 12 years of age, unless the court finds that the child has attained sufficient maturity of understanding to judge the nature and consequences of his or her conduct on the occasion.

The Criminal Procedure Code lays down, for all offenders under 15 years of age, detention in reformatories where facilities exist for discipline and training in a suitable craft, instead of confinement in jails. The Reformatory Schools Act of 1897 provides for the establishment of such institutions. This Act is in force in the whole of India except the territories which immediately before November 1, 1956 were comprised in Part B states. The Prisons Act requires the separation of male prisoners under the age of 21 altogether from other prisoners, and of those who have arrived at puberty from those who have not.

The Criminal Procedure Code provides a summary remedy to enforce the obligation to maintain both legitimate and illegitimate children. This is the only statutory provision enabling illegitimate children to obtain maintenance from the putative father.

The law restricts the employment of children in mines factories, plantations, docks, ports, railways and on ships. Employment of children is also forbidden in certain scheduled trades. Furthermore, the pledging of the labour of children is prohibited.

State Laws

There are Children Acts in the States of Andhra Pradesh,

former Bombay, Madhya Pradesh, Madras, East Punjab, Uttar Pradesh, West Bengal, Mysore, Kerala, Jammu and Kashmir and Delhi Administration. The two main objectives of the earliest Children Acts are to provide for the custody, control and punishment of youthful offenders and to ensure protection to children and young persons.

Then, we have the Borstal Schools Acts in the States of Andhra Pradesh, Madras, Bengal, former Bombay, Mysore, Punjab, Madhya Pradesh, Uttar Pradesh and Kerala. These Acts provide for special treatment for young offenders between the ages of 16 and 21 in special institutions where they are given industrial training and other instruction and subjected to such disciplinary and moral influences as will be conducive to their reformation.

To check the habit of smoking among the young, Juvenile Smoking Acts exist in the States of Punjab, West Bengal, Assam, Madhya Pradesh, Mysore and Rajasthan.

There are, besides, Suppression of Immoral Traffic Acts in most of the States. These deal also with minors in moral danger and provide for their rescue from brothels.

State Acts also prohibit the employment of children under the prescribed age in shops and commercial establishments.

Legislation Since 1951: What is important is not so much the enactment of goods laws as the enforcement of laws already on the Statute Book. It is neglect in respect of such enforcement that is at the root of many evils.

A considerable body of legislation, however, has been enacted during the past ten years. Article 39 (f) of the Constitution, as we have seen requires that the State shall in particular direct its policy towards securing childhood and youth against exploitation and against moral and material abandonment. Article 39 (e) calls upon the State to take measures to prevent the abuse of the tender age of children or their entering avocations unsuited to their age or strength. Article 45 enjoins upon the State to provide free and compulsory education for all children under 14 years of age within 10 years of the commencement of the Constitution. These are specific references to children in the Constitution.

We have already seen how the Hindu Minority and Guardianship Act and the Adoption and Maintenance Act, both of 1956, to some extent benefit children also. Attention was focussed recently on the widespread and increasing practice of kidnapping children and maiming them in order that they might be exploited as objects of compassion by beggars. Parliament in 1959 amended the Indian Penal Code, enhancing the penalties for kidnapping and maiming children.

Another piece of Central Legislation was the Women's and Children's Institution (Licensing) Act of 1956, since superseded by the Orphanages and Other Charitable Homes (Supervision and Control) Act of 1960. This, again, is an enabling measure as similar Acts for allied purposes have been enforced in States like Uttar Pradesh and West Bengal, with the object of regulating the activities of these institutions and bringing them all up to a particular standard, in the matter of the care, treatment and training of the inmates. There has, indeed, been a protest against regulating charity. But those familiar with the recommendations of the Advisory Committee on Social and Moral Hygiene set up by the Central Social Welfare Board must be aware that such legislation has not come a day too soon. For, while there are many good institutions run by persons inspired by the highest of motives, there are, unfortunately, many others where exploitation is rampant.

Lepers, Lunatics and Destitutes

The Lepers Act III of 1898 was undertaken by the Government of India as a safeguard against the "Imperial danger" for that was how it was referred to by the then Secretary of State for India in his despatches. It provides for the segregation of pauper-lepers by an order of the Magistrate, and of anyone certified by a medical practitioner as suffering from any form of leprosy in an asylum, provided the State Government has notified some place as such. It also prohibits persons suffering from any form of leprosy from being employed as teachers, barbers, dhobis, ayahs or nurses, and from being engaged in the preparation or sale of any article of food or drink. Lepers are not to have access to any public well or tank, nor are they permitted to use a public carriage. This law, however, has been found totally impracticable. Most of the State Governments have not notified places as asylums and what little leprosy relief work one comes across is performed by voluntary associations and individuals.

The Lunacy Act of 1912 authorised the establishment or the licensing of institutions for the care of the lunatics by State Governments. Though the Act was passed in 1912, it was not until 1922 that it was made obligatory for the asylum to provide any curative treatment at all. Here, again, it is for a magistrate to commit to an asylum a person certified to be a lunatic by a medical practitioner. Lunatics receive hospital treatment in advanced countries. But in this country, we have not provided for such treatment of the mentally ill. It is understood, however, that the Ministry of Health is engaged in drawing up comprehensive legislation and we may soon hope for the Mental Health Act embodying the latest researches in the subject.

The earliest attempts to check the practice of begging in a street or a public place are to be found in the City Police Acts of Calcutta, Madras and Bombay. These declare begging in such places to be an offence punishable with a month's imprisonment or fine. A ban on begging by itself can, however, achieve little; for all the sympathy that a mendicant still receives from people, there is no doubt that begging is an unsocial practice; the able-bodied beggar particularly deserves no sympathy. But the ban can be enforced only if special homes are established for disabled beggars and work houses for the able-bodied. The special Acts naturally call for the setting up of such homes and work-houses. Legislation of some kind or other for the prevention of begging is in force in Wet Bengal, Hyderabad, Travancore, Madras, Bombay, Bihar, Mysore and Punjab. To say that there are enactments on the Statute Book is not to say either that they are strictly enforced or that the problem has been eased to any appreciable extent. The cities of Madras, Bombay and Calcutta have comprehensive services, but even there, by reason of its vastness, the problems has only been partially tackled.

Prostitution and Immoral Traffic

It must be emphasised at the very start that the policy of the Government of India in respect of prostitution provides for abolition as distinguished from regulation; that is to say, the Government does not countenance prostitution and immoral traffic at all. As a signatory to the International Convention on the Suppression of Immoral Traffic in Women and Children at Geneva 1921, the Government of India had to undertake legislation to prevent this immoral traffic. The Indian Penal Code was accordingly amended in 1923 to make the procuring of a girl under 18 years of age for immoral purposes an offence.

Certain City Police Acts, the Municipalities Acts and the Cantonments Acts prohibited soliciting in streets or public places and banned the working of brothels with certain defined limits. Besides, the Children's Act enables the authorities to rescue minor girls who may otherwise be brought up for a life of prostitution. Certain sections of the Indian Penal Code also make provision for such rescue operations and certain laws as Prevention of Prostitution Acts and Suppression of Immoral Traffic Acts have been in force in Bombay, Madras, Bengal, Uttar Pradesh, Punjab, Bihar, Madhya Pradesh, Mysore, Kerala, Hyderabad and Ajmer. But they have now been superseded by a Central enactment, the Suppression of Immoral Traffic in Women and Girls Act of 1956.

The Association for Moral and Social Hygiene in India had repeatedly agitated for an all-India Act, the enforcement of which would be efficient and effective. The Bill, during its passage, was the subject of close and critical study by the Association as also by a committee appointed by the Central Social Welfare Board. It emerged in its final from after discussions in the Home Ministry at which the Central Social Welfare Board and many voluntary organizations and persons interested in the subject took part., The Act still suffers from several defects which make for its imperfect enforcement. It must be emphasised that this law, like other laws of this nature. Calls for proper education of public opinion. It has been repeatedly urged that little children living in houses of ill fame should be separated from their mothers or guardians, often fake "aunts" and "unless." Besides it is known that there are a number of women in the profession to whom, though their present mode of living is distasteful, no alternative is available. For such women some kind of hostel accommodation must be provided. The factors that made for half hearted enforcement of the Act, it was felt, were that the usual police machinery employed was wholly unsuitable and that proper benefits of rehabilitation were absent. These factors were kept in mind in finalising the Bill. The Act was ultimately enforced in May 1958.

Treatment of Offenders

Social justice demands that in the treatment of offenders we should substitute a correctional policy for the penal that is now pursued. The object of punishment, it was declared, was deterrence, retribution, reformation, repression and social utility. If social utility is acknowledged to be the true object of punishment, what is needed is a synthesis of deterrence and reformation. The treatment and training of convicted persons should be such as to implant in them the will to lead a good life on discharge and also fit them for some gainful occupation or other. There has been a steady improvement in the condition of jails in the country. Simultaneously, the principle of reformation has gained ground. It is gratifying to find that the Indian Jails Committee of 1919 has this to say on the ultimate object of prison treatment. "..... That prisoners while in prison should be brought under such influences as will not only deter them from committing further crimes but will also, have reforming influence on their character is the next principle which should, we conceive, be accepted. This proposition, though it was rejected by our distinguished predecessors (the Committee of 1863-38) has now been established by the general concert of penologists throughout the world, and is today questioned by hardly anyone. The general tendency of modern ideas is towards the view that severity alone has little effect in reclaiming the criminal, and that what is required is rather humanising and improving the influences which will lead to the prisoner's realizing the essentially evil results of crime on himself and others, and result in a real reformation of character and purpose. The place which the various reformatory agencies, religion, education, rewards for good conduct, the hope of release, the encouragement of industry, and the like should occupy in any scheme is a matter of detail."

Thus, there is urgent need to eliminate all that is negative and repressive in the system and to promote what is positive and constructive. The general deterrent effect of the penal system on potential offenders lies not in the rigours of life within a jail; it consists rather in the fear of detection, of public trial and conviction, and the certainty of punishment. For the individual offender deterrence means primarily the shame of being sent to prison with all that it implies, complete loss of personal liberty, separation from home, family, and friends, subjection to disciplinary control of 'forced' labour and deprivation of the ordinary amenities and intercourse a everyday life. Proof of the increasing awareness on this subject was the invitation extended by the Government of India to the United Nations expert on criminology, Dr. Walter C. Reckless, to study and report on the country's jail administration. He has made far-reaching recommendations, some of which have already been implemented.

The theory that punishment must be related to the offence must be replaced by the new theory that the punishment must be related to the offender. This calls for an understanding of the circumstances of the commission of the offence and a study of the offender's own mind, factors that are not excluded by the rigid rules of legal procedure. Different methods of tackling offienders must be employed and more extensive use mode of alternative to imprisonment of which not much is know even today. They are probation, judicial receive and the binding over and filing of cases. Further treatment should be individualised. Much would be achieved by a more extensive use of probation; for short-term imprisonment confers no benefit either on the offender or on society, but is fraught with serious consequences. There were probation acts in several States: Madras, Central Provinces (now Madhya Pradesh), Uttar Pradesh, former Bombay and Mysore. There were also provisions in the Criminal Procedure Code enabling courts to release first offenders on probation within limits. All this is now superseded by a recent Act of Parliament, the Probation of Offenders Act of 1958. Since then much water have flown under Ganges.

5

Social Welfare and the Free Market

Adam Smith outlined in a sustained critique of mercantilism, which was then the dominant economic doctrine in Britain and the other major nations of Europe. In one respect mercantilism was a political rather than an economic doctrine, since it placed the goal of national power above that of national prosperity. Lichtheim observed that the chief aim of mercantilist policies was not to maximize welfare but to promote the economic and political independence of the nation state'. The primary sources of a nation's power were held to be precious metals and a large population.

Protective tariffs, the prohibition of emigration and extensive governmental regulation of the activities of the economic market were considered to be the best policies for achieving national security and greatness. Mercantilist ideas became steadily more influential throughout Europe during the seventeenth and eighteenth centuries and they were closely associated with the rise of nationalist sentiments. Hicks suggests that mercantilism 'marks the discovery that economic growth can be used in the *national interest*'. Viner, however, points out that within the terms of mercantilist teaching it was possible to achieve a 'long-run harmony' between the ends of power and prosperity, 'although in particular circumstances it may be necessary for a time to make economic sacrifices in the interest of military security and therefore also of long-run prosperity'.

It was a fundamental tenet of mercantilist teaching that *Under prevailing conditions,* increases in heads would increase real income per head', and this proposition 'during the greater part of the eighteenth century' was, according to Schumpeter, 'manifestly correct'. As for the distribution of these increases in real income, the earlier mercantilist writers argued in favour of repressive poor laws and low wages. Given the choice, they argued, the poor would always prefer idleness to work, and habits of industry could best be enforced by keeping wages low. The larger the population, the easier it would be to control the level of wages without hindering the growth of industry. Consequently every effort was made in Britain, France, the German states and Russia to discourage emigration. (In Britain, for example, the emigration of skilled workers was prohibited between 1782 and 1824.)

During the seventeenth century, however, a more socially conscious version of the doctrine was developed by writers like Hartlib, Chamberlen and Goffe in response to the growing problems of poverty and social unrest. Wilson notes the growing concern of the Commonwealth and post-Restoration mercantilist writers with the 'chronic problem of poverty which affected severely somewhere between a quarter and a half of the whole population'. The declining demand for labor encouraged mercantilists to seek ways of diversifying the national economy and to propose new schemes for the employment of paupers and the training of pauper children. Hartlib believed that, if the poor could be rendered industrious, the nation would be preserved from dependence on foreigners. Hartlib, in company with Goffe, was among the most eminent of a number of Commonwealth authorities who wrote about social policy and provided, in Wilson's view, 'the basis of almost all later economic thought for more than a century. The recognition that the problems of poverty, employment and national welfare are all linked together was never subsequently lost sight of.'

In describing the major social and economic changes which had helped to bring about these modifications of mercantilist theory, Schumpeter emphasises the gradual breakdown of the medieval village community, which 'provided a berth for everyone whom it recognized as a member', and whose 'structural design excluded unemployment and destitution'. James draws attention to the social distress and economic upheaval which followed the Civil war in England from the collapse of local industries to the decline and corruption of charitable enterprises and the general increase in vagrancy. At the time, Hartlib recommended not an increase in poor relief 'so much as instruction in the doctrine and practice of self-help'. He therefore advocated both the suppression of vagrancy and a more systematic attempt to train the children of the poor. In his view it was not right for the vagabond to 'go whiter his lust as the manner now is' but to 'return to the workhouse from whence he came'. The Act of Settlement of 1662 came at the end of a period during which the increase in the number of vagrants had become a political as well as an economic danger.

During and after the Restoration the debate about national poverty continued in largely mercantilist terms. The traditional tendency of mercantilist thinkers to associate national welfare with 'the net amount of bullion gained or lost via the balance of trade' was broadened to include an active and genuine concern for the social needs of the community. Wilson recognizes that in practical terms few of the poor derived much benefit from these changes in outlook. At the same time he insists that 'The collective charge that a whole class was through several generations guilty of social irresponsibility must ... be rejected as non-proven.' Effective and humane social policies failed to develop, 'because the supply of those capable of organizing and administering (charities and poor relief) with reasonable efficiency, honesty and compassionate understanding was totally inadequate'. The same point is made by Hicks: the early mercantilists simply lacked the necessary economic and administrative expertise. The clearest indication of progress and the most explicit commitment to change were embodied in the provision of more education and schemes of apprenticeship for the children of the poor. The progress of social reform was, however, still held to be contingent on the maintenance of protectionist economic policies and the control of migration.

Charles Wilson summarises the main tenets of mercantilist theory by reference to Thomas Mun's major work, *England's Treasure by Foreign Trade,* which was published in 1664. He points out that, like the other mercantilist writers, Mun was concerned less with setting out a body of theory than with finding an answer to 'a pressing economic problem; not to amass bullion but to explain its loss. And, as Keynes pointed out in the 1930s, while economists might later have come to regard the favourable balance of trade as a "puerile obsession", those more immediately concerned with policy in the centuries that followed have continued to regard it as a prime object of practical statecraft.'

From this preoccupation with the trade balance developed the various strands of mercantilist policy — the imposition of restrictions and prohibition of certain exports; the encouragement of the immigration of skilled workers; the stimulation of the import of raw materials from colonies; the imposition of tariffs to check the import of foreign luxuries; and the passing of the Navigation Acts in 1651 and 1660 designed to give British shipping a monopoly of British trade. Behind these economic defences it was hoped that the national economy would steadily diversify and grow, to the benefit of all citizens.

In contrast to mercantilism *laissez-faire* was an internationalist doctrine. The classical economic theories on which the popular notions of *laissez-faire* were based sought to demonstrate that human welfare could best be enhanced if goods and services were allowed to move without hindrance between nations, if labor was allowed to move with similar freedom and 'find its own price in the market' and if the 'creation of money' was made subject to 'an automatic mechanism' of gold. Once these interdependent mechanisms were allowed to operate in a largely self-regulatory way, a natural coincidence would occur between self-interest and the welfare of all.

During the first quarter of the nineteenth century the conflict between mercantilist and *laissez-faire* doctrines centres upon a number of major issues, which included the Corn Laws, the Navigation Acts, the Settlement Acts and the future of the colonies. All of these issues had some bearing on the great debate about free trade and protection. The implications of this debate for social welfare are the subject of this and the following chapter.

It is true that this promised Utopia could not emerge unless the poor remained content with only a modest level of expectation; indeed Ricardo's iron law of wages promised little more than subsistence for the laboring classes. Nonetheless, as Polanyi reminds us, Adam Smith was confident that some of the increases in wealth which would follow industrialisation would filter down to the poor. Ricardo was also mindful of the ameliorating influence of custom on the definition of subsistence. There is a passage in *Principles of Political Economy* in which Ricardo suggests that 'the natural price of labor ... always depends on the price of food, clothing and other necessaries,; but that this price is never 'absolutely fixed and constant' since it depends upon 'the habits and customs of the people. ... Many of the conveniences now enjoyed in an English cottage would have been thought luxuries at an earlier period in history.'

The passing of the Corn Law in 1815 provided an issue over which the exponents of *laissez-faire* were able to begin cultivating popular support and to appeal directly to the rising class of manufacturers. Coasts reminds us of the disagreement which occurred between Ricardo and Malthus concerning the effect of the Corn Laws. Ricardo argued that enforcing an artificially high price for corn would not only raise food prices but would push up the level of money wages to the detriment of profits. A fall in the rate of profit would discourage capital accumulation, and in the resulting economic slump the living standards of the laborer would be catastrophically affected. Malthus, however, took the view that free trade in corn would destroy the landed classes and thereby undermine the political stability of the nation. Furthermore a nation overly dependent upon imported foodstuffs would be strategically at a disadvantage in time of war.

It is also important to recognize that very few of the classical political economists were committed in an unqualified way to what became the popularised doctrines of *laissez-faire.* They favoured free trade but were not indifferent to the need to afford some protection to the living standards of ordinary citizens in times of adversity. It was from the group of thinkers and political activists loosely termed the Manchester school that the most dogmatic and unqualified doctrines of free trade and individualism began to circulate and gain public support. An anti-Corn Law association was formed in Manchester during 1838, and under the leadership and inspiration of Richard Cobden this group formed the nucleus of the Anti-Corn Law League. Opposition to the Corn Law was only one part of the campaign of the Manchester school to make *laissez-faire* an internationalist doctrine in practice as well as in theory. It also adopted a strongly anti-colonialist policy, at a time when Britain was beginning to acquire a second empire.

Within the terms of mercantilist theory 'The colonies and the mother country were to supplement one another as producers of raw materials and of manufactured articles respectively,' which meant that Britain would retain 'a monopoly of the colonial markets and the inter-imperial shipping trade,' while the colonies would be granted 'substantial tariff preferences' in their trade with Britain. That policy would have been anathema to Cobden and the Manchester school, looking forward, as they did, to an ideal economic world in which every nation would eventually adopt free trade and live at peace with its neighbours. In contrast with mercantilism free trade was, as Fuchs describes it, an essentially cosmopolitan theory, 'the object of which is not so much the highest development of the nation and the national character, as the greatest possible levelling down of national barriers.' Its fundamental economic principle was 'buying in the cheapest and selling in the dearest market' within the context of an international division of labor. An essential part of the theory is the doctrine of the 'harmony of interests according to which it is impossible that one country can develop at the expense of another, or that the progress or advantage of one is not at the same time in the interests of all.' The case for free trade follows naturally from the very notion of reciprocal exchange: in every condition of free exchange both parties derive some benefit.

Free trade offered the possibility of an unlimited system of exchange, while protectionism accepted the necessity of limits which were determined by the conflicts of economic interest Titmussian problem of altruism did not exist, since a natural coincidence would occur under free conditions between self-interest and the welfare of all at both individual and collective levels. Nonetheless protectionism can be said to express a definite, if highly conditional, notion of altruism. This notion derives from the mercantilist argument that welfare is not definable in purely economic terms, in other words the maximization of exchange values. The prosperity of a nation depends on the achievement of a balance between the several productive processes of that nation, and only extensive governmental intervention can assure the achievement of such an equilibrium between the interests of agriculture, commerce and manufacturing. The free market could not be relied upon to bring about a natural reconciliation of individual and national interests. Only governmental regulation could ensure that the long-term needs of the nation were not jeopardised by the short-term interests of individuals and sectional groups. These were the central tenets of Friedrich List's defence of mercantilism and critique of Adam Smith. As Sir Eric Roll puts it, in List's view "The atomism of Smith took no account of the national bond: in considering man, the producer and consumer, Smith had forgotten the citizen.' Such an indictment, however, appears to have more relevance to the popularised versions of *laissez-faire* than to Smith's own work.

Adam Smith and Karl Marx

It was not only Marx who criticised Adam Smith's notion of civil society and human self-interest. There were other authorities who were greatly influenced by mercantilist doctrines, such as Daniel Defoe, John Cary and Jonas Hanway who argued that the claims of national security and social welfare must take precedence over the pursuit of profit.

A key point about classical economic theory is that in positing a natural coincidence between self-interest and collective welfare it seems to render altruism an irrelevant concept. The free market *was* he welfare society. In this sense it is pointless to judge the humanity of capitalism simply by reference to the new poor laws, because less eligibility and deterrence were only the negative insturments designed to force men and women to seek their welfare in the economic market. And it was only in this economic market that positive welfare could be found.

A part of the perennial attraction of Marx's social theory is that it does provide an analytical framework within which the student can seek to relate theory to practice. It is a system of thought in which the political theory derives from and acts back upon the social theory. It purports to tell us not only how societies change but something about the role of political theory as an agent in those processes ot change.

Marx conceptualised social reality as a man-made reality which was the product of human choice and action. Man was the product of his social relationships and at the same time he could experience his self-hood as an 'inalienable property' in its own right. In *Grundrisse* Marx elaborated this view of the self by comparing it with that of the classical political economists. 'The economists,' he suggested, 'express this as follows: each pursues his private interest and only his private interest; and thereby serves the private interests of all, the general interest without willing or knowing it. ... The point is rather that private interest is already a socially determined interest, which can be achieved only within the conditions laid down by society and with the means provided by society.'

We might remind ourselves at this stage that the perfectly competitive economic market was not and never could be some natural state of affairs which appears when all the unnatural restraints upon competition are removed. Both the creation and preservation of competitive markets depends upon extensive legislation and government controls. This point has been made clear by Polanyi in *The Great Transformation,* by Schumpeter in *Capitalism, Socialism and Democracy* and of course by Adam Smith himself.

For Marx the key agents in this creation and re-creation of social realities were social groups—especially social classes—rather than individuals. We find it very difficult to understand Marx's notion of praxis, that is, the union of theory and practice by which men make sense of their world, act upon it through the exercise of choice and experience in turn the counter effects of their own action. We find it easier to comprehend the relationship between individuals and their culture in Simmel's more fatalistic or tragic sense, namely, that culture will always deny freedom to those who seek it in any unconditional sense. Or one may take the functionalist view that men treat their culture as an entity over and above themselves because it is useful and necessary to do so.

Marx, as we know, took a contrary view. He saw the disposition of men to reify their culture—to treat, for example, the complete marketisation of social life under capitalism as a necessary fact of life regulating the conditions of life — as evidence of the way in which private property, the division of labor and the pursuit of profit alienated them from each other and the products of their own labor. Through such a process individuals lose control of their own lives and labor and thus become involved in 'a contradiction between the interest of the separate individual (or the individual family) and the communal interest of all individuals who have intercourse with one another.'

But both marx and Smith recognized the absolute centrality of the *productive process* in structuring the meaning and the sense of reality of the individual members of industrial societies. For Smith it was *through* the productive process that individuals sought their own interests. For Marx the key agents were social classes rather than individuals. Although both writers drew different conclusions regarding the outcomes of this competition, in terms of the consequences for human welfare and its enhancement, these differences should not be allowed to obscure the common emphasis which Smith and Marx placed on production.

Marx was, however, highly critical of political economists like John Stuart Mill who, in his opinion, drew a sharp distinction between production and distribution and then treated this model as if it were 'encased in eternal natural laws independent of history,' when in fact it only typified 'bourgeois relations.' Marx's 'very short answer' to this approach was that all production involved the 'appropriation of nature,' and that 'every form of production' created its own distinctive set of social and political relationships. But marx was not content to let the matter rest there. He went on the ridicule the 'syllogism' by which political economists treated production as 'the generality, distribution and exchange the particularly, and consumption the singularity by which the whole is joined together.' He was equally dismissive of the critics of political economy who argued that distribution was as important as production, only to fall into the same error of treating production and distribution as 'independent, autonomous neighbours.'

Marx contended that, although production, distribution,' exchange and consumption are not identical, they 'all form the members of a totality, distinctions within a unity. Production predominates not only over itself, in the antithetical definition of production, but over the other moments as well.' The fact that changes in demand influence the character of production only underlined the 'organic' nature of the whole process. As for exchange, Marx described it as merely 'an act comprised within production itself,' contingent on the division of labor, the forms of which are in turn determined by production. Similarly the forms of distribution were shaped by 'the existence of capital and landed property as independent agents of production.'

Smith begins *The Wealth of Nations* with an analysis of the division of labor. He argues that it is 'the great multiplication of the production of all the different arts, in consequence of the division of labor which occasions, in a well-governed society, that universal opulence which extends itself to the lowest ranks of the people.' The social inequalities which arise from the division of labor are defended on the same grounds as those used subsequently by Ricardo, namely, that 'the accommodation of a European prince does not always so much exceed that of an industrious and frugal peasant as the accommodation of the latter exceeds that of many an African king.' Smith attributes the division of labor to a natural human propensity 'to truck, barter, and exchange one thing for another.' This propensity to seek one's own advantage through exchange is constrained only by the limits of the market.

As Smith describes the means by which productivity is increased and goods and services are distributed, he distinguishes between 'productive' and 'unproductive' labor and between 'opulent' and 'poor' nations and cities. He concludes that 'The proportion between capital and revenue .... seems everywhere to regulate the proportion between industry and idleness. Wherever capital predominates, industry prevails: wherever revenue, idleness. Every increase or diminution of capital, therefore, naturally tends to increase or diminish the real quantity of industry, the number of productive hands, and consequently the exchangeable value of the annual produce of the land and labor of the country, the real wealth and revenue of all its inhabitants.' In *The Wealth of Nations* the relationships between production, distribution, exchange and consumption are interpreted in a manner and to an end quite at variance with Marx's analysis, but the emphasis on production is similar. Marx denied, however, that these relationships as they existed under capitalism, were immutable of that they were in any way a reflection of 'inviolable natural laws on which society in the abstracts is founded.'

Smith and Marx both wrote at times when social services, as we understand them today, did not exist—apart, that is, from charitable enterprises. In our time the proliferation of social services seems to provide *prima facie* evidence of the existences of a separate institutional entity, which can be termed the social market. If the social market is taken to include all those welfare goods and services which are allocated by reference to criteria of need rather than effective demand, it should properly be located in the sphere of distribution rather than production. It can of course be argued that social services are also productive forces, insofar as they contribute to greater economic efficiency. It is doubtful, however, whether the claims of the social market to institutional autonomy could be defended for long on such utilitarian grounds.

In short, if we argue from the position of either Smith or Marx, the social market can be seen to function as an agency of distribution, but its material scope and normative autonomy will always be prescribed by the nature of the productive forces operating in the economic market. Smith and Marx both offer a theoretical framework for the analysis of social policy in relation to the wider society, but the logic of their respective approaches consigns social policies to a very subordinate role.

Yet the emphasis which both authors place on production within the economic market has great relevance to students of social administration who may be tempted to differentiate what can be called the values of the economic market from those of the social market and to concentrate their attention upon the latter. The social market may perform certain handmaidenly functions in relation to the economic market, but it is in the last analysis an agent of distribution rather than production. In a subject like ours it is tempting to forget that wealth and hence welfare have to be produced before anything can be either distributed or redistributed.

This error of emphasis can be begin very early in the historical study of the relationship between industrialisation and social policy. The rise and survival of capitalism cannot be explained by reference to the poor law, and capitalism can no more be judged by reference to the poor law than Christianity by reference to the Spanish inquisition. Marx himself was foremost in recognizing the unprecedented capacity of capitalism to produce wealth, even as he indicted the human damage it might cause in the act of creation.

In seeking to understand the ways in which social welfare is enhanced—by whom and for whom — we must make use of theories which help us to understand better the relationship between the social and the economic markets. Both classical economic theory and Marxist theory can be used to this end. The normative content of the first insists that the two are indivisible and that the free play of the economic market is the best way to enhance welfare. Marxist social theory sought to demonstrate that the economic institutions and values of capitalism are destructive of welfare and that social policies can never be more than ameliorative, since their ends and values are always subordinated to and reflective of the competitive ethos.

Colonial Reformers and Free Trade

Of all the great industrialising nations of the nineteenth century, Britain came nearest to realizing the internationalist ideals of free trade and *laissez-faire*. Yet the logic of mercantilism offered a viable alternative prospect of international influence through the purposive acquisition and exploitation of colonies. The conflict between these two doctrines was temporarily resolved in the first half of the nineteenth century—before Marx published *The Communist Manifesto* and long before Marxism became an influential doctrine.

Both *laissez-faire* and mercantilism were compatible

with the rise of a capitalist mode of production but *laissez-faire* was far less compatible than was mercantilism with the development of collectivist welfare policies. The rise of welfare collectivism in Britain was to become associated with the subsequent revival of protectionist economic policies which owed much to the mercantile tradition. This relationship can be stated in more negative terms—the gradual loss of confidence in the capacity of a free economic market to enhance individual welfare was attended by a growing conviction amongst the citizenry that the state ought to play a more active role in the collective provision of welfare. As the terms of welfare obligation and entitlement at home became more generous protectionist trading policies became more popular. The protracted series of events through which these issues were resolved merit some attention because they help us to understand more clearly why British social policies developed as they did. In subsequent chapters we shall extend the analysis by comparison with other countries.

As it happened, the crucial years in the formation of Britain's imperial trade policies were those in which the doctrines of free trade were rapidly gaining political ascendancy. The turning-point occurred just before the repeal of the Corn Laws in 1846. By that date the imperial alternative to free trade was in temporary eclipse. In setting out the case against the retention of the colonies the leading free traders, Cobden, Bright and Goldwin Smith, argued that in any event separation was inevitable as well as necessary. First, the status of being a colony was in herently degrading and offensive to liberal principles. Secondly, expenditures on colonial defence were already high and were certain to go on rising, because colonies were a major cause of war. Thirdly, these costs of colonial defence fell upon the ordinary citizen and thereby necessarily diminished his welfare. Fourthly, the counter argument that the colonies provided free land for emigrants from the mother country was tendentious and irrelevant. The majority of British emigrants went to the United States and not to the colonies. After separation would not in itself deter those who wished to go to the colonies. Once granted independence, the former colonies would continue to trade with Britain, since it would be in their interests to do so. The lobby for the repeal of the Corn Laws was thus complemented by a far more wide-ranging campaign for the general liberalisation of trade and the separation of the colonies from the mother country.

During the 1830s these free trade views were opposed by a small but influential group of colonial reformers, which included Lord Durham, Charles Buller, Sir William Molesworth and Gibbon Wakefield. Durham's unpredictable temperament was one of the factors which were to deny him the highest political office, but he served as Lord privy Seal in Grey's ministry of 1830 and played a key role in drafting the 1832 Reform Bill. In 1838 he became Governor General of Canada and undertook an investigation of the serious discontent which continued to trouble the colony after the risings of 1837 in Upper and Lower Canada. Durham prepared a major report, published in 1839, which recommended the union of the two provinces and the adoption of a new set of principles on which might be based the future governance of the colonies. These principles directed, first, that through the institution of cabinet government a colony might be granted autonomy with regard to its internal affairs and, secondly, that British interests should continue to be protected by the maintenance of imperial authority in four main areas of policy, which were 'the constitution of the form of government, the regulation of foreign relations, and of trade with the mother country, the other British colonies, and foreign nations, and the disposal of the public lands.'

Under the Union Act of 1840 the provinces were united,

and Canada was granted responsible government. Durham, however, died before the year was out, and when Lord Elgin assumed the governor-generalship in 1846 he was given powers to implement the remaining recommendations of the 1840 Commission as he saw fit. By this time, however, not only were free trade doctrines in the ascendant, but even those who favoured the retention of the colonies feared that undue control by the metropolitan country might drive the white colonial settlers to secede. Fieldhouse argues that after 1848 'the British never stood on diarchy, for if they had done so, they would have forced ambitious colonial statesmen to opt for independence. The British preferred to throw out of the window all that they once thought vital to their own interests in a colony in order to retain at least some formal connexion with it.' This meant in the case of Canada that two of the four major principles recommended by the Durham Commission were swiftly abandoned. Imperial preferences were given up during and after 1846, and with the repeal of the Navigation Acts in 1849 Britain also surrendered its control of colonial shipping. In 1852 the control of the 'public lands was transferred to the Canadian government. Thereafter these two major policies were followed in the other colonies upon the granting of responsible government.

What determined whether or not a colony was granted responsible government? It was unlikely to be granted if the colony in question served a direct and particular metropolitan interest, for example as a military garrison or a penal settlement. Small or poor colonies would not qualify; neither would those without a majority white population. In practice the dominant criterion was a racial one. Other overseas possessions might be granted not responsible, but representative government, or they might be governed as crown colonies or, as in the case of India, as viceroyalties. Responsible government was granted between 1892 and 1890 to the Australian states, New Zealand, the

Cape Colony and Newfoundland, and with this status went control over trade and public land.

The decline in the influence of the colonial reformers is explicable partly by the effective lobbying of the Manchester school and partly by the fact that free trade was becoming the most advantageous policy from Britain's point of view. In its enjoyment of massive industrial and naval power Britain was able to contemplate the prospect of a great peace, while other nations remained highly sensitive to the reality or imminence of conflict. The American Civil War and the rise of Prussia in the 1860s were to justify these fears.

Yet another factor which may have contributed to the mid-century demise of imperial policies was the eclipse of the colonial reformers as an effective pressure group. Durham had died in 1840, and Buller in 1848, both of them in early middle age. Wakefield had been debarred from Parliament as a result of youthful indiscretions, and the greater part of his subsequent career was spent abroad, away from the centres of metropolitan influence. Molesworth died in 1855 at the age of forty-five. With the loss of these men, much of the direction and impetus went out of the movement for colonial reform in Britain.

While it cannot be argued that the defeat of the colonial reformers had any direct influence on the course of social reform at home, the success of the free trade movement is evidence of the growing influence of *laissez-faire* doctrines in their popularised forms among policy-makers and influential members of the general public. This is the period to which Dicey refers when he writes of the popular acceptance of classical political economy 'as a science containing very definite and certain principles, from which were logically deduced conclusions of indisputable and universal truth.' One of the fundamental principles of this doctrine was that minimal governmental interference in trade was the best way to enhance social welfare. In this respect free trade can be seen as the positive counterpoint to the deterrent policies which dominated poor relief during the 1840s and 1850s.

Burrow makes a point of further relevance regarding the complementary nature of certain aspects of utilitarian thought and political economy in the enhancement of human happiness. He observes that 'Much of the appeal of classical political economy for utilitarians lay in the fact that it provided in its own sphere what in the psychological sphere proved so difficult to obtain — namely, a means of determining what people wanted in an exactly measurable way. The price mechanism offered in the objective sphere of social life precisely what the Benthamite calculus failed to do in the subjective and inscrutable area of psychology .... a numerical index of relative wants.'

In keeping with the philosophical and economic spirit of the time it was inevitable that the role of government in the relief of destitution would remain a negative one. The new poor law was designed to force laborers to act positively on their own behalf. Yet for a brief period there had been a prospect that sponsored emigration and the settlement of the surplus poor in the colonial public lands might add a new and positive dimension to the enhancement of social welfare. In default of any government-sponsored initiative emigration became predominantly the concern of private enterprise, and the main flow of emigrants was towards the United States rather than the British colonies. The major intervention of government in this sphere, coming belatedly in 1842, took the form of the Passenger Act, which was designed to put a stop to some of the many malpractices which had become associated with the transoceanic shipment of paupers by private enterprise. The subsequent Passenger Acts, passed between 1847 and 1855, have rightly been described as representing a major stage in the development of effective regulatory practices in modern government. In terms of the pursuit of welfare, however, these Acts were a reaction against the excesses of the private market. A more positive role for the government in emigration policy was effectively precluded once the control of the colonial public lands had been allowed to pass under the jurisdiction of the new colonial governments.

The British transition to free trade was a gradual one, and its stages were dictated, according to Fuchs, 'step by step, according to the concrete necessities of English industrial life at the time of its introduction.' Given the advantages in industrial development and resources which Britain then possessed in relation to other nations this was a doctrine which was evidently attractive to the manufacturing classes. It was also a doctrine to which they were anxious to win converts abroad. Nonetheless the confidence of the free traders was such that they were fully prepared to see Britain converted to free trade on a unilateral basis, if necessary, since protectionist nations would only end up by raising their own costs of living, should they retaliate by erecting tariffs.

Despite these dire predictions this is exactly what the majority of other independent nations were already doing. Furthermore as soon as the colonies achieved the status of responsible government they also began to opt for protection rather than free trade and the regulation rather than the free movement of migrants. In 1859 Canada passed a major tariff law, which was designed to attract 'skilled settlers' and to nurture 'infant industries,' and thereafter Canadian trade policy became increasingly protectionist. In Australia all of the new states eventually adopted tariffs — once again in the interests of nurturing home industries — and the raising of wage levels by protecting their workers against the competition of cheap European Labor. Very similar policies were adopted by New Zealand and the Cape Colony, after they had been granted responsible government.

These trends were viewed with some alarm by the minority of colonial reformers who survived in British political life. Throughout the years between 1850 and 1870, however, separatism in either its 'active' or 'reluctant' forms dominated government policy and large sections of influential public opinion. It also became, as Bodelsen points out, the policy favoured amongst the leading permanent officials at the Colonial Office. Sir James Stephens, who served as Permanent Under Secretary during the period 1836-47, achieved the reputation of being an early supporter of the interests of indigenous peoples and he sought to protect their interests against prospective colonisers. Both Sir Frederick Rogers, who succeeded Stephens during the years between 1847 and 1871, and Herman Merivale were separatists. It is therefore not surprising that under the terms of the Colonial Laws Validity Act of 1865 it was laid down that laws passed by colonial legislatures 'should be void only in so far as they were clearly repugnant to an Act of the British Parliament.'

The most significant exception to these trends in British colonial policy was the case of India, in which cotton duties were abolished. India became the temporary salvation of Lancashire cotton industry which was already struggling to survive in an increasingly protectionist world. Lacking the status of responsible government, India had no choice in the matter. As Fuchs duly observes, 'A resolution of the English House of Commons, on August 30th 1877, declared that the cotton duties in India ... were, in their nature, protective; they were therefore in contradiction with the sound principles of trade policy, and should be abolished as soon as the condition of Indian finances permitted.' Thus, with the exception of India, Great Britain came to offer the world 'the remarkable spectacle of a country, anxious to convert all other nations to Free Trade, and yet unable to introduce it to its own colonies.'[69]

In his brilliant contemporary study of the British free trade movement Fuchs explores the complex interaction of international altruism and scarcely concealed self-interest which sustained this policy until the end of the nineteenth century. Fuchs's own biases are clearly expressed. He suggests that Cobden 'well knew how to cloak the special interests of England in the garb of a philanthropic cosmopolitanism and of an ideal aspiration after the welfare of mankind.' The same free traders who successfully campaigned for the repeal of the Corn Laws opposed trade union combination and the Ten Hour Bill. As it proved, the passing of that Ten Hour Act was the price paid for the repeal of the Corn Laws.

Despite the association of free trade with a general hostility to governmental intervention the popularity of free trade as a doctrine steadily increased within many sectors of the working class. The actual effect of free trade on their living standards, however, depended on a number of related factors, including wages. As Marx observed in his *discourse on Free Trade,* within the terms of Ricardian wage theory 'every means of cheapening ... The means of subsistence of the workers was bound to accrue to the advantage of the manufacturers,' 'and the poor would be better off so long as both wages *and* the price of corn remained high, since a little economy on bread would allow the purchase of other commodities.'

Nonetheless many members of the working class were won over to free trade not because of moralistic appeals to internationalism but because of the real and immediate attractions of cheaper food. In this respect there emerged a temporary coincidence of interests between workers and manufacturers. The economic and social casualties of free trade were the farmers and agricultural laborers. In reviewing the subsequent progress of free trade policy fuchs noted the difficulties in assessing its impact on living standards, apart from 'the continuous displacement of agriculture by other branches of economic production.' The increasing reliance on grain imports from Russia (especially in the periods 1866-70, 1871-5 and 1886-90), the United States and India had a disastrous effect on English agriculture.

The peculiarities of the British free trade system were such that some sections of the working class benefited significantly more than others. Under the terms of the Gladstone tariff of 1860, protective duties, that is to say, duties on goods which were also produced at home, were removed. Pure revenue duties — those on goods which were not produced at home such as tobacco, tea, spirits and coffee — were, however, retained, and Fuchs argued that by 1890 Britain was raising about a quarter of its national revenue by such duties, a far greater proportion than that raised by any other major power. The net effect of these duties was the imposition of taxes on the customary luxuries of the poor. Fuchs concludes, however, that it was the skilled rather than the unskilled members of the working class who were more positively disposed to free trade, because it enabled them to 'consume an increasing amount of cheap bread, cheap sugar, and the other cheap means of subsistence and enjoyment.'

The decision to repeal the Corn Laws was also, a Burnett remarks, a 'conscious decision against self-sufficiency,' an 'by the eve of the First World War British farmers supplied only half our meat and a mere one-fifth of our wheat requirements.' The most remarkable feature of the free trade movement was the confidence which inspired it, a confidence in Britain's capacity to win out in a competitive world and a conviction that international peace rather than war between nations would prevail and endure. At the time of the repeal of the Corn Laws Britain had already lost one overseas empire and was well on the way to acquiring another. In an earlier work we argued that the adoption of the poor law principles of 1834 represented 'one of the few occasions in the history of English social policy on which theory was allowed to take normative wings and find a legislative perch.' The complement to and indeed the rationale for this theoretical flight were embodied in the decision to adopt and maintain free trade policies, throughout a period during which every other emerging industrial power was becoming more protectionist, and during which the acquisition of a second empire was providing both the means and the incentive for Britain to do likewise.

From the 1870s onwards the trend towards protection gathered momentum throughout Europe and the United States as well as in the self-governing colonies of the British Empire. It was the raising of tariffs outside the Empire, however, which most seriously affected Britain. The McKinley Act of 1890, for example, had a particularly adverse effect on the British tinplate, cutlery and textile industries. By 1889 the American market was taking nearly one-eighth of the total value of British and Irish exports. Among the six major markets for British exports during the period 1860-90 the United States accounted on an average for 15.8 per cent of the total, France for 10.4 per cent, India for 9.9 per cent, Germany for 8.4 per cent, Australia for 6.1 per cent and Holland for 5.6 per cent. All these countries, with the exception of India, had adopted protection.

It was the onset of the Great Depression in world trade between 1873 and 1896 which more than any other event destroyed the general mood of optimism which had sustained Britain's confidence in free trade policies. Despite the brief periods of intermittent recovery this confidence was never to be regained. The rise of new industrial systems in the Untied States, Germany and France was depriving Britain of its privileged position in the international market. Every one of Britain's major industrial competitors was resorting to protection in order to survive the economic depression and quicken its rate of industrial growth.

Hinsley suggests that this general 'reversion to protectionism was more than offset by the constantly widening opportunities in international trade,' and that Britain's continuing commitment to free trade only served to encourage protectionism elsewhere. The trend towards protectionism in Europe continued throughout the last quarter of the century in Russia, Spain, Italy, Germany and France. At the same time it is possible to note throughout Europe an impetus not only towards protectionism but towards social reform and a more vigorous commitment to imperialism.

Polanyi argues that the one form of protection reinforced the other and was conditional on it. Agricultural protection forced up the price of food, so that trade unions clamoured for higher wages and welfare legislation. Industrialists demanded protective tariffs to meet these demands. It was becoming clear, as Robinson remarks, that 'the case for Free Trade as a benefit to each nation could not be made out. The weak spout in the analysis was in overlooking the implications of the assumption of universal perfect competition ... any one nation, within the conditions of the equilibrium model, may be better off with a smaller volume of trade at higher prices of exports in terms of imports than at the Free Trade position." Robinson goes on to observe that 'In the pre-1914 world Great Britain had everything to gain ... and very little to lose' in a free trade world, and that 'Marshall, the old fox, had known perfectly well that it was all a question of national self-interest' but had chosen to hide away his reservations in a 'rather boring appendix to the *Principles of Economics*.'

It is important to recognize the extent to which even Britain fell short of the ideal state of *laissez-faire* commended by the Manchester school. The liberalisation of trade never went so far that protection was completely abandoned at home. As late as 1870 there were still seventeen dutiable imports. Apart from these internal restrictions British trade had to contend with an increasing number of protected markets, as the century progressed. Given the central role of the City of London in the world money market, there was for a time a genuinely international free trade in capital. It was indeed vitally important for the working of the British economy that these exports of capital should be paralleled by opportunities to export paupers. For a relatively brief period there was an almost international market in labor, but this situation was changed by the increase in the number of nations which were imposing migration controls. Within Britain the internal movement of labor was also regulated by the sanctions of the poor law.

The Great Depression of the 1870s was to mark the beginning of the decline of free trade as the dominant British economic doctrine. In addition, although there was a brief revival of the full severities of the new poor law during this decade, the remaining years of the century were ones in which the advocates of more generous policies of social welfare were to find unexpected support amongst the imperialist and protectionist elements of both major political parties. In reviewing the major economic trends of the period between 1870 and the First World War Ashworth attaches greater importance to changes in real income per head than to price movements. He concludes that 'Despite the qualification that must be made about its later years the impression of the whole period from 1870 to 1914 is one of great economic advance."

A contrary view is taken by Hobsbawm. He recognizes that 'So far as the working people are concerned, it [the

Great Depression] cannot compare with the cataclysm of the 1830s and 1840s, or the 1920s and 1930s,' but he goes on to propose that 'If "depression" indicates a pervasive—and for the generation since 1850 a new — state of mind of uneasiness and gloom about the prospects of the British economy, the word is accurate." Hobsbawm draws attention to the adverse impact of the Great Depression upon the living standards of the poor and the confidence of the business community. Thereafter, he notes, we enter a period characterised by intensified political activity on the part of the working classes and exemplified in the formation of a Marxist International, and an increasing disposition on the part of business interests to call 'on the state not only to give [them] a free hand, but to save [them].'

REFERENCES

Adam Smith, *The Wealth of Nations*, Vols. I and II, Everyman Edition, Dent Dutton, 1937.

A.W. Coats, 'The Classical Economists, Industrialisation and Poverty,' in Institute of Economic Affairs, *The Long Debate on Poverty*, IEA Readings 9, London, 1972.

C.A. Bodelsen, *Studies in Mid-Victorian Imperialism*, Glydendalske Boghandel-Nordisk Forlag-KJQ Benhaven, Kristiana, London and Berlin, MDCCCCXXIV.

Carl Johannes Fuchs, *The Trade Policy of Great Britain and Her Colonies Since 1860*, Macmillan, 1905.

Charles Wilson, *The Other Face of Mercantilism*.

Charles Wilson, *England's Apprenticeship, 1603-1763*, Longmans, 1965, pp. 60 et seq.

David Ricardo, *The Principles of Political Economy*, Everyman Edition, Dent Dutton, 1929.

David Thomson, "The United Kingdom and Its World-Wide Interests,' Ch. VIII in J.P. Bury (ed.) *The New Cambridge Modern History*, Vol. X, *The Zenith of European Power, 1830-1870*, Cambridge University Press, London, 1967.

Eric Roll, *A History of Economic Thought*, Faber and Faber, 1973.

Hinsley, Introduction to *Material Progress and World-World Problems*.

Jacob Viner, 'Power versus Plenty as Objectives of Foreign Policy in the Seventeenth and Eighteenth Centuries,' in D.C. Coleman (ed.), *Revisions in Mercantilism,* Methuen, 1969.

John Hicks, *A Theory of Economic History,* Clarendon Press, Oxford, 1969.

Joseph A. Schumpeter, *History of Economic Analysis,* Allen and Unwin, 1963, pp. 251-2.

J.W. Burrow, *Evolution and Society: A Study in Victorian Social Theory,* Cambridge University Press,, 1979.

Karl Polanyi, *The Great Transformation: The Political and Economic Origins of Our Time,* Beacon Press, Boston, 1968.

M.R. James, *Social Problems and Policy during the Puritan Revolution, 1640-1660,* George Routledge and Sons, 1930.

Oliver MacDonagh, *A Pattern of Government Growth 1800-1860,* MacGibbon and Kee, London, 1961.

Werner Coze, "The German Empire,' in Hinsley (ed.), *Material Progress and World-Wide Problems.*

6

Social Reform and Welfare

Compared with the right and the radical Left, the Centre-Left tends to be much more eclectic and diffuse doctrinally. It represents essentially a pragmatic and practical, rather than a theoretically rigorous and systematic tradition. In this tradition is included Fabian socialist (*e.g.* Titmuss) interested in the pursuit of equality through social policy as well as moderate collectivists (*e.g.* Beveridge) concerned with using the state welfare services to guarantee a basic minimum. Their approach to collectivism and welfare differs more in degree than in kind. Both groups have a commitment to the welfare state and to political democracy and freedom.

A convenient British label for this genre of reformism is 'Fabianism' and will be used in this chapter more or less interchangeable with 'social democratic' to indicate this Centre-Left position. Although the term Fabianism is not directly transferrable to countries outside Britain, including the United States, the assumption made here is that in almost all western industrial countries intellectual and political orientations akin to it can be identified. In Britain social scientists such as Richard Titmuss, T.H. Marshall and Peter Townsend represent this genre of thinking and collectivist approach. True, they (and others discussed below) differ in many important ways in their thinking. Many, moreover, might not wish to wear the label 'Fabian' or 'social democrat'. Be that as it may, the main point is that the reformist tradition of enhancing social welfare through pragmatic state intervention is seen here as a distinctive approach, paralleling the neo-conservative, Marxist and the corporatist views outlined already. Here our main concern is with the intellectual standpoint largely associated with the post-war welfare state. The impasse in which the Keynesian managed economy found itself from about the mid-1970s and the resulting implications for social welfare have left the Fabians in a quandary. As Donnison points out, post-war Fabian thinking about social policy took economic growth for granted. Social policy was therefore seen as 'dealing with the *redistribution* of the fruits of economic growth, the management of its human effects, and the compensation of those who suffered from them.' There was little concern with the *productive* aspects of welfare capitalism. This did not seem unreasonable in the 1950s and 1960s when by all accounts it looked as if the pre-war problem of economic recessions had finally been solved.

But once capitalist economy was confronted with stagflation, and Keynesian recipes proved ineffectual to overcome it, the situation changed radically. As growth and full employment ceased to be valid assumptions, the argument for higher social expenditure and redistribution began to look increasingly unrealistic. In any case rising unemployment was a cruel reminder of the importance of 'economic welfare', which could no longer be guaranteed by the welfare state. In Britain, Thatcherism capitalised on the hiatus between Labourite stress on distributive collectivism, and the sorry state of the British economy and its productive base. Thatcherites emphasised their own 'realistic' appraisal of the needs and priorities of the British economy, contrasting it with the 'mindless' collectivism and the economically disastrous growth of social expenditure favoured by the Fabians. In the United States Reagan politics capitalised on a similar disjunction between the nation's apparent desire for higher consumption (for private & public) as well as lower taxes on the one hand and the precarious state of the economy on the other. By and large, in English-speaking countries, the policy initiative has been seized by the Right while social democracy finds itself in disarrary.

But where does this leave the Fabian Centre—the main intellectual support of the post-war welfare state ? What has been its response to the 'crisis' so far ? Perhaps the most revealing thing about the Fabian response is that it is virtually a non-response. What Rustin has noted recently *a propose* Britain has wider validity; namely, that the Centre seems to have collapsed without a fight in the face of political and intellectual onslaught of the new Right. Rustin believes that the radical Left must take some of the blame for this. He writes, the 'discrediting of welfare reformism, and the failure to maintain much believe in its further potential, has surely help to clear the way for the attack on it from the Right.' Rustin's point is well taken. But quite apart from the peculiarities of the British situation, he fails to address the more fundamental issues involved. There are two. First, the key role of Keynesian economics in underpinning the mixed economy, which in turn formed the mainstay of the social welfare services. It is not so much the attack on reformism by the radical Left as the increasing difficulty of the mixed economy and the crumbling of its intellectual prop, namely Keynesianism, that has silenced the Centre. What recent events have also underlined is the extent to which social democratic reformism and strategy of change depended on the smooth functioning of the mixed economy. Moreover, this is a point that social Fabians such as Titmuss and Townsend not only did not come to terms with but scarcely acknowledged. Successful economic management and growth were taken for granted. The market economy, therefore, tended to be seen either as an engine of inequality and privilege, or else ignored as irrelevant to the moral case for egalitarianism and social justice. In any case the arguments centred largely on distribution and collective consumption. But once the economy moved into a no-growth situation public attention shifted towards the problems of production, inflation and the like. Moreover the distributive struggle became so intensive as to threaten the very conditions of production (hyperinflation, reduced profits, bankruptcies, etc.). The situation in which value conflict over distribution could be waged around social expenditure in a civilised sort of way vanished robbing the Centre of much of its appeal. The Centre has been rather more vulnerable in Britain in part because the country's steady economic decline is associated with the post-war period of welfare consensus and also because by the end of the 1970s the economy was really in bad shape.

The second and more basic point to be made from the perspective of this book is that Fabianism lacks an articulated theory of the welfare state. Indeed, as already pointed out, its approach to social reform has been piecemeal and pragmatic, based on a range of economic, political and social assumptions which have not been made explicit, and with little recourse to theory. Moreover, a similar lack of fundamental thinking about social democracy more generally has been characteristic of the 1960s and the 1970s. Perhaps the last systematic statement of the theoretical standpoint of post-war social democracy came from Anthony Crossland. Recent years have seen a spate of books about social democracy and socialism but lack the elegance, verve and weight of his influential treatise. Through-out the 1960s and for a good part of the 1970s both welfare statism and parliamentary socialism have relied on a mix of technocratic and moral arguments (*e.g. ad hoc* statements in favour of welfare).

It is hardly surprising that the Centre which intellectually speaking never really had much coherence and weight should 'collapse' as problems began to mount for which neither Keynesianism nor a roused social conscience had any solution.

The atheoretical tradition dominant in the study of social welfare, the empirical study of discrete social problems and their solution through administrative reforms, has often been noted. Yet it would be wrong to suggest that thirty years of welfare statism and the study of social problems has failed to generate any theory whatsoever. But this theory is largely concerned with what might be called social problems located *within* the framework and practice of the welfare state. Social research and theorising have often been of an applied kind concerned with poverty, stigma, selectivity, universality, and territorial justice. In this approach—and this is the nub of the matter from the viewpioint of the current crisis—there has been very little concern with trying to understand the welfare state as a whole, as a *social system*. The focus has been almost entirely on social policy and administration, whilst the wider social-structural context of state welfare activity has been ignored.

Writing recently Robson, a veteran British Fabian, bemoans the absence of a clear rationale of the welfare state—a theory or vision that would both elicit *moral* support from the people and act as a guide to policy-makers. 'There is at present no philosophy of the welfare state', writes Robson, 'and there is an urgent and deep need for such a theory.' For Robson, the welfare state cannot simply be an instrument for distributing and allocating resources through collectivist channels. If it were to be merely that then it would become an extension of the capitalist market-place, an arena for grabbing what different groups can be exerting pressure on the government rather than a system which serves the community as a whole in accordance with nationally-based priorities. The latter, however, presupposes a welfare *society* which, in turn, demands a measure of national consensus or unity.

This unity was present in Britain after the war, but Robson finds little evidence of it in the 1970s. The result is a void. The welfare state is not based on a broadly accepted altruism grounded in a social philosophy : 'Political scientists have not provided a theory of the proper province of state action in the contemporary world.. The term welfare state offers no guide to the proper limits of individual freedom or governmental action.' Robson, moreover, raises the question of duties or obligations (corresponding to rights) within the welfare state. For example, given the interrelationship between the economic and social sectors of society does free collective bargaining by workers, professionals and others, aimed at maximizing sectional interest, make sense ? Robson believes that maximizing self-interest in this way is more 'appropriate to a *laisser-faire* state'. It is scarcely 'compatible with a welfare society', for 'in such a society welfare is not only something created by the state through the action of public authorities, but is also generated by the actions and attitudes of individuals, groups and institutions.' In fact, Robson seems to be drawing attention, *inter alia*, to the weaknesses of a plural welfare state (DWS) and some of the issues he raises, for example the need for restraint and for consensus over national goals and priorities, point towards a corporatist solution (IWS). But it is not a a solution that Robson consciously looks at.

Robson's book is important because of the questions it asks rather than the answers it provides. It is one of the rare attempts by a British Fabian to look at the welfare state as a whole, critically, and as a social system linked with other institutional aspects of the society of which it is a part. Robson's principal thesis is that 'we are vainly trying to have a welfare state without having achieved a welfare society. *i.e.* without generating those attitudes and outlook necessary to sustain the ideal of a welfare state. Despite important differences in method and objectives,

Robson's work is comparable to Janowitz's elegant sociological study of the crisis of the welfare state in the US.

Others, notably Bell in the USA and Hirsch on the other side of the Atlantic, have also raised the question of an adequate theory, normative and positive, of the welfare state. These writers believe that piecemeal social engineering and *ad hoc* collectivism are not enough. Without the necessary intellectual and moral underpinning, the welfare state far from being integrative, becomes anomic. Bell notes that while the state's role in managing economic and social affairs has grown enormously there is neither an adequate sociology nor social philosophy of the 'public household' (*i.e.* government revenue and expenditure). Meanwhile the combination of a market economy, a democratic polity and a growing public sector is proving fatal. For Bell, contemporary economic dilemmas confronting Western societies derive from the fact that we have sought to combine bourgeois appetites which resist curbs on acquisitiveness, either morally or by taxation ; a democratic polity which, increasingly and understandably, demands more and more social services as entitlements; and an individualist ethos which at best defends the idea of personal liberty, and at worst evades the necessary social responsibilities and social sacrifices which a communal society demands. In sum, we have had no normative commitment to a public household or a public philosophy that would mediate private conflicts.

The upshot is that the public household 'is not a community but an arena, in which there are no normative rules (other than bargaining) to define the common good and adjudicate conflicting claims on the basis of rights.' Bell, in the manner of a latterday Durkheim, looks for 'some transcendent tie' that would bind individuals in a society 'sufficiently for them to make, when necessary, the necessary sacrifices of self-interest.'

In the course of a novel and elegant thesis on the social limits to growth, Hirsch poses a similar problem. The growing collective regulation of the economy and public provision of goods and services is, nonetheless, taking place in the context of individualism and the pursuit of self-interest. Without a social ethic that would legitimise existing regulations and distributive patterns the public sector tends to be less a community and more an arena concerned, like the private or market sector, with egotistical and sectional interests. Hence in the public sphere technical manipulation alone is no longer effective. For in the absence of the appropriate motives and attitudes on the part of the factors (restraint, acceptance of a social ethic) technical measures, (*e.g.* those aimed at inflation) do not work. Ratherepessimistically for the liberal capitalist society, Hirsch concludes that we 'may be near the limit of explicit social organization possible without a supporting social morality. Additional correctives in its absence simply do not take.'

The absence of a macro-theory of the welfare state is, in one sense, an indictment of post-war Fabian thinking about welfare which has tended to neglect, if not altogether avoid, the systematic analysis of the welfare state as a social structure. The empiricist, practical and largely atheoretical approach prevalent in the study of social welfare has been noted already. However, at least two post-war social scientists, Titmuss and Marshall, who have made outstanding contributions to the analysis of welfare, merit attention. However far is their work relevant to the development of a theory of the welfare state ? We begin with Titmuss.

It is no secrete that Titmuss, though outstandingly original and incisive in his analyses, was not a systematic thinker. In fact he had little patience with theorising and did not even care much for a schematic approach to the study of welfare. His was a critical intelligence which illuminated specific issues in social policy supremely well, but never sought to comprehend the 'welfare state' as a macro-social system. He never explored its relationship with the rest of the society systematically whether at the level of values or functions. 'Titmuss was not a theorist ... He was suspicious of attempts to construct broad, general theories of social policy development or the roles and functions of social services.' It is a pity that this was so, for more than anyone else working within the academic tradition of social administration, Titmuss took a wide, societal view of social welfare. His account of the development of social policy in Britain during the war years, the study of income distribution and social change, the Fabian lecture on the 'irresponsible' society, and above all the idea of social welfare as an expression of social solidarity and community all attest to his interest and insight into the society-welfare relationship.

Unfortunately there is too much in Titmuss's writing that is *ad hoc*, improvised and eclectic, and too little that is worked out systematically to be able to provide the foundations of a theory of the welfare state. Much of his work was a polemic against the ideology and practice of economic *laisser-faire*. In the economic climate of the 1950s and 1960s his defence of the 'institutional' approach against the 'residual' was in important contribution to the debate then taking place around policy issues. Titmuss had the good fortune (or misfortune) not to see the end of the Indian summer of the Keynesian mixed economy and the welfare state. How he would have responded to the intellectual challenge to Fabianism posed by the political economy of stagflation can only be guessed at.

Unlike Titmuss, Marshall is primarily a theoretical sociologist interested in the social analysis of the welfare state. His concerns are academic and analytical rather than practical and reformist. Among social democratic thinkers, Marshall is virtually unique in his attempt to analyse the welfare state as a social system, especially in relation to capitalism. He sees the welfare state largely as the institutionalisation of social rights in a capitalist society. It is a part of the development of the idea and institutions of citizenship-encompassing civil, political and social rights-in western democratic societies. In this sense capitalism, democracy and state welfare institutions form a part of the evolutionary development of the West. None the less Marshall, somewhat like Titmuss, also notes the conflict of values inherent in a social system comprising a market economy, a democratic polity and a state welfare sector. For instance, there is the problem of reconciling the value of inequality inherent in the market with the egalitarianism implicit in the idea of meeting needs. But whereas for Titmuss the values underlying the economic and the social sectors-capitalist market economy and social welfare-are diametrically opposed, for Marshall they are not so. Rather the problem is one of achieving a judicious mix of values. The copresence of differing values and principles within a social structure is not necessarily a source of weakness. In fact it could be the opposite. Marshall believes that if the respective spheres of the market economy, the polity and the welfare system are clearly demarcated and respected, no major problems need arise.

We may point out that this presupposes a good measure of social consensus and discipline concerning the nature and functioning of social institutions. It is more likely to be achieved in the corporatist rather than the plural welfare state. In any case Marshall fails to address the problem of how, given the sociopolitical dynamics of a pressure group polity and the competitive ethos of the economic and political market-place, a neat division of labour between the various sectors of society could be maintained? Yet in recent writings Marshall reiterates the view that current difficulties are largely due to the confusion between the respective role of the market and welfare sectors. These writings also reveal Marshall as a 'moderate' collectivist, one who subscribes, more or less, to the Beveridgian concept of welfare based on the idea of a 'national minimum' available as of right. For Marshall, that principle provided a clear rationale for the scope of state action but postwar developments have led away from it. We shall return to this point.

Marshall's approach has the merit of looking at the welfare state (a) in a systematic rather than an *ad hoc* and empirical manner, and (b) in relation to its wider social context. But it too suffers from some of the limitations associated with Fabianism. First, it centres largely on *values* and *value conflicts* within welfare capitalism and ignores the *functional* relationship involved between different parts of the social structure of democratic-welfare-capitalism. Thus Marshall maintains that value pluralism might be beneficial, or at least need not be detrimental, to the social structure. yet the issues raised by Robson, Bell and Hirsch, for example, throw serious doubt on this proposition. And quite apart from that, institutions are not simply *value realms* but also *material entities* that are interrelated and interdependent. 'Dysfunctional' relations could therefore develop between them (*e.g.* abolition of poverty could seriously affect the work ethic and the profitability of industry) resulting in a loss of effectiveness overall. Unless the welfare sector is so modest and small as not to interfere with the market economy, and the major political parties agree to maintain such a stable system, it is difficult to see how a balance between the economic, political and welfare elements of the social structure could be maintained.

As we have seen in earlier chapters, current problems of the welfare state seem to have a lot to do with dysfunctions arising out of the relationship between the various sectors of democratic welfare capitalism. The Marshallian approach does not come to grips with this problem. Nor does it point out the basis on which a consensus about the respective role of state welfare, market economy, party politics and the like (Marshall's mix of values underlying the 'hyphenated' society of democratic-welfare-capitalism) can be developed within the pluralist welfare state. A second weakness of Marshall's approach is that, in common with Fabians such as Titmuss, he too looks at social welfare largely from the standpoint of *consumption* and *distribution* and fails to explore its connection with *production*, at least in any direct sense. The result is a failure to graph the problems specific to a capitalist market economy-profitability, accumulation, investment, international competitiveness and the like-which together with political pluralism and state welfare enable us to make sense of the current difficulties (including the problems of budget deficits and taxation). In his recent writings Marshall notes that the political economy of the post-war welfare state is in a 'precarious and somewhat battered condition', but shies away from any explanation.

In short, neither Titmuss's nor Marshall's intellectual legacy is of much help in coming to grips with the current problems of welfare capitalism as a social system and indicating possible lines of solution. Nor do we find social democrats outside Britain, at any rate in English-speaking countries, able to offer anything of substance on this score. The objectives of social welfare, whether they be maintaining a national minimum standard of living achieving greater equality, or promoting altruism and community, need to be spelled out clearly and the prospect of their being achieved in the context of welfare capitalism also needs to be argued in detail. The relationship between economic and social welfare, and more generally between the requirements of a profit-oriented market economy and the values and institutions of social welfare, likewise need to be clarified. The relationship between the normative and the positive aspects of welfare, in particular the implications of the institutional dynamics resulting from the relative autonomy of the market economy, the plural polity and the welfare sector also need to be explored systematically. Put another way, the problem of the unintended consequences of one institutional sector for another must be addressed. These are among some of the major questions that need to be answered by a social democratic theory of the welfare state.

It is indeed something of a paradox that over three decades of successful welfare statism has not produced a 'Centrist' theory of the mixed system comparable to the analytical perspectives of the market liberals and Marxists. A part of the problem seems to be that the very pragmatism and reformisms underlying the welfare state militates against a systematic theory of a mixed system comprised of market and state regulation. it is not easy to theorise about a system whose boundaries remain extremely fluid and whose paternity ranges from Bismarckian conservatism to modern social democracy, from Ne Deal liberalism to the 'political economy of the working class'. Morever, if the welfare state is largely a product of piecemeal social (and moral ?) engineering, then it may be futile to search for theoretical and normative coherence behind its patchwork quilt.

As Furniss and Tilton observe, 'To date no coherent and persuasive case for the welfare state exists. Its appeal is pretheoretical.... Instead of one satisfactory justification for the welfare state, a variety of partial and mutually inconsistent arguments circulate in the political debate of advanced industrial societies.' Moreover, as they rightly point out, the absence of a clearcut logic to the welfare state is an intellectual rather than a political disadvantage. In modern democracies, to be persuasive a political argument must 'appeal to a variegated audience of citizens entertaining distinct and often contradictory fundamental assummptions.' What is required therefore 'is not strict logical consistency, but the capacity to elicit general agreement and support ... current arguments for the welfare state have this broad, eclectic quality.' What Furniss and Tilton forget to add is that these political advantages have the edges so long as the welfare state 'works'. When it runs into difficulties (as at present) then the lack of scientific and normative coherence becomes a distinct disadvantage (as at present)—at least as far as the *intellectual* defence of the middle ground is concerned.

Social Democratic Perspective

Whilst the current crisis has not evoked any major intellectual responses in defence of the post-war welfare state it has not been without its impact on social democratic thinking. In the following pages we shall look at some of the recent social democratic writings, relevant to our concerns, whether meant as a response to the current crisis or not. These may conveniently be grouped under four main headings : (*i*) Fabian socialism, (*ii*) moderate collectivism, (*iii*) neo-Keynesianism, and (*iv*) theoretical defence of the welfare state. Let us look at each of these briefly drawing mainly upon British works.

Fabian Socialism

In the post-war years, social democratic strategy of change crystallised around a distributive and welfare-oriented socialism. Behind this strategy was the assumption of a post-capitalist Keynesian economy which would provide full employment and economic growth. Developments from about the mid-1970s have undermined this assumption. Chronic stafflation, rising unemployment and the failure of Keynesian techniques have dealt a body-blow to the strategy of financing social expenditure from economic growth and effecting some measure of redistribution of the growing national income in favour of the poor. More generally, the Fabian hope of using universal social services and progressive taxation as the means to a more equal society have been largely disappointed. Since about the late 1950s social scientists of varying shades and opinions have been unanimous in their view that taken together taxes and social services do little to reduce the inequality generated through the institutions of the market and private property. Repeated attempts by Left Fabians in Britain to pressurise Labour governments into adopting redistributive tax policies appear to have yielded meagre results. Thus increasingly the poor have been asked to shoulder the burden of financing public expenditure.

The picture is no different when we turn from taxation to the social services. By providing education, health care and pensions on a universal basis it has been possible to avoid the stigma and low standards associated with a selective service; but it has also become quite clear that in a highly stratified society univerally-available services often benefit the middle class more. Moreover, while free education and health care have been available for more than three decades, they seem to have had little effect in reducing class differentials in respect of educational and health outcomes. Overall, it would seem, the pursuit of equality and redistribution through universal services has not been particularly effective.

Thus, after a massive survey of poverty in Britain, Townsend concludes that redistribution is 'not much of a reality and the social services can increasingly be seen to ... reinforce rather than reduce poverty and inequality.' While social expenditure in Britain had risen appreciably as a percentage of the GNP, a great deal of poverty has persisted none the less. Le Grand's recent study, focused specifically on the redistributive impact of the services, reaches a similar conclusion : 'Public expenditure on the social services has not achieved equality in any of its interpretations. Public expenditure on health care, education, housing and transport systematically favours the better off, and thereby contributes to inequality in final outcome.'

Le Grand believes that behind the social democratic strategy of providing universal services was the desire to 'avoid the nettle of income redistribution'. It was an attempt to 'achieve such redistribution via the back door' which has clearly failed. He concludes that in so far as equality is the aim, the problem must be tackled at its roots, *i.e.* the distribution of cash incomes must be made more equal.

Among the other weaknesses of the welfare state we might mention the adverse consequences of the growth of state bureaucracy and professional power. Over the years, the growing centralisation and bureaucratism involved in the provision of social security, health care and other services has come under increasing criticism. More recently, the success of the populist demagoguery of the Right against the encroachment of the state over people's lives has added a fresh point to this problem for many Fabians and friends of the welfare state. The relentless professionalisation of the services has also presented its own problems. Fabians have traditionally revered professionals-the 'Enlightened Ones'—and seen them as the progressive allies of the reformers. They have tended to associate professionalism with the idea of a service ethic and commitment to the disinterested use of knowledge for the benefit of the community. Indeed, the englightened paternalism underlying the Fabian approach, itself has a close affinity with professional orientation. Despite some criticism, therefore, on the whole a positive view of the professional role has been a part of social democratic thinking an social development.

Beginning from about the late 1960s radical sociology, which saw professionalism more as a strategy for the enhancement of income, status and power than as a reflection of a set of objective attributes of occupations, began to cast a critical eye on the professions. Other arguments and evidence also began to accumulate to show that professionalism had a lot to do with vested interests. In the context of the social services, the professionals (especially the higher professions) are now seen as groups driving a hard bargain with government on salary and service conditions and trying to maximize their own sectional interests. Professionalism thus not only contributes to the rising cost of the service but by monopolising the provision and delivery of services, also makes the clients and lay people dependent on the professional.

Increasingly, Fabians are coming to recognize the force of these criticisms. Thus Townsend acknowledges the error and naivety of the belief prevalent in the 1960s that 'the more professionals we had the better ... the needs of democratic socialism would be served.' It has taken a long time—the 1960s and the 1970s—to 'began to appreciate the kind of problems posed by managerialism and professionalism.' Elsewhere, Townsend speaks of the role of the professions in reproducing inequality and privilege within the social services.

Frank Field, an ex-Labour MP and a well-known publicist on welfare issues, wrote in 1981 of the undesirable consequences of growing state power. Under the strong influence of Crosland's pen social democracy had been equated with the pursuit of equality through state intervention. This process has given the state increasing power over the individual. Field does no deny that state regulation and provision of services may have promoted equality. But the same measures have also deprived individuals of the freedom to spend money as they like. They have been provided with more and more services—which they do not control, and on whose running they have no say. 'By ignoring the lessons of the technical limits on what the state can effectively do. Labour directly assists the Tories who have not been slow to capture public fears of state power and to fashion them into a campaign for a night watchman state.'

Field, rather in the manner of a socialist Friedman, would like to see the state redistribute cash resources in favour of the lower income groups, rather than go on providing more and more services. Field believes that the state can be an effective instrument for transferring (redistributing) income and wealth. He goes on to propose a substantial reform of the taxation and social security systems which would eliminate poverty and redistribute income from the rich to the poor. We shall return to this later. But let us note that in switching the emphasis from the services to the redistribution of income Field seems to be suggesting a fundamental re-orientation of social policy, for the provision of universal, as-of-right social services has formed a major plank in post-war social democratic policy. Unfortunately, Field does not discuss the services in his reform proposals and it is not clear if he favaours their denationalisation so that, with more equal incomes, people might be free to choose and shop around as they do with other services at present.

But it is significant that Townsend, Le Grand and Field are all disenchanted with universal social services and favour a much more direct assault on inequality. Thus Townsend sees social policy in terms of three models: (*i*) 'Conditional welfare for the few', (*ii*) 'minimum rights for the many', and (*iii*) 'distributional justice for all'. These roughly form a continuum extending from the residual welfare of the conservatives to the 'national minimum' of Marshall and Beveridge, through to a socialist distributive approach which Townsend himself favours. Townsend finds that the principle of a national minimum, the model of social policy underlying the British welfare state, has proved difficult to put into practice. For 'there is an in-built tension, and even contradiction, in the application of the principle of a national minimum to a market economy. A minimum is hard to establish alongside or underneath a wage-earning and property-owning hierarchy—except at a very low level.' In other words, the principle 'falls far short of the expectations of its advocates.'

Townsend's survey of Britain showed that poverty (relative deprivation) was widespread. He recognizes however that the conquest of poverty in this sense, and more generally the acceptance of the policy of 'distributive justice for all', would require a massive restructuring of society. It would involve, for example, the abolition of excessive wealth and income, abolition of unemployment (the institution of a legally enforceable right to work) and similar radical measures. By relating poverty to the wider structures of privilege and power, associated *inter alia* with occupation and property, Townsend shows that abolition of poverty would require a far deeper social change than has generally been believed. In this sense Townsend's work goes far beyond the bounds of social democratic thinking, based on modest redistribution of incomes and the provision of generous social services financed out of growth.

In differing ways Field, Le Grand and Townsend all seem to be moving away from what might be called Crosland's welfare socialism. at the same time, however, some of the basic elements of the Fabian approach persist. First, there is no link between the social and economic in the social structure, or more precisely between distribution and the productive organization of society. Thus Field proposes a thorough reform of virtually the entire system of income distribution and taxation in order to bring about greater equality. Yet he makes no attempt to consider the implications of such a distributive strategy for the system of production which, presumably, is to remain in private hands and function through the market mechanism. Townsend, too, while grounding his analysis of poverty in the class structure and the market economy fails to consider the relationship between radical changes in distribution of the kind he proposes, and the system of production based on profitability, material incentives and the freedom of an international market economy.

Consider, for example, the implications of the legal right to employment, which Townsend advocates, for the capitalist market economy. Such a measure would have massive implications for the productive system. In short, is it possible to socialise distribution while production remains in private hands ? The implications of the current crisis of capitalism, which has brought back mass unemployment and shown itself incapable of even providing 'minimum rights for the many', seem to be that no radical programme of social distribution can be taken seriously if it fails to address the problem of production and the control of economic resources. Indeed many democratic socialists have become increasingly aware of the need to attack the problem of inequality at its roots, *i.e.* in the very system of production, specifically at the level of wages and the organization of work. The current crisis of welfare capitalism has underlined the need to address the problems of the economy, above all those of production and growth, if distributive issues are to be solved and social justice secured. Thus, it is not enough to say that 'far from putting economic objectives like solutions for inflation or economic growth at the head of the list of national concerns, we should put social objectives like social equality or the abolition of poverty at the forefront of our national effort.'

Another weakness of Fabian thinking has been the tendency to ignore 'subjective' facts about the social structure. Since Fabianism has meant essentially *administrative* (rather than political) solutions to social problems, only facts relevant to such an approach have been looked for and emphasised. Social facts have referred almost exclusively to occupation, income and demographic characteristics rather than to the attitudes and beliefs of the subjects themselves, the poor, the deprived, the workers. It is to the credit of Townsend and his researchers that they did probe into people's own attitudes toward poverty. What they found however offers cold comfort to Fabian reformers. As Townsend admits, there is 'much more inclination among the working class to have individualistic explanations of poverty and to imagine that people are poor because of personal mismanagement rather than the institutional structures of society.' Indeed, it appears that the British take a much more personalised view of the causes of poverty compared with the Swedes and other Europeans. As Townsend concedes, 'It's clear that political education has been far less influential in the history of the labour movement than many of us supposed.'

Many Labourites now recognize the importance of popular attitudes and beliefs, and of consciousness and ideology for social reform. Le Grand writes:

The lesson is clear. If greater equality of whatever kind is desired it is necessary to reduce economic inequality. To do this successfully, however, it is necessary to reduce the hold of the ideology of inequality on people's value and beliefs ... Ideology is a much more important determinant of social processes than is often supposed.

Clearly the agenda for changing people's beliefs and values about inequality, in a society steeped in hereditary privilege and social deference beginning with the monarchy and the court, is a much wider one than that of administrative reform. Field, in more traditional Fabian vein, asserts that there is a 'moral case for a significant vertical redistribution of income from the rich to poor'. This may be evident to Field and his fellow Fabians, but is it to the majority of British people ? After all, Field's own book tart with observation that 'laziness' and 'drink' were among the most frequently cited causes of poverty by the British in a recent survey of EEC countries.

The election to power of Thatcher, with the support of

skilled manual workers concerned about eroding wage differentials, the large support for the middle-of-the-road Social Democratic Party in Britain, and the jingoism connected with the Falklands invasion in 1982 are hardly portents of growing egalitarianism. Meacher, for example, recognizes the importance of the problem. On the prospects of democratic socialism in the 1980s he writes:

> At present little is being done to educate and mobilise socialists in Britain, as is illustrated most strikingly perhaps by the virtual absence of a socialist press. Until much more is done, it is certain that the grip of the dominant value system will be strengthened further still, and the ideological supremacy of the establishment will be even more firmly consolidated.

Meanwhile Fabian collectivism can do little more than maintain its moral stance and reiterate what social policy in Britain *ought* to be doing ('we *must*', etc.), and propose administrative solutions, even while the gap between these noble sentiments and expectations and the harsh reality under Thatcherite capitalism grows wider every day. Fabianism, largely a form of administrative and distributive socialism, seems to be at its best when times ar good economically. For then its chief method, namely social engineering through *consensus*, in turn based on fact-finding and a diffuse appeal to the values of community, justice, compassion and the like, seems to work. These favourable times also nurture the belief that more might be achieved through such means. The crisis of capitalist economy alters the situation radically, making it clear that what are at bottom structural problems (rooted in the economic system and class power) cannot be solved administratively. Every major capitalist crisis—that of the 1930s, for example—therefore cuts the very ground from under the feet of Fabian collectivism. The current crisis is no exception.

Moderate Collectivism

A rather different response to the problems of welfare capitalism has been to advocate a moderate form of collectivism, one that will have a clear rationale within the context of a market economy and would therefore 'fit' the system better. In Britain the names of Marshall, Robson and Pinker are associated with such a view point. While these writers differ in many ways in their approach, the thread of moderate collectivism running through their recent work provides an obvious link.

Marshall, as we noted earlier, finds that the composite social formation of democratic-welfare-capitalism has not been working well for some time. The welfare idea has been degraded as well as downgraded, largely because the respective spheres of the market economy and social welfare have been increasingly blurred. Marshall believes a thriving market economy to be a vital component of an efficient, democratic society. At the same time social welfare, especially in the form of universal services (*e.g.* health care and education) remains a necessity, providing a framework of prevention against poverty and helping to create a civilised community. Here Marshall's idea that the state welfare services are a part of the status of citizenship in modern society provides the underlying rationale for a national minimum. However, the gentle prose in which he speaks of 'Strengthening... the civilising power of welfare' tends to gloss over such features of these services as increasing professional dominance and rising costs. Health care is the prime example here, although to a lesser extent education and the personal social services are relevant too. If a citizenship approach requires that these services be provided to everyone at an optimum standard, then it is only the income maintenance programme, consisting of cash transfers, that emerges as one that might be scaled down in terms of scope and expenditure. But the exact policy implications of moderate collectivism in the area of income maintenance remain unclear.

Unlike the Left Fabians Marshall openly acknowledges, indeed emphasises, the economic component in welfare. Not only the social services but the economy too contributes to welfare in the wider sense. Social welfare, therefore, must not be allowed to interfere with or hinder the economy. And if the division of labour between the two sphere is generally accepted (consensus over the role of social policy ?), then the composite social system of democracy-welfare-capitalism might not only survive but also be strengthened. Clearly, Marshall has a great deal of sympathy with the national minimum view of welfare, embodies for example in the Beveridge Report, which fits in with the notion of citizenship and the ethos of an egalitarian civic culture. This has little to do with the pursuit of equality and redistribution which, for Marshall, belongs to a very different area of social action. To confound these various objectives is to dilute and degrade the essence of welfare.

Marshall uses the same distinction in his attempt to rescue poverty from the embrace of inequality. In the ideal democratic-welfare-capitalist society, 'poverty is a disease' but inequality is 'an essential structural feature'. Poverty can therefore be abolished in such a society. marshall admits that poverty forms a part of the wider social question of inequality, but rejects the notion 'that one could not eradicate poverty without solving "the problem of inequality".' Selectivity and means tests again are instruments that Marshall would not reject out of hand: they are not necessarily stigmatising. Marshall has held some of these views publicly for a long time. Others he has come to espouse more explicitly only in recent years.

Robson, too, is concerned with the degradation of the welfare idea, with the loss of direction of the welfare state. As noted above, he is greatly distributed by the lack of a normative (and by implication also scientific) theory of social welfare. Not unlike Marshall, he believes that some form of national consensus on the objectives of social welfare is essential if the welfare state is to constitute a stable and viable social system. Moreover, Robson stresses the importance of popular attitudes and feelings concerning social issues in their bearing on welfare. This is a welcome emphasis all too rare in the administratively-oriented literature in this area. Commenting on the dearth of ideas about the objectives of the welfare state Robson notes that the advocacy of equality has become the conventional wisdom of the Left. But how widespread is the belief in equality in British society ? Fabian advocates of equality rarely ask that question. Moreover, observes Robson, relative definitions of poverty have merged almost imperceptibly with those of inequality. Whereas the idea of a national minimum has been the 'cornerstone of welfare state policy', the pursuit of equality introduces a radically different aim within the fabric fo the welfare state. He too believes that 'genuine' poverty can be (has been ?) abolished within the welfare state. Like Marshall he maintains that the mixed economy and the various economic liberties that go with it has to be seen as desirable features of these societies. Unfortunately, Robson's own normative view of welfare, couched in extremely general terms, does not take us far. What, for example, are we to make of the statement that the welfare state is (*i.e.* ought to be) concerned with the 'well-being of the whole society' ? or that it is (*i.e.* ought to be) 'Committed to a continuous improvement of the social services in regard to their scope, adequacy and quality.' In short Robson, like Marshall, finds it difficult to be precise about the role of the welfare state.

Pinker, a leading British social administrator, has also broken with Titmuss-type collectivism and the idea of the pursuit of equality through social policy. He favours moderate forms of social protection which instead of being at daggers drawn with the market economy will live in harmony with it and be more in keeping with the sentiments and feelings of the British people. For Pinker too an efficient and healthy market economy, personal liberties and democracy are essential parts of the broader fabric of welfare. he evokes the Keynes-Beveridge tradition of thinking about welfare quite explicitly in support of his position.

What moderate collectivists leave out of account, however, is the social dynamics of the welfare system. It is one thing to advance moderate collectivism as a normative proposition, although a we have seen there are problems even at this level. It is quite another to demonstrate that a delineated sphere of social welfare could, as it were, be sustained within the context of a market economy and plural polity without either degenerating into a residual form of welfare or simply continuing to grow (as the post-war welfare state did from its modest Beveridgian beginnings) under the pressure of demography, relative price effect political market, professional-bureaucratic interests, and the like. Put simply, these views are plausible at the normative level but not at the level of practice.

A part of the problem is that note of these social scientisits really examines the dynamics of a social system which comprises a market economy, a pressure group polity and a state welfare sector. Since market capitalism and interest-group politics are pre-eminently about the pursuit of self-interest (in the economic and political market-place, respectively) the social welfare sector (the junior partner in this trio of economics-politics-welfare) simply becomes a part of the value system and structure of the wider society. Is this not the problem identified, for example, by both Hirsch and Bell? In sum, the moderates fail to address the *institutional* problem of how to build and maintain consensus in a pluralist welfare state.

Moderate collectivism has other weaknesses. First, it fails to see the role of the state and the social welfare system in relation to changing technological and economic factors. Thus, in the 1980s, the possibility of large-scale unemployment and the inability of the market economy to provide jobs for millions has to be considered when arguing for moderate collectivism.

Second, the implications of moderate collectivism or a 'national minimum' concept for the various services (*e.g.* income maintenance, health, education, housing) need to be spelled out.

Third, the reasons for advocating a limited role for social welfare must be made quite clear. There is sometimes an assumption, more or less implicit, behind these arguments that rising social expenditure and the attitudes generated by the security of full employment and social welfare more generally are responsible for Britain's ills, especially her economic decline. the dubious nature of this assumption is obvious. A cursory glance at big spenders like West Germany or Sweden makes it amply clear that public expenditure on health, education and welfare does not *ipso facto* lead to a decline in productivity or economic growth. Indeed judged by the proportion of GNP spent on the social services in advanced industrial countries Britain's collectivism is now definitely modest. Thus there is a need to clarify the nature and rationale of moderate collectivism.

Fourth, and a related point, is that the issue of national consensus over welfare (social and economic) is quite different from that of the degree of collectivism. As countries like Austria and Sweden amply demonstrated consensus, stability and growth can be achieved within welfare capitalism at a fairly high level of collectivism. the issues of consensus and the degree of collectivism must not be conflated.

Neo-Keynesianism

While some social democrats have been repeating their moral prescription about what must be done to further social justice and equality others have been reaffirming a belief in neo-Keynesianism. A recent collection of Fabian writings. Provides a good example of this approach which involves essentially a reflationary strategy ('reflation in one country'- based on increased public expenditure. This is expected to create jobs and generate demand for the output of private industry. But is also admitted that 'improvements in living standards, including the standards of public services can only come about through increased efficiency and productivity.' The anti-inflationary thrust of this warning is quite clear. Moreover, it virtually affirms the Croslandian approach to social expenditure, based on growth and higher output, in contrast with the Left Fabian approach which looks for a redistribution of incomes (from the rich to the poor) through the social welfare system. It is also acknowledged that we cannot 'expand public spending by as much as we like for ever.' Thus some sort of a limit on government spending, however unspecified, is recognized as well as the mixed nature of the economy. More important, it is assumed that 'the promise of a commitment to bring back full employment will make the advantages of greater productivity clear to everyone. It should remove the fear that one man's productivity gain is another man's job loss. This is wishful thinking when we know that precisely the opposite seems to have been true of Britain's thirty years' experience of full employment. In the main, neo-Keynisian thinking of this kind relies on the strategy of generating economic growth, part of which could then be allocated to social programmes and priorities. Hence a scheme of investment and industrial development through the National Enterprise Board is also seen as important.

It is difficult to take such facile solutions to the problems of British welfare capitalism (unemployment, inflationary wage settlement, over-manning, productivity, growth) seriously. There is a distinctly *deja vu* air about these pronouncements. Despite some new features (*e.g.* import tarrifs) relevant to the 1980s it is, in essence, a plan (not unlike the Mittrand programme in France) that the British Labour Party has tried before. its spproach to social expenditure is also a familiar one, although it recognizes fully the scarcity of resources as well as the need to restrain, or even reduce, social spending in some areas.

This neo-Keynisian — and one might add also Croslandian — approach, for example, informs Labour Party's outline of economic and social policy, *Labour's Programme 1982*. It is based on a strategy through which it is hoped that growth will be resumed, full empiloyment restored and social policy objectives met. yet this approach, and the attendant optimism, flies in the face of the general trend of rising unemployment and economic stagnation in most European economies. In the absence of growth, increased productivity (one of the objectivieies of the programme) is likely to result in higher unemployment. Indeed it looks as if large-scale unemployment will continue to be a feature of British and other western economies. As Jordan points out, 'Labour, while seeming to have turned away from the optimism of Anthony Crosland's vision, has in fact clung on to many of its most unrealistic features. Above all, *Programme 1982* continuously asserts that there are no hard choices to be made; that redistribution will occur painlessly, through growth, and with the restoration of full employment.' Clearly British Fabianism, like a great deal else in Britain, seems to be mired in traditionalism and can offer little that is new. It is nor surprising that Mrs Thatcher not only champions the cause of the people against the Big State but also takes pride in her 'realism' compared with the facile optimism of many of her political opponents.

Against orthodoxy, from the somewhat jaded Old World Fabianism, we turn to a refreshingly original as well as hard-headed analysis of the current impasse by Lester Thurow. Thurow's work merits attention for a variety of reasons, not least for being one of the most impressive arguments put forward by an *American* political economist from a Centre-Left position. Thurow focuses on the US economy, but his reasoning applies more generally to advanced capitalist economies. His main point is that the US has reached a point where further economic growth requires major adjustments, in respect of energy use, industrial investment, and the like. In this process of structural change some groups stand to lose while others stand to gain. It is a zero-sum game in which there are no winners without corresponding losers.

But thanks to the political economy of the welfare state-post-war developments in democracy, government responsibility for protecting living standards, and the growth of interest groups including those representing the underprivileged—it has become increasingly difficult if not virtually impossible to impose the costs of change on any particular group in society, at least not of the magnitude necessary for economic growth to be feasible. That is the essence of the current impasse. In Thurow's words,

> For most of our problems there are several solutions. But all these solutions have the characteristic that someone must suffer large economic losses. No one wants to volunteer for this role, and we have a political process that is incapable of forcing anyone to shoulder this burden. Everyone wants someone else to suffer the necessary economic losses, and as a consequence none of the possible solutions can be adopted.

Thurow examines a range of issues including energy, inflation, government regulation of the economy, growth and income distribution. he is able to argue quite convincingly that big government and budget deficits are not at the root of inflation and economic stagnation. Hence the nostrums of the Right, including lower taxes for the wealthy reduced public spending, and so on, as well as being inequitable, are irrelevant to the main problem. He points out, for example, that many European countries have a far bigger and more pervasive government than the US but nonetheless, have achieved a high level of economic growth. 'Government absorbs slightly over 30 per cent of the GNP in the United States, but over 50 per cent of the GNP in West Germany. Fifteen other countries collect a large fraction of the GNP in taxes.' Nor have the United States' competitors 'unleashed work effort and savings' through increased income differentials. Using the earnings ratio between the top and the bottom decile as an index, 'the West Germans work hard with 36 per cent less inequality . . . the Japanese work even harder with 50 per cent less inequality.' Indeed, among industrial nations only the French surpass Americans in inequality of earnings.

Furthermore, the history of such countries as West Germany and Sweden, as well as the United States' own experience (since the New Deal), shows that far from hindering growth, government intervention and social welfare programmes seem to have aided it. As regards inflation, Thurow believes that the major influence in the 1970s was the sharp rise in oil prices (OPEC decisions) albeit the Vietnam war and the US government's energy policy were also to blame. Inflation in later years, it is true, reflects the inability (or unwillingness) of governments to impose the costs of oil price rises on any one segment of society (although inflation has its own redistributive impact). But the idea that inflation is caused largely through government growth, budget deficits and high wages is both simplistic and misleading. The situation is rather more complex:

> Energy, growth, and inflation are interrelated on many fronts. Without growing energy supplies, economic growth is difficult, and rapidly rising energy prices provide a powerful inflationary force. Inflation leads to public policies that produce idle capacity and severely retard growth.

But economic growth in the 1980s requires, above all, major structural changes. New industries have to rise and old ones decline. Thus investment as well as 'disinvestment' (*i.e.* running down old unprofitable industries), becomes essential. Yet interest-group politics and government intervention makes disinvestment difficult : 'Instead of adopting public policies to speed up the process of disinvestment, we act to slow it down with protection and subsides for the inefficient.' Many industries in the USA enjoy protection in one form or another. Shipbuilding for example is 'completely dependent upon subsidies'. All such actions are meant to provide economic security, but lock the economy in low productivity areas. Without effective disinvestment it is virtually impossible to compete in the modern growth race. Moreover, workers fear that technical change will take their jobs away and alternative work will be hard to find. They therefore push for more restrictive work rules to stop technical progress. 'The end result is a stagnating economy with a productivity slowdown.'

For Thurow, it is this issue of interdependence between capital and labour that goes unrecognized in facile, free-market solutions. If the labour force is indifferent or uncooperative then investment in new plant and equipment may not prove very productive (and therefore not profitable).

> New skills and higher earnings depend upon a co-operative work force. Simply raising the income of capitalists, with tax cuts that must be paid for with tax increases for workers, is unlikely to achieve either more investment or a higher growth of productivity

> ... Starting a class war is hardly the way to proceed.
>
> Thurow uses the Japanese lifetime employment system, where technological change and higher productivity do not threaten either jobs or earnings, based largely on a mixture of seniority and profit-related bonus, as an example of a positive relationship between job security on the one hand and technological change and productivity on the other. In pointing this out, however, Throw's main objective is to illustrate 'the complexity of the problem and the irrelevance of simple one-factor solutions'.

Thurow offers no penacea for the ills basetting US capitalism, let alone for welfare capitalism more generally. If anything his insistence on the 'societal' or 'systemic' nature of the issues warns us against quick fixes and miracle cures, such as those touted by monetarists. Rather it is his stress on the inter-related and interdependent nature of the problems (and their solutions) that commands respect. For example, he does not treat either production or distribution in isolation from each other.

As a social democrat Thurow believes that the costs of social change cannot be allowed to lie where they fall. In order to free the economy from the impasse in which it finds itself, the impact of change must be cushioned. The government has an important role to play in spreading the burden of change equitably and sheltering individuals from the negative impact of change.

Thurow believes that since the US prides itself on the work ethic the government must take responsibility for providing everyone who wants a job with one, if necessary through a federal guaranteed job programme. Moreover, the government should act to reduce, or at least prevent from worsening, the level of inequality of incomes, mainly through progressive taxation. Unlike many Fabian and Leftist writers on welfare who purport to show that the social services do not help the poor and then proceed to ask for more state welfare, Thurow maintains that without transfer payments and forms of welfare assistance, including food stamps, the standard of living of the elderly, the poor and other low income groups would have been much worse. He give other examples of the progressive nature of the public sector. For example, because of its equitable practices blacks and women stand a much better chance of being hired and their pay differentials, compared with white males, also tend to be smaller.

Thurow does not, however, favour government regulation of everything. Eschewing dogma, he argues that the choice is not between regulation or its total absence but between the right and the wrong kinds of regulation. Echoing the arguments of Bell and Hirsch, Thurow believes that decisions concerning equity and distribution can no longer be fudged. Unlike these writers, however, he does take a stand. He offers his own version, admittedly somewhat pragmatic, of equity principles. For example, he suggests as the effective poverty line half the average income as the level below which no one should be expected to live. He argues for a more progressive tax structure. He suggests a differential of 5 : 1 between top and bottom quintile of earnings, existing at present among *white males* in full-time work, as the maximum for *all* workers. This compares with a current differential of 27 : 1 for the American labour force as a whole, that is including women and blacks. To cushion the impact of economic and technical change Thurow advocates giving help to individuals (retraining, relocation, financial assistance) rather than subsidising industries or firms. These principles are important, for unlike orthodox neo-Keynesians Thurow does not believe in a miraculous return of growth which will automatically benefit everyone. Nor does he look for corporatist solutions as such. He rejects mandatory wages and prices control arguing, quite rightly, that these measures can only work if voluntary.

Moreover, he notes, only about a quarter of the labour forcé is unionised in the USA, a level of unionisation rather low to be conducive to a corporatist approach.

Yet there is little doubt that, overall, Thurow's approach represents a move away from the pluralist welfare state towards one that has elements of corporatism. Unlike the pluralist (DWS) approach which differentiates social policy clearly and sees it as something apart from economic policy (*e.g.* Titmuss, beveridge, Marshall, etc.), Thurow sees them as closely interrelated. Secondly, in line with the corporatist approach (IWS), he sees institutional or systemic integration as interdependent with group integration. In other words, if economic problems are to be solved successfully then inter-group relations, centred on distribution and equity claims, must be resolved.

In this sense his approach to social management is systematic (as in the IWS)(rather than piecemeal (as in the DWS). Thurow does not discuss the social services (*e.g.* health care and education), as such. But in the area of economic investment, job creation, transfer payments, progressive taxation and the like he envisions more rather than less government responsibility. Unlike neo-conservatives. Thurow does not believe a return to *laisser-faire* either possible or desirable. Neither does he believe moderate collectivism to be the answer. His analysis shows quite clearly that social welfare can no longer be meaningfully isolated from economic welfare. Morever, if equity considerations are not to be set aside then government must involve itself more (or rather differently) not less with economic regulation and welfare in its wider sense. In these key respects his thinking goes beyond post-war Keynesianism. Unlike many neo-Keynesians and orthodox Fabians he recognizes that the option of generating full employment and economic growth through a managed market economy and then using social welfare (the role of social policy in post war years) to redistribute and socialise growth is no longer available. The problems of democratic-welfare-capitalism cannot now be solved in the manner of Croslandian social democracy, or for that matter a Beveridgian national minimum.

Thurow's main weakness lies in his ability to specify the institutional mechanism through which consensus, or at least major support, could be built around the kind of approach he advocates. He bemoans the absence of a European-style political system in the USA in which the ideological divide between parties is clear cut and governments are elected with a mandate to carry out a clearly identifiable set of policies. He has a point here in that the absence of a Social Democratic Party in the US frustrates certain kinds of development. But the experience of Western Europe makes it quite clear that without a broad consensus among the major economic power-holders economic growth, equility and welfare, and apolitical democracy cannot be combined successfully.

However, these critical remarks should not detract from the boldness, originality and sociological realism of his analysis. The label neo-Keynesian may be quite inappropriate for his economic and social approach. But the attempt to go beyond prevailing orthodoxies in the analysis of contemporary problems, an openly espoused value position, the attempt to link means and ends clearly, the belief in a mixed economy and liberal democracy, and lastly the insistence on value choices are all reminiscent of Keynes's response to the crisis of capitalism in the 1930s. In any case, what matters is the content rather than the label. And there is little doubt that the political economy of the welfare state presented by Thurow is one of the most original (without being idiosyncratic) and persuasive to appear in the Centre-Left tradition in recent years.

Theoretical Defence of the Welfare State

In recent years the intellectual foundations of social democracy and the welfare state have come under heavy critical fire. Generally speaking, criticisms of the welfare abound, whereas its systematic defence is hard to come by, From this viewpoint the recent contributions of Room, and Furniss and Tilton merit particular attention. From somewhat differing perspectives and concerns they advance a range of arguments in defence of the Centre-Left view of social policy. We shall consider these arguments in some detail and comment on their validity as well as adequacy, beginning with Room's work.

Room examines the view of social policy in modern western society held by three major theoretical perspectives-liberalism, Marxism and social democracy. He looks at the interpretation of social policy and social change offered by each from an historical perspective. The development of social policy in modern British society forms the testing ground, the laboratory so to speak, for the interpretation offered by these theories. Overall, Room finds the social democratic perspective to be the most convincing of the three. In so far as he is sympathetic to the social democratic paradigm of social policy and also considers its merits and demerits in some detail his work is most timely. A critical defence of the social democratic position could be of considerable interest especially in the light of the current difficulties of the welfare state.

Room maintains that economic growth no longer depends on the rate of investment and profitability (accumulation of capital). Rather in economies like the British, which have reached a position of labour scarcity (!) it is the skill and expertise of the labour force that becomes crucial for economic growth. Therefore Room concludes that it is the social policy of the state, which helps create a healthy and skilled labour force, that is now crucial for growth rather than investment and profitability. Room admits that rising unemployment seems to question Kaldor's view of increasing labour scarcity in advanced capitalist societies. But he suggests that 'if we regard the current international recession as short run and as signifying no necessary fundamental change in the pattern of western economic development' (a massive assumption which, to put it mildly, looks increasingly unrealistic) then Kaldor's 'emphasis on labour scarcity in manufacturing industry as a developing constraint in economic growth will remain valid.'

The point is this: even if the recession had turned out to be a temporary one (in the manner of previous post-war recessions), thus validating Room's assumptions, there would still remain serious problems with his argument. Writing in the 1970s, it is somewhat unreal to put forward labour scarcity as the major reason for Britain's poor economic performance compared to other industrialised economies. Rather, one would have to speak of labour market rigidities, over-manning, trade union attitudes towards new technology and lack of investment in advanced technology in British industry. Here one could argue that the policies of full employment and social security combined with traditional defensive trade union attitudes may have a lot to do with the poor state of the British economy. In short, far from helping the cause of growth social policy may in fact have been hindering it.

But quite apart from the problems of British economy, what happens to social democratic argument about state's role in promoting growth when the recession turns into a long drawn stagnation, if not an outright depression (after Room has dismissed Marx's gloomy prognostications as outmoded) ? In the 1930s the Webbs, those quintessential Fabians, eventually turned to Soviet-style communism as the only solution to capitalism's ills. Time and time again the capitalistic nature of western economies has proved to be the bane of social democratic hopes of an evolutionary socialism. The 1980s seem to be no exception.

Room's own view of the prospects for a social democratic advance, in the light of current difficulties of capitalism, is quite pessimistic. 'In the present situation of recession and public expenditure cuts.... The Social Democrats' hope of translating privileges into universal social rights are rendered increasingly difficult.' Furthermore, 'what has for several decades been taken as perhaps the most well-established universal social right-that to employment-has increasingly been translated into a privilege of the more powerful.' Finally, to cap it all, these and other developments 'seem to signify the erosion of altruism and moral solidarity in the face of the shared [?] adversity-an erosion that political leaders and those groups wielding power in the wider society (including the trade unions) have promoted, whether by intent or neglect.' Here we seem to be back to square one with Marx's reserve army of labour coming to life, altruism disappearing, and a *sauve qui peut* mentality taking over with social welfare facing a bleak prospect.

Room draws attention to many shortcomings and problems connected with the practice of the welfare state either ignored or not foreseen by social democrats, *e.g.* vested professional and bureaucratic interests, opportunism of political leaders, the ability of vested interests more generally to thwart reforms, the 'unprincipled nature of the wider distribution of power and advantage' and its implications for altruistic social policies. But he is unable to offer any solutions apart from pointing out that if the prospects for a 'social democratic common wealth', look bleak such a development is not inevitable. Such 'a future will not have come inevitably, but to some degree will rather have been the fruit of decisions by political leaders and, indeed, by the citizenry at large that centre in their lack of commitment to a promotive [?] social policy.' Thus, in the long haul, the social democratic view of society and social policy may have the edge over liberalism and Marxism. But in the short haul social democrats (actual and potential) are left more or less to fend for themselves (theoretically speaking) in the midst of rising unemployment, growing sectionalism and shrinking altruism.

Although Room's approach to his subject-matter is comprehensive and the treatment systematic, his analysis none the less suffers from a number of defects. First, it focuses almost entirely on problems of social integration (and that too from the viewpoint of citizenship and the democratic polity while neglecting the cash nexus entailed in industrial and property relationships under capitalism), and fails to consider problems of system integration adequately. In other words, the focus is almost entirely on values, social relationships and the moral basis of community, while problems of the technical-economic functioning of society are largely ignored. The book scarcely mentions the Depression, the trade-cycle and other awkward capitalist entities which brought the economy to near collapse in the 1930s, contributed mightily to the growth of Fascism, and eventually led to the outbreak of war. Faced with the crisis of capitalist economy in the 1930s, British social democracy could offer little.

More serious still is Room's omission of any reference to Keynesianism. (The index contains no reference to Keynes, and as far as we can see the importance of Keynesian techniques in maintaining full employment — one of the 'social rights' of citizenship — is completely overlooked.) Admittedly, a sociological work such as Room's cannot be expected to discuss economic issues in any detail. It remains true none the less that Room falls victim to the cardinal sin of Fabian writings on welfare-namely, the failure to consider adequately the productive aspects of capitalist economy and their relationship to social reform and the welfare state. The failure to acknowledge the centrality of the market economy for capitalist society and the failure to consider problems of system integration mean that the importance of the relationship between system and social integration, for the success of the 'middle path' of mixed economy and the welfare state, is missed completely. Despite attempts at a social structural analysis Room's approach to his subject-matter remains essentially idealist. He focuses on values and the ability of the social democratic movement to persuade the citizenry and the organized interests to choose the right values. Support for the appropriate values and policies then emerges as the 'solution' to the difficulties facing the welfare state-not exactly a helpful analysis for social democrats, or others for that matter.

A cogent defence of the modern welfare state, typified by Sweden, is offered by Furniss and Tilton. It is based on the rejection of both the 'liberal strategy of free and unregulated markets' as well as the 'traditional socialist nostrum of nationalisation'. The free-market economy fails to achieve equilibrium, provide full employment and ensure social justice and efficiency. Nationalisation, on the other hand, as the experience of Britain and other countries shows quite clearly, does not help realize the traditional socialist aspirations. Moreover as Soviet block countries amply demonstrate 'state socialism can be more tyrannous than private capitalism.' By focusing on Sweden as the model welfare state Furniss and Tilton are able to present a strong case for the irrelevance of nationalisation, since in Sweden the extent of public ownership of industry is extremely limited. Social democracy has chosen the path of regulating private economy and providing social welfare rather than extending public ownership.

Furniss and Tilton use a threefold typology to analyse modern forms of state intervention in economic and social affairs: the 'positive state', the 'social security state', and the 'social welfare state'. Only the latter two really qualify as welfare states. Of the three types, the USA provides an example of the first, Britain the second, and Sweden the third. The 'positive state' aims 'primarily at insuring economic stability and thus the self-interest of existing property holders'. The 'social security state' aims at 'a guaranteed national minimum'. The 'social welfare state', with which Furniss and Tilton's sympathies really lie, aims at furthering 'greater social and economic equality' and collective participation in the making of public policy. These are ideal-type formulations and the USA, Britain and Sweden are seen as empirical cases more or less approximating these three forms of state intervention.

Furniss and Tilton spell out the values underlying the social welfare state and also seek to demonstrate the technical viability and success of countries like Sweden in moving towards the model of the social welfare state. They also consider, rather briefly, some of the major arguments, levelled against the welfare state by its critics, both conservative and radical, but tend to dismiss them rather lightly. Be that as it may, Furniss and Tilton's work deserves to be recognized more widely in social policy literature, as it is one of the few examples of a systematic defence of the welfare state. Moreover it is admirable in its clarity, economy, balance between the empirical and ideational, and openly-stated value premises underlying its arguments. It also offers an interesting typology of state intervention. As we suggest below, the notion of the 'social welfare state' has distinct affinity with the idea of the corporatist welfare state. Yet despite its many strengths, Furniss and Tilton's work remains weak on contemporary relevance. Essentially it pre-dates the present crisis and therefore does not confront some of the key issues that have arisen within the last five years or so which have forced the welfare state very much on the defensive. For example, Furniss and Tilton defend state intervention in the market economy on the Keynesian grounds that the capitalist market economy is not self-regulating and therefore needs 'a visible public hand to steer it'. They counter the conservative critique by referring to the success of the mixed economy and the welfare state. The 'end result of the superiority of public and private co-operation over a reliance on private rationality alone has been demonstrated concretely in the upsurge of prosperity since World War II, by the disinclination of any major political party in any western nation to revert to pre-Depression economic practices, and by the advent of the "post-market" economy. To use Shonfield's phrase, "widely managed capitalism" has become the order of the day with the emphasis as much on "managed" as on "capitalism".' Here we are still in the golden age of postwar affluence and the welfare state, with staglation no more than a small cloud over the horizon. Indeed Furniss and Tilton's reference to inflation is primarily academic and concerns the modest inflationary pressures typical of the 1960s.

Their rebuttal of the Left (*Radical*) critique suffers from a similar defect. It does not take into account the economic recession and the crisis of production facing the capitalist economy which has given fresh point to the Marxist critique of social democracy and welfarism. Thus they belittle the problem of profitability in a capitalist economy. They also misunderstand the nature of the Marxist argument in suggesting that it is based on 'a faulty psychological assumption', that 'the capitalist's fundamental desire... is to make profits.' The systemic problems of the capitalist market economy, as evident in the decline of profitablility, does not feature in their discussion. The issue of 'fiscal crisis', (*i.e.* mounting budget deficits, rising public expenditure, high rates of taxation) is similarly played down. More generally, they endorse the classic social democratic tenet, namely, that distribution can be socialised while leaving production in the hands of private capitalism albeit of a managed kind.

Finally, we should mention that Furniss and Tilton seem to assume too readily that the state apparatus functions is a *rational* instrument of policy. They dismiss the notion of vested professional and bureaucratic interests somewhat lightly. They also fail to consider the general problem that in a pressure group polity the state, rather than being a guardian of the public interest, becomes a vehicle through which sectional interests realize their aims. Virtually nothing is said about the feminist charge of patriarchy against the welfare state.

Penultimately, given the 'pre-crisis' nature of Furniss and Tilton's study it fails to address the emergent problems of welfare capitalism in some crucial areas—the failure of Keynesian techniques, and the advent of staflation and unempiloyment. The key assukmptions underlying the book-the success of mixed economy and the efficacy of Keynesian management techniques-give it a somewhat *passe* flavour.

Both Room, and Furniss and Tilton produce cogent arguments in support of the social democratic view of social change by way of the welfare state. But these arguments rely on either an historical view of the evolution of capitalism (Room), or on the success of Keynesian welfare capitalism (Furniss and Tilton). Neither takes into account the contemporary failures of the mixed economy. Yet the intellectual challenge facing social democracy is precisely that of providing convincing answers to the current ills of welfare capitalism.

These authors do not address this task. Not do they confront systematically the many problems of welfare statism that have arisen over the years, including the apparent failure of redistributive and egalitarian policies, persistence of poverty, growth of professionalism and bureaucracy and the relation between economic and social welfare. While Room acknowledges a range of shortcomings related to the practice of social welfare policy he is unable to show how these might be tackled in the context of political pluralism, market economy, and institutionalised inequalities of power and privilege of the kind that Townsend, for example, focuses on. Furniss and Tilton, on the other hand, arguing from a value-committed standpoint, tend to gloss over many such criticisms levelled both from the Left and Right.

In taking Sweden as their model welfare state, and in distinguishing it as a type different from the 'social security state' such as Britain, the authors come close to taking a corporatist (IWS) view of Sweden's success. For example, they stress the importance of an active labour market policy, responsible wage bargaining and the concern for efficiency in Sweden's success. But writing from a pre-crisis perspective, they fail to grasp the importance of these features in the light of the recent tribulations of welfare capitalism.

Summing Up

This chapter has been concerned with the intellectual response of the 'Centre-Left' to the current difficulties of the welfare state. The middle-of-the-road reformist tradition represented by the Centre-Left is based on practice and pragmatism rather than theoretical coherence and systematisation. A moderate collectivist wing associated with social liberalism and a Fabian socialist wing associated with social democracy were distinguished. Neither has been able to formulate a clear rationale of social welfare in a capitalist society. Both presupposes a Keynesian-style mixed economy but cannot suggest a way out of the current impasse. In recent years, some Fabians have come to recognize that the pursuit of equality through social welfare and progressive taxation has failed and that in order to create a more equal society alternative means, such as the manipulation of primary income distribution, may have to be adopted. Others realize the limits of administrative egalitarianism in the absence of appropriate popular attitudes. Writers such as Thurow and Furniss and Tilton suggest that the Centre-Left position can be articulated more systematically and given intellectual coherence. Meanwhile, Fabians must face up to the unenviable, if necessary, task of defining the limits of Abianism clearly and deciding to work within them.

7

The Social Division of Welfare

The various schools of thought on social welfare agree in recognizing the 1834 Poor Law as epitomising a social policy supportive of laissez-faire capitalism. As a distributive system, it was to rely on the twin principles of 'less eligibility' and the 'abolition of outdoor relief'. This reformed system was intended to be not the challenge to the dominant market order its predecessor had been, but, rather, subordinate to that order: the gradient of life chance outcomes between employed and idle would be restored; the elimination of the possibility that those in employment might secure outdoor relief ensured that market valuations of different employed individuals would likewise be restored to the pre-eminence that was properly theirs. Nor did the Poor Law challenge the disregard by the cash nexus of variations in the number of dependants of a bread-winner, and its disregard of the very existence of the unemployed.

For, on the one hand, it did not acknowledge the possible failure of the dominant market order to guarantee adequate employment opportunities at a wage level sufficient for subsistence needs; on the other hand, it did not recognize that there might be any contradiction in principle between providing each pauper family with its subsistence needs and ensuring that the cost of the latter was less than the labour market rewards which the family's chief breadwinner could earn in independent employment. Thus, the overall pattern of distributive outcomes in the society as a whole would express and embody the values of the market place: those values would not only reign unchallenged over the life chances of the employed, but would also define the parameters for provision of relief to the destitute.

Neo-Marxist writers typically view contemporary social policies as a distributive mechanism no less subordinate to the dictates of the dominant market order than was the social policy legislation of 1834. In the criteria of eligibility, in the level and quality of benefit granted and in their impact upon distributive outcomes, such social policies reflect and reinforce market values. Moreover, following Marx's immiseration thesis and his more general view of the inequities suffered by the proletariat, neo-Marxists argue that it is precisely the section of the population—namely the working class—experiencing disproportionately the depradations of capitalism that *also* receives least favoured treatment. Social policies and the market place constitute a single, well-integrated distributive system, within which access to life chances is, for the mass of the population who own little or no property, heavily dependent upon the market value of their labour power. An individual's position within the social division of welfare therefore remains derivative of his position within the social division of labour, which continues to define individual and class interests.

Contemporary market liberals propose a definition of need and a level of provision for social policies that accepts, like the 1834 legislation, the priority of the market as a distributive mechanism and measure of values. Their discussion of the distributive role of social policies is, therefore, often couched in normative terms, critical of what they see as the significantly different role actually played by contemporary policies. We may, however, in part re-state their arguments in terms that appear in principle amenable to empirical investigation. First, they postulate that a sufficient criterion of need for state aid, in cash and in kind, is a specified low level of income. Unlike the Poor Law provisions they do not, of course, advocate entry to the workhouse as a condition of relief that will deter those not truly in destitution; rather, they typically favour rigorous means-testing. Here, then, as in the 1834 legislation, the cash nexus and the valuations of the labour market are to be pre-eminent: an individual's money income from that market is taken as indicating either his inclusion among the minority of the population requiring state assistance or else, in the case of the majority, the life chances distributed by the market to which he, on grounds of equity and social efficiency, is entitled. As for the level of provision that state social policies should ensure, market liberals advocate a basic minimum or 'safety-net': an argument harking back to the 'less eligibility' principle of the Poor Law. Expressed in less normative terms, market liberals are arguing that for any of the benefits distributed to individuals through social policies, it is possible to distinguish—and to justify this distinction—between that basic level of provision strictly necessary for social existence and supplementation of the latter. Finally, in regard to the overall pattern of distributive outcomes in such a market-dominated society, an optimism prevails as to the long-term consequences of economic growth in a capitalist market system. In particular, such growth may be expected to eliminate need and poverty without the aid of redistributive social policies; the safety-net provided by present-day Welfare States will be required by a declining proportion of the population. Some writers appear to go even further, arguing that such growth may additionally be expected to produce a more general trend towards equality in life chances.

Political liberals tend to be less concerned to demarcate the appropriate realms of the market and state social policies: The distributive justice that, for the market liberal, is the fruit of continuing dominance of the cash nexus, is seen by the political liberal as being the result of free access, not so much to the economic market place as to the political 'marketplace'. Moreover, such free access to the political arena is a sufficient condition for the elimination of political value-judgements from social policy definitions of need and of the appropriate level of provision. As to the overall patterns of distributive outcomes in the life chances with which these social policies deal, an optimism is prevalent at least as great as that of market liberals. As barriers to meritocracy are progressively removed and an equality of opportunity realized, a trend to greater equality in life chances may confidently be expected and is, indeed, already apparent. By neither group of liberals, therefore, are the social policies appropriate to a modern advanced urban—industrial society seen as involving distributive principles fundamentally and necessarily in conflict with the wider market society. They are, rather, seen as subordinate or complementary to it. As such they promote and reinforce an identity of interests among all citizens, who enjoy free access to the economic and/or political arenas.

For the Social Democrats, it is neither methodologically sound nor empirically very illuminating to treat the distribution of life chances in our society as being dictated by a unified, coherent distributive system. Rather, the overall pattern of distributive outcomes must be understood and accounted for as the net result of individuals' access to, and outcomes within, a variety of distributive institutions. These include two of particular importance: the market and social policy agencies. Within the former, individuals exercise their civil rights; within the latter, their social. The subordination of the exercise of one set of rights to exercise of the other—and hence the existence of a unified and relatively well-integrated overall distributive system—cannot be assumed *a priori,* but must, rather, be a matter for empirical investigation.

What then, are the principal differences in perspective and argument from the neo-Marxist and liberal standpoints summarised above?

(*i*) First, it must be conceded that Social Democrats have been somewhat uncertain and varied in their reactions to the neo-Marxist claim that class gradients in distributive outcome have not been reduced by the advent of the Welfare State. They seem in general to have held optimistic expectations at its institution; but subsequent investigation and evaluation suggested that, notwithstanding an apparent egalitarian trend, 'ancient inequalities had assumed subtler and more sophisticated forms' (Titmuss, Introduction to Tawney, 1964, pp. 10-11). Thus, as we saw in previous chapters, over the post-war period they have tended to lose confidence in the sufficiency of universalist services to reduce inequalities, while continuing, however, to insist on their necessity. Over the last fifteen years, theirs have been among the foremost investigations that have furnished ammunition for the neo-Marxist case (see, for example, Titmuss, 1962).

Nevertheless, their arguments do differ significantly and fundamentally from those of the neo-Marxists. One difference concerns the criteria by which the significance of inequalities in life chance outcomes is to be judged. In classical Marxism, such inequalities derive their significance principally from their implications for individual and class interests. The immiseration that accompanies capital accumulation ensures that this conflict of objective interests progressively increases in intensity. For the neo-Marxist, it is sufficient to point to the continuing class gradients in outcome as evidencing at least no reversal of the process of immiseration. For the Social Democrat, in contrast, the significance of these persisting inequalities is more problematic: they are the net result of individuals' experience of a variety of distributive agencies, whose systemic integration cannot be presupposed. Consequently, it becomes necessary to explore the definition of individuals' interests and the loci of conflict in these various milieux. The free exercise of civil tights, whose peculiar domain is the market place, may indeed tend to promote an increasing conflict of objective interest between those owning property in the means of production and those whose only marketable commodity is their labour power. In respect of social tights, however, a fundamentally different delineation of interests may in principle be possible. More particularly, the Social Democrats argue that universalist social policies establish areas of common interest. In this case, the inequalities deriving from individuals' differing market and work situations will not necessarily have the same significance as inequalities in the enjoyment of social tights.

Second, the Social Democrats affirm, no less than the neo-Marxists, the desirability of the distributive principle 'to each according to his needs'. They argue, however, that the prior socialisation of the means of production is neither a necessary nor a sufficient condition for the realization of this principle. Rather, it is through the attempted extension and enrichment of social rights that the specific character of market-imposed obstacles to its realization are laid bare and a programme for such socialisation and public control as may be necessary is actively developed. Hence, such attempted enrichment represents the immanent practical critique of market values and distributive principles demanded by classical Marxism, avoiding the utopian tendencies of many neo-Marxists.

(*ii*) The Social Democratic arguments also contrast with those advanced by liberals. First, Titmuss has been a particularly strong critic of liberal expectations of the elimination of need through the automatic development of a market-centred urban—industrial society. He argues, on the one band, that the inequalities of income and wealth generated by the market appear to have diminished little in this century (Introduction to Tawney, 1964), and, on the other hand, that the depradations and social costs generated by accelerating socio-economic change are likely to be increasingly fateful for individuals' life chances. Without preventive and redistributive social policies, therefore, he sees no evidence that greater equality of life chances is likely. Yet he also fears that even such policies tend to be accompanied by the expansion of 'fiscal welfare' distributed through the personal taxation system and of 'occupational welfare' enjoyed unequally by different categories of employee. Both tend to be regressive in their impact.

Second, the Social Democrats deny, *contra* the market liberals, that need for state aid is sufficiently and validly indicated by criteria of income; and, *contra* the political liberals, that need and merit in respect of access to social services are sufficiently indicated by apolitical, technical criteria. The political liberal errs in neglecting the value-judgements implicit in the unavoidable ranking of different needs; the market liberal fails to make explicit the value-judgement implicit in surrendering this ranking to the dictates of market power. Finally, the Social Democrats refuse to accept that some basic minimum level of provision can, even in principle, be defined in absolute terms as the appropriate standard for state aid, in contrast to the market liberals in particular. They argue, rather, that the substantive content of social tights is unavoidably determined by continuing political value-judgements over the quality of that common life to which all citizens should be guaranteed access.

The first line of enquiry appropriate to this chapter is, therefore, an exploration of the distributive principles and outcomes in different branches of social policy, although for reasons of space, we must confine ourselves to detailed examination of only one, namely health care. Extrapolation of our conclusions must therefore be cautious. However, a second line of investigation is also relevant. Instead of focussing on some branch of social policy, we consider the overall life chances typically enjoyed by individuals variously situated in our society. More specifically, it was the poor—or, more strictly, the destitute paupers—whose overall circumstances of life were the particular concern of the Poor Law. Since, therefore, all the schools of thought in which we are interested take the 1834 policy as a criterion for evaluating that of today, in section II we focus on the overall life situation of the poor in the contemporary Welfare State. We leave to the start of that section any rehearsal of the competing perspectives on such poverty and its treatment.

THE SOCIAL DISTRIBUTION OF MORBIDITY & MEDICAL CARE

Health policy has preventive, ameliorative and curative functions. There may be inequalities in the extent of need, i.e., in morbidity, as well as inequalities in the treatment of need, i.e. medical care. The former may be affected by preventive and promotive measures, such as environmental improvements and health education. The latter, on the other hand, concern ameliorative and curative measures. The health of a particular individual or group, and thus the extent of his or their continuing need for medical care, will depend, first, on the morbidity of that group and, second, on access to, and quality of, treatment for that particular morbid condition.

There is an extensive literature on the distribution of health needs and treatment but we do not attempt any extended review. Rather, we limit ourselves to the empirical evidence of relevance to the contrasting arguments set out in section I on the definition of needs, the level of state provision and the overall pattern of distributive outcomes. This then permits some evaluation of these various theories' analyses of the implications of contemporary social policies for individual and group interests. Two principal impressions emerge from such recent surveys: (*i*) the data available are of only limited use and do not permit confident and reliable judgements to be made; (*ii*) there appear to be continuing marked class inequalities in morbidity and care, notwithstanding several decades of a National Health Service. Both points are relevant to our present concerns.

(*i*) Three main types of information on the pattern of morbidity are available (Morris, 1964, has here been a seminal work). In the first place, mortality statistics provide relatively reliable information on the age, sex and class distributions of death from various specified causes. However, by themselves such data are likely to be of only limited use as indicators of the general morbidity of different social categories, for many diseases and disabilities can of course vary greatly in their severity and in fatalities. Second, information (collected principally by the various branches of the health service) is available on the use of health service facilities—for example, General Practitioner consultation rates among different social categories. Yet such data may be unreliable as indicators of morbidity: different social groups may have different self-medication practices, different abilities to recognize symptoms, different tolerances of pain and different attitudes to the available National Health Service facilities—or even knowledge of their existence. Programmes of multiple screening of the general public have revealed considerable unrecognized morbidity (Cooper, 1975, p. 13). Furthermore, there may be medically irrelevant factors influencing consultation rates: for example, working-class patients are more likely to need sick notes for employers. Moreover, studies that rely on information concerning the use of a single branch of the health services (e.g. GP consultation rates) will have their reliability further reduced if different social groups differ in their preferences among these various branches. That these two measures, morbidity and consultation rates, have little systematic relationship to one another is suggested by Rein's comparison (1969), for diseases with a class mortality gradient, of the death rates and consultation rates; his results indicate no clear pattern whatever. Neither of these two indices, therefore, seems adequate by itself; possibly some combination might be of value (Cf. Culyer *et al.* 'Health Indicators' in Shonfield and Shaw, 1972, pp. 100-2). Third, surveys have been undertaken to ascertain people's own assessments of their morbidity. Yet again, the reliability of this information will be vitiated to the extent that members of different social groups vary in their typical perception of symptoms and their tolerance of pain.

The information available on health care and its distribution among different social categories is of similarly limited reliability. The quality and effectiveness of treatment would appear intractable to reliable direct measurement. Instead, studies of the distribution of health care typically rely upon measures of inputs of various kinds—medical personnel, hospital beds, etc.—and assess input variations among different specialisms and medical conditions and among different regions and social classes.

(*ii*) Two main aspects of inequality in morbidity and treatment have received particular attention in the literature: those among different regions and those among different social classes. In addition, the relative resources devoted to different morbid conditions have been of concern. It is the differences among social classes that are of initial interest here, given the criteria of relevance developed in section I. We consider in turn the available measures of differential class morbidity and of treatment received.

Morbidity

It seems clear that different disabilities exhibit different class distributions: there are 'diseases of the rich' as well as 'diseases of poverty' (Arie, 1966). The latter, deriving principally from economic and environmental deprivation, include ulcers, hernia, bronchitis and pneumonia. The 'new' diseases of the rich, such as coronary disease, in part owe their increasing prevalence to increased life expectancy: chronic degenerative disease is more common in the upper and middle classes, with their older age structures. In addition, however, occupational stresses of men in these classes—in particular, nervous strain and sedentary work situations—seem to be a contributory factor. (This is suggested also by the fact that middle-class women suffer coronary disease relatively little, yet at an increasing rate, paralleling the rising female labour force participation ratio.) For some disabilities, the class pattern appears to vary markedly among different age groups. Logan, for example, finds that the class gradient for mental illness involves higher rates for lower social classes in younger age groups, but a reversal of this gradient above the age of sixty-five (Logan and Cushion, 1958-62; cf. Rein, 1969); which suggests—perhaps not surprisingly—that the principal causes may be significantly different for these different age groups. Morbidity, therefore, must be recognized as a multi-dimensional phenomenon, with class gradients varying a great deal for different disabilities. Nevertheless, as already noted, it is the older age structure in higher socio-economic categories that accounts in some measure for the concentration of degenerative conditions in these groups. That classes differ in their patterns of morbidity does not, therefore, necessarily imply that for any given age group the class gradients for these various forms of disability exhibit similar variations.

The foregoing generalisations may be supplemented and supported by reference to findings based on the various indicators of morbidity discussed earlier. Parker finds significant class gradients in mortality for several major forms of disability; although for coronary disease, no clear gradient appears. Overall mortality rates exhibit marked class gradients, although the change in these since the 1930s is a matter of dispute (Parker, 1975, pp. 73-4, covering the period 1930/2-1959/63) So also do infant mortality rates (Parker, 1975, p. 74, for the period 1949-64; cf. Halsey, 1972b, Table 11.9) and stillbirth rates, and the latter gradient appears to have widened in the post-war period (Parker, 1975, p. 74, citing evidence on the period 1949-64). In contrast, the social class gradient in childhood deaths narrowed considerably during the period 1930-50 (Arie, 1966).

Evidence of differential class usage of health services—such as General Practitioner consultation and hospitalisation rates—serves to supplement such comparisons of mortality, although problems of interpretation and validity are especially great. The establishment of the National Health Service involved the formal elimination, but for the retention of a small private sector, of the cash nexus between patient and doctor. Among the reformers' intentions was that consultations should henceforth reflect medical need rather than ability to pay. In addition, therefore, to investigation of class consultation rates and changes in these over recent decades, there has been a continuing debate over the extent to which the reformers' intention has indeed been realized, with consultation rates providing valid indicators of morbidity. This debate has led on to investigations of the social processes whereby such validity may be undermined even in the absence of a cash nexus. For the moment, however, we simply record some of the broad conclusions on consultation rates, as an indicator—of greater or lesser validity—of morbidity.

For General Practitioner consultations, highest rates in the mid-1950s seem to have been among members of social class III (Parker, 1975, p. III 76; Halsey, 1972b). However, fifteen years later it was the lower social classes that exhibited the highest rates (Parker, 1975, p. 76, citing the *General Household Survey*). Class gradients in consultation rates vary among disabilities. They are marked in the case of bronchitis and cancer, where lower social classes consult considerably more frequently than the upper, but are not in evidence for various other complaints (Halsey, 1972b).

Hospitalisation rates are another indicator of facility use whose relationship to morbidity is debatable. During the first decade of the NHS, Abel-Smith and Titmuss found that hospitalisation rates corresponded to social class proportions in the population (1956, p. 149). In contrast, Carstairs' data on Scotland give a strong class gradient both for admission rates and for mean stay. Carstairs argues that this greater use of hospitals by lower social classes reflects a lack of home amenities and/or greater prevalence among the lower social classes of certain *chronic* diseases—hospitals become a substitute for better housing, etc. (1966; the data refer to 1963). The influence of such non-medical factors upon need for and use of hospitalisation is also highlighted by Abel-Smith and Titmuss, when they argue that for the aged and mentally ill 'the existence or otherwise of surviving husbands, wives or children is perhaps the most important single social factor governing the amount and distribution by age and sex of demand for hospital care' (1956, pp. 146-7). That is, hospitalisation rates for these categories are especially high for the single, widowed and divorced.

Finally, the morbidity of different classes is to some extent revealed through surveys of people's own assessments of their state of health. Over a wide range of chronic illnesses, the *General Household Survey* indicates strong class gradients in reported disability. Resulting absenteeism exhibits similarly strong gradients (Gough, 1970, p. 213). Overall, then, notwithstanding the inadequacies of the available information, there are grounds for suggesting that, while the morbidity of each age group has been reduced for all social classes over recent decades, class gradients have changed little in respect of many major disabilities. Without giving any detailed treatment, because of their limited relevance to our present concerns, we may observe that regional variations in morbidity are also marked and persistent—although in some measure regional and class variations overlap, inhabitants of the South and East suffering least debilitation (Parker, 1975, pp. 74-6).

Levels of Treatment and Allocation of Health Care Resources

Prior to the establishment of the National Health Service, such resources were very inadequate and were maldistributed both geographically and functionally. Hospitals and consultants were highly concentrated 'in metropolitan areas, accessible (at least geographically) to the lower classes; but General Practitioners and other non-institutional services were more concentrated in middle-class areas, partly because of their reliance on a private patient clientele for an adequate income. Functionally, there were shortages of hospital and specialist facilities for chronic illnesses, and surpluses in other fields. These defects were exacerbated by the lack of coordination of voluntary and public hospitals and many of the former were very small, unable to enjoy economies of scale. Moreover, such charitable foundations were unable to exploit to the full the rapid advances that were taking place in medical science, on account of their limited funds; public institutions were likewise constrained by the limitations of local authority funds. For the General Practitioners, few of whom worked in partnerships, the costliness of new equipment incorporating the latest medical advances meant that clinical conditions were often severely deficient. Reliable information on the class distribution of treatment is again limited and fragmented. Access to health care, however, was class dependent in two particularly obvious ways: first, the middle class was excluded from the National Insurance Scheme; and second, the voluntary hospitals, which included all the teaching hospitals, came to be associated with technical sophistication, a contrast being apparent between the standard of treatment they offered and that granted in public institutions to a predominantly lower-class clientele.

Attempts under the NHS to deal with such regional disparities appear to have met with only limited success. Designation of under-doctored areas produced some improvement in the 1950s, but this proved only temporary (Parker, 1975, p. 77; Butler and Knight, 1974); other resources have no better a record. In general, it is the South and South-East that are most privileged across a wide range of medical care resources: regional disparities in one resource appear not to be counterbalanced by compensating disparities in others, but rather reinforced (Cooper, 1975, pp. 60-72).

Within this general context of marked regional variations (which, favouring the South and South-East, probably also favour the middle and upper social classes), significant inequalities are evident in the treatment accorded to different morbid conditions, as also in the treatment received by members of different social classes suffering the same disability. Within the hospital service, long-standing inferiorities in geriatric and psychiatric medicine and mental care are especially glaring (Townsend, 1974). Of course, different forms of disability require different forms of treatment, which in turn require different combinations of health care resource. Strictly speaking, the relative extents to which different morbid conditions are being relieved are, therefore, intractable to objective comparison; particularly when those conditions are chronic and amelioration, rather than cure, is the most that can be achieved. Nevertheless, certain components of need, such as the quality of wards and food provided in hospitals, are common to patients with diverse medical conditions; and in these respects it is geriatric and mental patients who receive markedly inferior treatment (Crossman, 1972b). The relatively low numbers of skilled manpower devoted to them may then, perhaps, be plausibly interpreted as resulting more probably from a similarly low priority being accorded to the medical needs of these categories, rather than from their conditions requiring lower skills. Alternatively, it may suggest that many of these aged and mentally ill patients are being hospitalised *faute de mieux*—a dearth of community health services and personal social services hinders the community care that would be more appropriate. As seen in the previous chapter, it is in these terms that the development of community health services and cooperation with local personal social services has been emphasised in the recent NHS reform.

Finally, there is evidence that middle-class patients are more able to obtain desired treatment from NHS facilities than are members of the lower classes with the same need. Townsend (1974), for example, finds that among the geriatric cases to whom we have just referred, there is a marked class gradient in the quality of care. Feldstein undertakes a special study of the hospital treatment of maternity cases. He finds that this ability to manipulate the medical services sufficiently outweighs the poorer home conditions of lower-class mothers (implying a need for hospital delivery) for the higher classes to have a higher probability of admission, longer stays and greater likelihood of being in teaching hospitals. Even when Feldstein controls for the doctor and the hospital care, and for the woman's age and parity—the number of children she has already borne—duration of stay is found to decrease monotonically from the highest to the lowest social class. Howlett and Ashley (1972) investigate the higher quality of care available in teaching hospitals. They find that in the case of prostrate gland operations it is the older and the lower class patients who are least favoured. However, Carstairs (1966), while acknowledging that middle-class patients are more likely to enter small hospitals, and that their General Practitioners are more likely to have access to hospitals' diagnostic facilities, sees that as being largely a result of area variations in NHS facilities; little difference in treatment occurs while the patient is in hospital. But she *does* see the upper and middle classes as having a more positive attitude to elective surgery and preventive care. The need for further studies is agreed by all these writers.

The change in life chances as a result of some disease will depend on the success of the treatment, together with the opportunity cost of the disease for the individual (i.e. any cost of treatment, loss of earnings while ill and changes made in future occupation as a result of the disease). Cartwright's hospital study demonstrates the striking class differentials here. Thus 77 per cent of the middle-class heads of households obtained full wages while in hospital, as compared with 20 per cent in the case of working class; and only 12 per cent of the middle class received no payment from an employer—and presumably many of these were self-employed—compared with 55 per cent of the working-class patients. Few middle-class (10 per cent) but more than half of the working-class patients had suffered moderate to severe financial strain.

There was also a marked class differential in the proportions who felt that their work had contributed to their illness—especially in the case of long illness. Yet more than half of these returned to the same job, owing to inability to find an alternative job or because of family responsibilities. Little help was, given by hospital almoners. Their class situation thus made likely the need for recurring hospital treatment. In those cases where recovery is incomplete, such a likelihood is increased; while if an easier—and probably lower-paid—job is taken, poverty may foster general health deterioration. Thus the chronic sick tend to be downwardly mobile. Here, then, are displayed some of the constraints upon the potential, even in principle, for a health service from which the cash nexus has been eliminated to render independent of class situation the consequences for an individual of succumbing to some morbid condition.

This discussion of the dependence of treatment upon class membership has been confined to the facilities of the NHS. The persistence of a private sector, however, particularly in the hospital service, appears to involve the perpetuation of the cash nexus for the highest quality of health care. The extent to which two standards of treatment indeed prevail is difficult to judge in the absence of adequate empirical studies; but the differential would seem to be not insignificant. The manner in which the elimination of the private sector would affect the total resources available to the NHS is even more difficult to gauge on the basis of available information—it would, of course, depend crucially on policy decisions by the government of the day. Nevertheless, that the private sector's persistence and current expansion reinforce the class gradient in treatment obtaining in the NHS can hardly be doubted (Parker, 1975, pp. 78ff.).

Theoretical Implications

The foregoing discussion of morbidity and medical care in Britain may serve as the basis for an evaluation of the competing arguments summarised in section I.

Neo-Marxists

Neo-Marxist propositions pertain first to the distribution of disabilities and morbidity among members of the population, harking back to Marx's depiction of the proletarians' debilitating work situation and Engels' account of their living conditions (1969). That class membership continues to be significantly associated with morbidity lends some *prima facie* support to neo-Marxist contentions that relative immiseration of the working classes under capitalism can be reversed not by the health policies of the Welfare State, but only by the humanisation of living and working conditions that socialisation of the means of industrial production would permit.

However, as we have seen, the relevant evidence is incompletely available; and where it is, closer examination prevents unqualified acceptance of these neo-Marxist arguments. First, it may indeed be the case that certain important disabilities are caused principally by characteristics of work situation, by poor housing conditions and nutritional deficiencies and by inadequate health education and improper self-medication practices. Nevertheless, our discussion suggests that the association between work situation and health can only very crudely and superficially be expressed in the neo-Marxist terms of class gradients. Likewise, when in the previous chapter we investigated access to adequate housing, the neo-Marxist assumption that civil rights to dispose of property in the market place were of overwhelming importance proved inadequate. Lastly, one can hardly infer from these occupational and environmental determinants of morbidity that no changes are possible without the prior fundamental changes in the ownership of industrial property that the neo-Marxists demand. Rather, these findings have encouraged increased attention to industrial and community health policies (Arie, 1975). Whether such policies must prove politically unacceptable to the-powerful can hardly be decided *a priori,* but must be a matter for empirical investigation. While this is not an issue to which we shall directly address ourselves, we do explore, in previous chapters, the political acceptability of preventive social policies aimed at reducing the social costs of urban—industrial change imposed upon the powerless.

In regard to the personal health services, the neo-Marxists argue the continuing dependence of access upon class membership. Evidence that within the NHS middle-class patients obtain better treatment suggests that the formal abolition of the cash nexus has been of little significance. The mediation of the professional may determine the *type* of treatment, but not its *quality*. The indicators used in deciding the latter are in practice merely a surrogate for individuals' market power; and overall health outcomes among different social classes are no less clearly monotonic in gradient than is the hierarchy of rewards distributed through factor markets (cf. Westergaard and Resler, 1976, p. 183).

Nevertheless, our discussion again suggests that this is too crude and superficial an inference. First, class differences in treatment seem to arise in part from patients' own role in identifying their needs and prescribing treatment. Carstairs' study, for example, highlights the more positive attitudes to preventive care typical among the middle and upper classes. Douglas and his colleagues find, similarly, that working-class patients are less likely to seek out preventive services provided by local authorities for their children (cited in Arie, 1966). The empirical studies we have surveyed also suggest there are considerable variations among patients from different social classes, regions and age groups in tolerance of pain and expectations of health. Second, Arie (1966) argues that the '"social distance" between doctors and patients has important effects on the type of care that patients receive'. Together these points suggest, therefore, that we must think of the prescription of treatment as arising from negotiation between patient and doctor, with the patient seeking to put a 'health project' into effect, within the context of his more general life project. As Cooper comments, 'Probably the most important factors determining [treatment] are the patient's persistence, his ability to articulate his symptoms in a form understandable to the doctor and the resource constraints' (1975, p. 22; see also Stimson, 1976).

Here, then is a process of need definition fundamentally different from that obtaining under the Poor Law, which was meant to be 'self-acting' and unambiguous, deriving not from a negotiation between professional experts and patients engaged in the attempted realization of their health projects, but rather from the clear valuations of the market place. In a modem socialised health service, the negotiation that appears to take place between professionals and patients over diagnosis and treatment requires that the resulting inequalities in treatment be accounted for, not in terms of the subordination of the definition of medical needs to the values of the market system, but rather in terms of differences in health projects and individuals' capacities to realize them.

To maintain a distinctively Marxist position, it would be necessary to demonstrate, first, that there are systematic differences in the health projects of individuals in different social classes, adequately accounted for in terms of their market and work situations; and, then, that individuals' differential capacities to realize their health projects may be accounted for in terms of their relationship to the ownership and control of the means of production. The available evidence is scanty. However, that individuals' life *goals* cannot adequately be seen as deriving from their work and market situations is a principal conclusion of the *Affluent Worker* studies. Moreover—to turn to the second of the above propositions—the final volume of the Luton studies includes discussion not, admittedly, of health projects but rather of the educational projects these workers have for their children. A principal conclusion is that differential capacities to realize these projects spring, not from the relationship of parents to the means of production, but rather from differential knowledge and understanding of the education system, of the selection mechanisms at work within it and of what constitutes a conducive home environment. As we shall see in the next section—and in previous chapters—the degree and social distribution of such understanding is itself in considerable measure an outcome of existing social measures. Health projects and the capacity to realize them may well be susceptible to modification through health education, with positive discrimination towards less articulate groups, or through the development of collective action that results in criticism of the professional and political organization of health care and of the inequalities it reproduces. Thus serious doubt is thrown on the neo-Marxist theses rehearsed above.

Market Liberals

In the opening section, we summarised the market liberals' arguments in a threefold form:

(*i*) in respect of the definition of need for state aid, they postulate that a sufficient and valid criterion or indicator is a specified low level of income, applied through rigorous means-testing;

(*ii*) they argue that, for each of the life chances distributed through social policies, there exists a basic level of provision necessary for social existence, which can be determined by objective study;

(*iii*) they display a measured optimism as to the trends in the pattern of overall distributive outcomes generated in a market-dominated society and anticipate the elimination of need without the aid of redistributive social policies. Let us examine these arguments in turn.

(*i*) We saw earlier that the chronically sick are likely, in a private health insurance scheme, to be subject to increased risk-rating and premia by virtue of their chronic condition. This reduces the effective demand for the private sector to provide a quality of service for chronic degenerative disease superior to that of the state. At the same time, their probable downward mobility, in search of less demanding jobs, renders them decreasingly able to afford private treatment proportionate to their likely requirements; and, if a specified low level of income is taken as indicating need for state aid, these chronic and degenerative conditions will tend to become the concern primarily of the state's safety-net provision—as, indeed, was to a considerable extent the case in the inter-war years (for a personal account, see Aronovitch, 1974). Yet, as we saw in previous chapters, with advances in techniques for dealing with acute and infectious illness, chronic degenerative conditions have become increasingly prevalent, partly as a concomitant to increased life expectancy. Consequently, it is for no small number of the population that private medical care services cannot be expected to provide a high quality of treatment. Moreover, the accidents of chronic disablement would be at least as significant as the individual's taking out of health insurance policies in determining his health outcome. Such nullifying of the individual's 'responsible' choices in the market place is hardly consonant with the market liberal's own prescriptions for social organization. Furthermore, this effect of a market organization of health care could hardly be reversed by procedures for legal compensation from the agent responsible for the chronic disability; for, as Titmuss has frequently argued, it becomes increasingly difficult, in a complex and rapidly changing urban—industrial society, to identify such agents.

(*ii*) These liberals affirm that there exists a basic level of health care provision that can be determined by objective study and that they prescribe as the limit of the state's proper role; above this, a market organization ensures equity, efficiency and individual choice. Our earlier empirical analysis suggests a fourfold criticism. First, the very definition of health and health needs is recalcitrant to precise specification and cannot but be seen as a social construct. The probability that different social classes and age groups have differing tolerances of pain and health expectations was noted earlier. Moreover, as medical techniques advance and increased resources are made available, medical conditions hitherto regarded as untreatable become susceptible to alleviation. We might, therefore, say that demand and need for medical care are, in principle, unlimited, and that as new techniques and additional resources become available, so expectations as to standards of health are likely to rise (Cooper, 1975, Chs 2, 3). Among the empirical studies cited earlier, this is, for example, a principal conclusion of Feldstein's analysis of hospitalisation: 'in health care,...appropriate standards of provision cannot be determined by reference to levels of "need" inherent in or manifest by the co nmunity' (1967, p. 201).

This insatiability of need also has implications for the likely distribution of health care resources between public and private sectors if health services were organized on the lines the liberals advocate. Jewkes and Jewkes, in their study of the NHS, while not denying that the immediate effect of an expansion of the private sector might be to redistribute resources towards the middle and upper classes, argue that in the medium and long term such a reform would call forth a sufficient increase in health care resources to produce an improved service for all groups. The queues in the NHS testify to the excess of demand over supply; and 'it may be that the NHS, because of its form, has positively discouraged the allocation of resources to the purposes of medicine'. If, however, private provision were encouraged as a complement to the public sector, 'everybody [would get] a better service. As more people move over to the private supply, the pressure on the public supply is reduced and waiting time there also becomes less' (1961, pp. 37-8). In contrast, our evidence on the seemingly unlimited character of medical need suggests that, whatever new resources may be called forth by the presence of a private sector, they will not satiate the effective demand emanating from that sector. Rather, the result would seem likely to be a starving of the public sector resources no less perpetual then the existence of unmet medical need. The traditional liberal thesis that the pursuit of individual self-interest within the market place cannot but promote the collective interest and the interest of others is here shown to be incorrect or even meaningless. This discussion also undermines liberal attempts to depict the process of health care allocation in a market system as a competitive equilibrium determined as much by actors' varied preferences as by their economic resources. Rather than some harmonious systemic equilibrium being attained, what is apparent in our foregoing empirically oriented discussion is a power contest in which actors' economic resources are of crucial significance in determining an outcome that can in no meaningful or useful sense be termed an 'equilibrium'.

It is convenient at this point to examine a related argument advanced by some market liberals in recognition of this potentially unlimited demand for medical care. This is that a market organization of health care services discourages excessive demand by imposing an opportunity cost upon the potential patient: prescription charges render less likely the wasteful use of drugs; consultation fees prevent pressures upon medical professionals building up intolerably. The introduction of the NHS fostered a debate over the consequences for consultation rates, etc., of the elimination of the disciplines of the cash nexus. Titmuss agrees that in the early years of the new service, following the austerity of war and post-war reconstruction, it had to face a 'back-log of needs...most vividly depicted by the demand for spectacles, dentures, hearing aids and other postponable adjuncts to better health' (1963, p. 153). However, he also marshals evidence suggesting that the establishment of the NHS not only did not lead to any excessive demand for GP services, but that it saw, rather, an actual decline in GP consultations as between the nationally insured labour force in the 1930s and the same age group of men in 1949-50. Cooper, moreover, observes that even in the absence of a cash nexus there do exist opportunity costs to seeking health care: 'Deterrents include the necessary expenditure of time and energy, inconvenience, travel costs, leisure forgone, the discomforts of the doctor's waiting room....' (1975, p. 16). The more fundamental question that arises out of these considerations, however, is the distribution among different medical needs of the reduction in effective demand for health care, as a result of market allocation on the one hand or the costs mentioned by Cooper on the other. Only in the light of a value-judgement on the desirability of these distributions can either of these two methods of restricting effective demand be evaluated. The value-ladenness of the liberal argument we have been examining in this paragraph must, therefore, be recognized.

The final criticism of the second liberal proposition also derives from our empirical discussion of the character of need for medical care. The diagnosis of medical need, we saw, is essentially an esoteric task, notwithstanding the patient's participation in the pursuit of his health project. That a market organization of health care widens the citizen's choice, as in the neoclassical economist's model of competitive markets, must therefore be questioned. The esoteric definition of need by professionals means, rather, that no realistic choice can be said to exist for the patient, as among different patterns of treatment, even in a market system. True, each individual would be exercising choice as to the proportion of his income to be devoted to health care; yet the most significant choice that the market would introduce is for those with substantial financial resources to command equally substantial health care resources.

(*iii*) The market liberal typically anticipates that the 'natural' development of a laissez-faire market system will ensure the elimination of basic need without the aid of redistributive social policies. In so far as these market liberals expect this to result from a reduction in the occupational and environmental depradations of advanced capitalism, there seems only limited supportive evidence.

It is true that over wide ranges of morbidity, rates for all classes have declined, even though class gradients have often remained broadly unchanged. That this is due to post-war prosperity may well be true. Nevertheless, this has of course been the era of state-managed capitalism, raising the much wider question of the viability of a laissez-faire advanced market system. Moreover, at least some of this reduction in morbidity must surely be attributed to preventive health policies and to the impact of other aspects of post-war social policy, such as housing.

However, market liberals also look to developments in the personal health services for the elimination of basic unmet need. That the objective specification of this 'basic' level of medical need is in principle impossible has, however, been argued above; and it renders this third liberal proposition somewhat vacuous. Second, we have also just argued that with a substantial private sector alongside the public, the latter would be starved of resources; it might be said to suffer probable immiseration, in relative if not absolute terms. Third, as also already argued, a market organization of health care would seem likely to concentrate the chronically sick in a low-quality public sector. The chronically sick would be disproportionately represented among the objects of this immiseration.

Political Liberals

The arguments of the political liberals recalled in section I related (*i*) to the meritocratic equality of opportunity that free access to the policy-making arena could be expected to promote; (*ii*) to the technical and apolitical character of the resulting indicators of need and merit; and (in) to the greater equality of life chances that such meritocratic social policies—themselves increasingly guaranteed by the logic of industrialism—might be expected to produce.

(*i*) The first of these propositions may be criticised on three grounds. To start with, 'free access 'is not, for those political liberals who emphasise it, an unqualified presumption. Rather, there is typically the caveat—explicit or only implicit—that such access be granted to all *legitimate* interest groups. Such legitimacy is itself problematic, of course, but is typically applied to established interest groups only, with no formal provision made for the legitimation and political inclusion of any new groups that may develop in the society at large. Interests not subsumed in the objectives of 'legitimate' interest groups are not, therefore, heeded in the bargaining process of which social policy formulation is supposed essentially to consist. Clearly a more general critique of such a political theory cannot be attempted here. Nevertheless, particularly in our discussion in previous chapters of recent debates over consumer participation, we have seen that the question of the legitimacy of consumers as an interest group to be admitted to health policy formulation has been put into sharp focus. The Conservative government's *Consultative Document* counterposed efficient management to participation by consumers; and its modification of the Labour proposals on such participation must be seen as a refusal to admit advocacy of their interests, save by their 'legitimate' political representatives in Parliament and government. Since reorganization, the experience of the Community Health Councils has involved continuing challenge by medical professionals to the councils' competence and legitimacy to pronounce on consumer and community interests (Klein and Lewis, 1976, pp. 124-34).

This proposition may additionally be criticised in terms of its assumption that free access to the policy-making process is a *sufficient* condition for advocacy of the interests of all legitimate groups. Our earlier discussion highlighted the need to account, for inequalities of treatment in terms of typical differences in health projects and individuals' capacities to realize them. Yet, consistently with this, it was also seen that it has been precisely those categories of patients most lacking in such capacities—namely the aged, the chronically sick and the mentally ill and handicapped—who have been accorded least favoured treatment of all the various morbid conditions. In a situation where such medical conditions seem to be growing in their prevalence, the insufficiency of equal access to the policy-making process as a condition of equitable treatment—however the latter may be defined—is especially evident.

A final criticism centres on the assumption that social policy formulation may adequately be conceptualised as a bargaining process in the course of which a systemic equilibrium is achieved, the just outcome of an interaction of group interests. On the one hand, the discussion, in previous chapters, of the evolution of health policy revealed some of the ways in which the struggle of diverse interest groups in pursuit of their goals has involved a perennial promotion of substantive irrationality in health care services. Similarly, to take an example from the inequalities discussed in the present chapter, 'the distribution of [consultant awards], associated as it is with high professional status, must surely influence the choice younger doctors make about the area of medicine in which they practice' (Parker, 1975, p. 82). On the other hand, to speak of a systemic equilibrium presumably requires that there be some central values to which policies increasingly tend, in the course of the bargaining process. It is, however, the perennial diversity of values and conflict among them that is evident in our investigation—where by values one is here referring to the priority rankings of different health needs.

(*ii*) The political liberals suppose that political value-judgements may be eliminated from social policy formulation: criteria of need and merit, and decisions over the allocation of resources become increasingly the proper concern of scientific and professional expertise. That such a proposition has much plausibility in the field of health care follows from our earlier empirical survey. The esoteric nature of medical need, especially with the advance of diagnostic and clinical techniques, finds its obverse in the expertise of highly trained medical personnel.

However, our empirical discussion also revealed the existence of value-judgements in health policy irreducible to technical questions of medical diagnosis and prescription. As we have seen, the social construction of definitions of health and the seeming insatiability of needs for care render health care resources inherently scarce. But for such scarcity, it might in principle be possible to envisage a service meeting all health needs; decisions in health policy would be wholly of a technical and administrative character. Yet the inherent scarcity that in fact obtains requires that priorities be specified for resource allocation—whether it is through a market or through professional and bureaucratic criteria that such a ranking of priorities is achieved. Such priorities concern the relative treatment of different needs and, therefore, of different individuals. It is in this sense, then, that the ranking of priorities involves value-judgements in a most fundamental sense—judgements on the degree to which the needs of different individuals should constitute the ends or objectives of social policy. This unavoidable specification of priorities has been at least partly responsible for continuing friction between medical practitioners and the state, as a provider of resources, over the relationship between clinical freedom and service planning (Klein, 1977). Placing this discussion within the context of the more general view of urban—industrial society held by the political liberals, the question arises as to whether this set of value-judgements may be resolved in terms of society's evolving 'needs', i.e. by technical judgements, albeit not by *medical* experts. One of the conclusions of previous chapters was that no such reduction was possible.

Likewise, it was evident in previous chapters that the problems of, and the need for, improved planning and effectiveness have increasingly been felt in the NHS. Such recognition has grown *pari passu* with awareness of the need for more adequate information and data collection. Alderson argues that the integration of the three branches of the NHS permits the creation of a unified health information service, not service-oriented but 'population-based and problem-oriented', enabling *inter alia* a comparison of the costs of different methods of treating a given condition (in Maunder, 1974, section 7). Feldstein's study of the hospital service (1967) exemplifies the latter analysis. He first develops several production functions relating inputs to treatment. He is able to assess the cost-effectiveness of an input for any category of patient; this enables both the analysis of the efficiency of resource use, and rational decisions on changes in policy, if it is desired to change the weights given to various illnesses when allocating resources. Cooper surveys recent attempts to engage in cost—benefit analyses of different forms of treatment. Methodological problems are often substantial; nevertheless, he sees such investigations as promoting 'a very critical self-examination of current practices and a ruthless pruning out of the ineffectual' (1975, p. 124). Neither Feldstein nor Cooper, however, sees such technical analyses as removing the need for value-judgements and priority rankings in respect of different needs and different categories of patient; such investigations, rather, can properly serve only to *inform* these judgements.

(*iii*) The final argument of the political liberals is that the meritocratic social policies that are developing as part of the logic of industrialism may be expected automatically to produce greater equality in the overall distribution of life chances. However, our foregoing discussion suggests three grounds for doubt. First, we have argued that political value-judgements over the relative priorities to be accorded to different medical needs are perennial and are irreducible to technical judgements. No trend in the pattern of health outcomes can, therefore, be deemed 'automatic'; it will, rather, in principle at least, be or have been a matter of political will. Second, the trends in class gradient we have reviewed give no clear indication of growing equality. Lastly, as among different categories of medical need, our discussion suggests that the aged, the mentally ill and handicapped, and the chronically sick continue to receive poor quality treatment; and that, while recognition of this may have informed recent attempts to redefine the objectives and priorities of the NHS, there can hardly be said to have been any obvious trend in the post-war era towards equality of treatment among these various need groups.

Social Democrats

Such criticisms of liberals and neo-Marxists are broadly consistent with the position adopted by Social Democratic writers. For them, the NHS has provided perhaps the clearest example, in both its birth and its aims, of a universalist social policy making a reality of the 'needs nexus'. Nevertheless, within our discussion are pointers to the inadequacy of such universalism, requiring at least some modification of the Social Democratic position as enunciated in the euphoric 1940s. First, we have traced persisting inequalities in realizing the right to equal treatment—reflecting the priorities and perceptions of medical professionals, patients' varying expectations and tolerance of ill-health and the historical patterns of resource distribution and institutional organization. Whether positive discrimination—for example in health education and resource allocation—is technically and politically feasible, as a means of reducing such inequalities, is at best an open question. Second, it has become increasingly evident that for social inequalities in morbidity to be reduced, preventive policies are necessary that involve new social controls on industrial and urban milieux— and hence upon those enjoying power there. A social right to health—rather than merely to treatment when ill—cannot be realized by universalist social services alone. Third, this universalism may indeed compensate unconditionally the victims of urban—industrial change, recognizing that the agents of depradation are often invisible. However, as neo-Marxists affirm, it may also thereby discourage investigation and preventive social control of such agencies. Equally invisible socially are the costs, in terms of poorer treatment, that the articulate and informed are able, through their manipulation of medical professionals within a universalist service, to impose upon their socially less competent fellows. The conditions under which the visibility of such processes and outcomes may be increased will be a major theme of previous chapters.

Consider now the implications of the foregoing for the definition of interests.

Liberals

For contemporary liberals, *free* access to either the economic or political arenas suffices to define an identity of interests among citizens, irrespective of social class. Such free access ensures that the pursuit of self-interest will not conflict with, but will rather promote, the collective interest; distributive outcomes will be determined through the establishment of a systemic equilibrium. However, our empirical criticisms of both market and political liberals included a demonstration that such 'free access', as conceived of by these writers, cannot be seen as establishing a value-free 'equilibrium'. Rather, our discussion revealed that within any health care system there is bound to be perennial conflict over the priority rankings of different medical needs, and that a market organization of care resolves such conflict only by subordinating its outcome to differentials in market power. This lends support to the Social Democrats' criticism of liberal analyses of individual interests. For, *contra* the liberals, the Social Democrats argue that an advanced urban—industrial society cannot, even in principle, be organized in such a way that individuals' pursuit of their self-interest need not necessarily be mutually opposed.

Neo-Marxists

Contemporary neo-Marxists, while admitting the absolute improvement that may well have occurred in the life chances of manual workers, affirm a continuing trend to relative immiseration, and deny that contemporary social policies affect the implications of this threat for the definition of class interests. The earlier empirical discussion suggests at least three lines of criticism.

(*i*) Consistent with the Social Democrats, there are certain respects in which there exists a common interest among all classes in state interference with the market. (Marx himself acknowledged the common interest of different social classes in such measures. Yet this acknowledgement, far from demonstrating that such measures are consistent with the capitalist market economy depicted by Marx, shows rather that such an economy was taken by Marx as an ideal type, and that he saw such community-oriented measures as representing a movement of English society away from that ideal type; Avineri, 1968, pp. 159-62). Thus we have referred to the impact of preventive policies upon morbidity and the new importance ascribed to community medicine, particularly its preventive aspects, in recent reforms of the NHS. However, it cannot be assumed that all preventive measures will significantly benefit *all* social classes, still less that such benefits will be perceived as *evenly* distributed. We have, for example, seen that the lower socioeconomic groups tend to be inarticulate and lacking the understanding required to appropriate the treatment that the middle classes obtain. Therefore, measures aimed at health education and early presentation of symptoms or at enabling medical professionals to overcome cultural barriers of class and ethnicity may tend, in the absence of significant increases in overall health care resources, to threaten the standards of care that those middle classes have come to expect. This in turn threatens the Social Democratic confidence that such measures will typically and immediately evoke widespread popular acquiescence. Or, alternatively, it makes especially clear how different their approach must be from the liberal reliance upon self-interested acquiescence in societal functioning: emphasising, instead, not only that such acquiescence must involve some subordination of this self-interest to the common interest, but also that imperious definition of this common interest is a matter for political leadership. However, these considerations (central to Weber's concerns) have been left implicit or only superficially explored by our Social Democrats.

A further area of common interest among social classes is apparent when one considers the prevalence and consequences of chronic illness of various kinds. Under a market distribution of health care, we argued earlier, such illness is likely to receive low priority in the allocation of resources. No private insurance scheme will guarantee members full cover against the risk and costs of chronic illness of unlimited duration. To the extent, therefore, that the risk of chronic illness or disablement is significant through all social classes, and to the extent that the resource costs of providing the quality of treatment technically available are high, there is defined a common interest among the members of all social classes in the establishment and promotion of services free to the user. The growing costs of medical care, apparent in this section and previous chapters, together with the growing prevalence of chronic illness among different social classes, suggest that such a common objective interest is today not insignificant.

We may, therefore, recognize that such common interests do objectively exist and that class interests are not wholly opposed. Nevertheless, these counter-arguments might meet with a twofold rejoinder from the neo-Marxists. First, such areas of common interest in universalist social policies extend only to the lower—and middle-income groups; the wealthy, encouraged by tax relief on private health insurance schemes, have no such interest. This, then, suffices merely to support the thesis of the 'proletarianisation' of the middle classes. Second, we have failed to make explicit the more fundamental common interest that the mass of the population shares in eliminating the substantial ill-health that is the fruit, directly or indirectly, of a capitalist organization of the division of labour. Against the latter retort, however, we have conceded that politically contentious changes may indeed be required; but we have insisted that their form and their manner of realization cannot be defined *a priori.*

(*ii*) A second criticism of the neo-Marxist analysis of class interests is that the processes of care allocation within the NHS create common interests that transcend considerations of class. We earlier argued that the treatment an individual receives appears typically to depend upon his health project, upon the negotiation between doctor and patient over the definition of need and the prescription of treatment, and upon the priority granted to that need category by political decisions on resource allocation. For those with a common need, as defined by the medical professionals, there is therefore a common *immediate* interest in altering the priority ranking of that need within the political resource allocation process. Admittedly, for certain wealthier individuals receiving NHS treatment, they might prefer to 'opt out' of the NHS, paying less taxes and taking out private health insurance. Their objective interest is class related. Once, however, health care is distributed in accordance with medical need, as a social right of citizenship, and charges are levied upon the healthy as a social duty of citizenship, the common interest is created that we have just delineated. Thus as Titmuss argues, 'the middle classes...have not contracted out of socialised medical care...their continuing participation, and their more articulate demands for improvements, have been an important factor in a general rise in standards of service' (1968, p. 196). As argued by Social Democrats, the pattern of immediate interests generated by social rights may therefore be fundamentally different from that generated by the exercise of civil rights. It follows, then, that the Social Democratic critique of the neo-Marxists here depends on the readiness of even the wealthy to embrace the social rights and duties of citizenship that such a universalist service embodies. These writers have, perhaps, increasingly acknowledged the fragility and vulnerability of such readiness in face of the acquisitive individualism enjoined by other social milieux. This will be a major theme in the next chapters.

(*iii*) The neo-Marxists imply that while the working class may have an immediate interest in the extension of social rights realized through universal social services, such extension has little prospect of major success; for it comes into conflict with the interests of the dominant capitalist class. The trade unions and the labour movement cannot, therefore, reasonably see the extension of such social policies as a new means to their long-standing aim of withstanding the threat of immiseration and even establishing a socialist distribution of treatment according to need. We have, however, argued with the Social Democrats that, at least in the case of health policy, it has been through the attempted extension and realization of common social rights that the immediately necessary modifications of free exercise of civil rights have been revealed, in an immanent practical critique of market influences. An essentially historical conception of the realization of social rights is necessary, rather than the relatively static systemic approach of the neo-Marxists, with its utopian tendencies.

It may, of course, be that, as the neo-Marxists predict, such efforts lead to authoritarian reaction by the ruling class, if such may be said to exist. For the Social Democrats, however, this is essentially an empirical question. Moreover, they would argue that it is through attempts at social policy reform that such potential areas of conflict are revealed; that since such revelation is in the interests of the working class, so too is such attempted reform; and, finally, that such revelation promotes a subjective appreciation of objective interests. On the other hand, as we have noted elsewhere, the Social Democrats have insufficiently explored what social groups are available—or can, by appropriate political leadership, be created—having both the will and the capacity to voice and implement this critique.

Finally, in bringing our empirical findings to bear upon the liberal, neo-Marxist and Social Democratic arguments, we have laid bare important differences in the significance they attach to the social division of welfare. For liberal writers, the distribution of life chance outcomes is of only secondary interest. What is of primary importance in judging distributive processes—and in predicting their implications for group formation and action—is their formal equity among individuals enjoying free access to the economic or political market place; although liberals do use evidence of distributive outcomes as indicators, first of how meritocratic in some objective sense—and hence how equitable—our society is, and second of the elimination of need defined in some basic or absolute sense. For Marx, the investigation of trends in inequalities was significant in indicating the development of the objective conditions of immiseration that, as they were subjectively apprehended, would impel the working class to active transformation of capitalist society. Yet many contemporary neo-Marxists seem, in contrast, to see the documentation of continuing inequalities as serving primarily to demonstrate the continuing validity of Marx's portrait of capitalism. Indeed, both liberal and neo-Marxist writers sometimes seem content to take measures of such inequalities as sufficient evidence of wider social processes—for example, some automatic trend to meritocracy or a hardly less inevitable immiseration. Or they may even take these measures as adequate indicators of the 'species' to which our contemporary society belongs. In both cases they betray the ahistorical systemic view of society that we criticised in previous chapters. For Social Democratic writers, the elucidation of inequalities—of an 'abnormal' social division of welfare—is significant primarily for continuing redefinition or the state's role in enunciating and realizing the social rights of citizenship: a role that is necessary for social cohesion in particular (see Terrill, 1974, pp. 217, 275).

Following this comparison, note that neo-Marxists commonly take class gradients in, for example, morbidity, as the significant measure of inequality. This seems consistent with their inherited interest in immiseration: they are comparing the proportions of the lower socio-economic categories suffering debilitation relative to society in general and to the upper categories in particular. However, with such class gradients unchanged, a reduction in the absolute rates of morbidity for all social classes logically implies that for the lower social classes the proportionate increase in those not suffering ill-health is greater than in the case of the middle and upper classes. It is *this* definition of inequality that liberal writers seem commonly but implicitly to embrace; it is consistent with their interest in progress to a society of competent and self-sufficient individuals—with incompetence or incapacity conceived of in absolute terms. Social Democratic writers seem ready to take the improvements in the health of all classes as indicating, in part and *contra* the neo-Marxists, the efficacy of social policies, and to take the persisting class gradients in ill-health as indicating, *contra* the liberals, the need for further intervention including, for example, positive discrimination and preventive measures, if the appropriation of these social rights is to be universal. What might appear, then, as a merely technical problem of defining indicators of inequality turns out to involve fundamental value-judgements and theoretical interests. What measures of inequality are most appropriate will, therefore, depend upon the ability of the theories utilising them to provide adequate explanations of the empirical consequences of inequality. Among such consequences, we have argued, the implications for group formation and action have been accepted by all schools as particularly important; these form the subject of the next chapter. There we shall investigate the influence of inequalities in the social division of welfare upon the values and goals to which individuals and groups orient themselves.

There are, however, at least three major limitations to the approach we have adopted in this section. First, for reasons of space we have investigated the pattern of needs and outcomes in only one branch of social policy. Had we considered educational inequalities, for example, we would have been drawn into the growing literature on the stratification of opportunities and provisions, and the strategies that differentially advantaged groups may employ to control and monopolise the more privileged sectors and, via them, similarly privileged positions in the wider society. At least until recently, as we saw in previous chapters, the ideology of equal opportunity has provided a widely accepted legitimation for the individualistic acquisition of formal qualifications within this unequal society—an acquisitiveness oriented to the preservation or improvement of credentials *relative* to those of others. Here the apparently unending expansion of demand for the life chances distributed through the social services is exposed as expressing not so much rising expectations of common standards of provision, but rather inherently unrealizable—because universal—demands for access to positions of privilege. Here then, still more strikingly than in the case of health care, the divergence is revealed between pursuit of self-interest and promotion of the general quality of a universalist service, and, hence, the political task that securing popular commitment to such promotion must entail. At best, therefore, our limited focus has provided an exemplar for further studies and raised issues relevant to other chapters; at worst, however, it may encourage misleading and invalid generalisations.

Second, even within medical care, we have focused upon the public sector and largely ignored the private. The latter is, admittedly, used by only a small minority of the population (Parker, 1975, pp. 89-91). Yet the resources it attracts, its prospects for growth—particularly in the form of occupational fringe benefits—and its dissolution of a universal interest in improving the quality of public provision may be more significant. Titmuss and the other Social Democratic writers have been as vociferous as the neo-Marxists in their criticism (see Wilding, 1976, pp. 159-62). On the other hand, this choice of perhaps the most 'socialised' sector of social policy may, by the same token, have enabled us to examine most dearly how far life chance distribution can in principle be extricated from the cash nexus historically dominant in our society—exposing most dearly, therefore, such new processes of inequality as tend to emerge in nominally universalist services.

Third, we have neglected the social distribution of the burden of financing health care. This would have involved consideration of the national insurance and taxation systems, and the latter discussion would need to have included fiscal incentives to private health provision. We have, therefore, perhaps given insufficient attention to two of the three elements distinguished by Titmuss in his seminal essay on the social division of welfare—namely, occupational and fiscal welfare (on these, see Sinfield, 1978, and references therein). Had these findings then been used in a judgement on the distribution of the costs and benefits of health care, it would, of course, also have been necessary to take account of the longer life expectancy—and higher use of facilities for chronic illness—among the middle—and upper-income groups.

Returning then to the first of these limitations, it is an investigation of the need for, and the distribution of, benefits in cash that would have been an especially desirable addition, had space permitted. In recent decades the payment of direct taxation has extended to most of the population, at the same time as social security benefits have developed a concern with earnings-related benefits. There have in consequence been various political proposals for rationalisation or unification of the two systems (most notably the Conservatives' *Proposals for a Tax Credit* System—Treasury and DHSS, 1972), and several important recent studies of the net impact of the social security and taxation systems on those with different incomes and domestic responsibilities. These have exposed the non-progressive character of direct taxation, its increasing burden on the low paid and on those with families in particular and the lack of any redistribution among broad income categories via the two systems taken together (Kincaid, 1973, esp. Chs 5-7; Field *et al.,* 1977, esp. Chs 2, 4, 9). They tend, therefore, to challenge the confidence of political liberals that the state has, through these institutions, effected such redistribution to a significant degree. Yet the pattern of interests to which these systems give rise is hardly what the neo-Marxists would predict. Rather, as in our discussion of health care, common interests arise among those in common situations *vis-a-vis* such public bureaucracies. Hence, for example, the Child Poverty Action Group is currently seeking to establish a family—rather than a poverty—lobby by those with families, who, whatever their levels of income, have a common immediate interest in the expansion of universalist child benefits (Field, 1977; contrast Field, 1976). Here, then, as the Social Democrats argue, social rights may tend to generate areas of common interest—and, indeed, new lines of conflict—distinct from those defined by the market place, notwithstanding the apparent failure of such rights thus far to promote any marked income redistribution among classes. Nevertheless, the articulation of such interests involves political leadership and does not arise spontaneously; to this the Social Democrats (like their rivals) have perhaps given insufficient attention.

DEPRIVATION IN THE WELFARE STATE

The second type of investigation appropriate to this chapter focuses not on some arm of social policy—for example, morbidity and health care—but rather on the overall life chances typically enjoyed by individuals variously situated in the society. More particularly,, the classical and contemporary perspectives on industrial society and social policy explored in Part I alert us to the situation of the poor, who have been a perennial political concern. For example, it was on alleviation of their lot that the Beveridge Report on post-war reconstruction centred: it looked to the abolition of those apparently most gregarious of giants—Idleness, Want, Disease, Squalor and Ignorance.

Following in a long tradition of British empirical social science, there has been a rapid growth in the investigation of poverty over the last two decades. Some of this literature has attempted an overall assessment of the extent and distribution of poverty in contemporary Britain. It has tended to emphasise the financial or economic aspects and to take individuals or households as the units of its analysis. We focus instead, however, upon the other main arm of this expanding literature—the study of local communities exhibiting long-term multiple deprivation. The studies we use may not immediately permit an assessment of the extent of such multiple deprivation in the society as a whole, but they do afford insight into its aetiology.

We recall, first, that for *neo-Marxist* writers the analysis and explanation of poverty must be firmly rooted in an understanding of the class situation of the poor, i.e. their position within the mode of industrial production. They are those who bear disproportionately the social costs of capitalist development. For they consist principally of an industrial reserve army ensuring adequate supplies of cheap unskilled labour as capitalist employment levels fluctuate, the technologically unemployed, as new techniques displace human skills, and such unemployables as the aged and handicapped, incapable of being rendered productive within capitalist enterprise. The continued dependence of housing allocation upon market power tends to result in the concentration of such poor in blighted zones of falling house values; political decisions over housing allocation, notably by the local authorities, have tended if anything to reinforce such zoning (Castells, 'Advanced Capitalism, Collective Consumption and Urban Contradiction' in Lindberg, 1975, esp. pp. 182-5). Attempts to redress the social ills of such areas through social policies will bear little fruit unless combined with an attack on capitalist property relations. Yet programmes under the auspices of the capitalist state by definition exclude such an attack.

Liberal writers have generally predicated their diagnoses of poverty upon a vision of society as a collection of atomised individuals—a vision that the market liberals see as threatened by the twentieth-century growth of collectivism but that the political liberals see as increasingly taking the form of a competitive meritocracy. Poverty is therefore seen as deriving either from the motivational—or even moral—inadequacies of the poor themselves, or else from incomplete realization of the liberals' vision of the good society. More specifically, there has on the one hand been a variety of diagnoses and policy proposals focussing on some alleged 'culture of poverty' that inhibits the capacity of the poor to take up opportunities for full participation in the wider achieving society. The prescription is remedial policies directed at the familial and community processes that foster and perpetuate such inhibitions. Alternatively, diagnosis and prescription may look to the peripheral malfunctioning of the wider society. Market liberals decry the welfare bureaucracies that sap incentives for self-help. Political liberals emphasise the need to equalise opportunities as between the poor and the *non-poor—inter alia,* through sustained efforts by local and national government to improve service delivery. The ultimate goal in each case is that the poor should be enabled individually to deploy their resources and to appropriate common opportunities within an open society. The optimistic liberal prognoses we saw in the previous section recur here. Benevolent 'treatment' of the poor together with improved efficiency in public services, involving only modest resource costs, are tending and will suffice to incorporate the poor into the mainstream of the improving wider society.

Tawney and T.H. Marshall, in his earlier essays, may have been overly optimistic as to the impact of the Welfare State upon poverty. Titmuss, however, is alert to the new—and not-so-new—intergroup struggles that determine life chance allocation, and he uses a broadly actionist perspective in exploring individuals' strategies and successes—or failures—in realizing their life projects. The deprived then appear as those who have suffered persistent exclusion from resources and from power to realize their life projects. For example, they suffer disproportionately the 'social costs and social insecurities which are the product of a rapidly changing industrial—urban society'; social programmes intended to discriminate according to need are perennially in danger of stigmatising recipients, thereby reinforcing their exclusion and their inability to define themselves as full citizens (Titmuss, 1968, pp. 133-5, 158-9). The *Social Democratic* perspective is, therefore, distinguished from liberal views by its refusal to embrace a naive optimism as to any benign trend in our society towards the elimination of poverty, and in its emphasis upon a diagnosis in terms of differential power and advantage in inter-group struggles. It differs from the neo-Marxist accounts in wishing to distinguish the political, community and production milieux as potential arenas of such conflict, and in denying that it is the situation of the poor *vis-a-vis* the means of production that is invariably, necessarily and unambiguously dominant in the generation of deprivation.

Recent anti-poverty programmes have been predicated upon various of these theories and have incorporated a research commitment, with continuing diagnosis of deprivation and evaluation of different strategies for its extirpation. We have chosen to focus in this section upon the long-term multiple deprivation of local communities. It seems sensible, therefore, to concentrate upon the research findings of these projects in attempting an evaluation of the foregoing theories and of the role that social policies have played and can play in the elimination of deprivation. We focus on the findings of the Community Development Projects, which are located in areas of multiple deprivation and have been recently producing their final reports.

First, then, what do the findings of these action—research projects suggest in regard to the generation of deprivation? Their initial remit seems to have been implicitly predicated on a broad acceptance of the liberal diagnoses outlined above: the neighbourhood basis seems in part to have expressed official confidence that deprivation was a problem peripheral to the society as a whole. That problem, furthermore, was seen as deriving either from characteristics of the populations concerned, or else from technical malfunctioning of Welfare State agencies which were functioning satisfactorily as far as other sections of society were concerned. At the same time, some deliberate selection was attempted, to include a variety of areas for such action—research—ranging from isolated settlements in South Wales and Cumbria to inner-city neighbourhoods, and from contexts of prosperity such as Coventry to others of general decline (National CDP, 1974, paras 2.1, 3.3).

Yet the clearest conclusion to emerge from the national experiment is the inadequacy of this diagnosis. Typical have been the findings of the Coventry CDP. Hillfields, the area in which it was located, simply did not contain an abnormal share of 'inadequate' families. The most obvious problems of the area were ones of social circumstance rather than individual competence. Moreover, low incomes, poor housing and planning blight afflicted the mass of residents, and were similar in kind, if different in degree, to the problems of other inner-city areas (Coventry CDP, 1975a, para. 5.4). Nor could the assumption be maintained that it was the merely technical malfunctioning of public services that permitted the persistence of deprivation, and that improved communication would suffice to effect a significant change. For the technical and managerial skills of Coventry Corporation are second to none.

Rather, the Inter-Project Report, drawn up approximately midway through the originally intended life of the national experiment, concludes that, while improved service coordination and communication might 'achieve some greater flexibility in the face to face delivery of services', for issues like redevelopment such strategies are by themselves largely futile, since 'there need to be basic changes of policy'. Likewise, the 1975/6 Forward Plan for those projects still in operation rejects 'accounts (of area deprivation].., based on social pathology', as also any hopes that 'improved coordination of existing social and welfare services can...make [more than]...a marginal impact'.

The CDP experiment points, therefore, to a diagnosis of deprivation that sees it as the precipitate of society-wide processes—a diagnosis that is, therefore, necessarily historical in orientation. Rapid urban—industrial change has widely varying consequences for different social groups: it tends to produce virtuous and vicious circles of advantage and disadvantage, with only those groups already relatively advantaged able to convert such advantages into the power on capacity to escape new forms of disadvantage. Thus some CDP neighbourhoods are reception areas for unskilled and semi-skilled newcomers to city regions enjoying rapid industrial growth. Yet these are groups likely to be badly organized, to include high proportions of non-whites exposed to racial discrimination, and to be especially vulnerable to redundancy in times of recession (National CDP, 1974, para. 3.14). Others are areas of population decline, with the skilled and the young among the first to depart, leaving behind those least able to arrest the general decline of the neighbourhood (para. 3.15; cf. National CDP, 1975, p. 2; Payne and Smith, 'The Context of the Twelve Areas' in Lees and Smith, 1975). In both cases, growing need is likely for public services to the dependent; but a shrinking rate base coupled with lack of political power for the residents affected instead typically promote a reduction in such services. Yet in general such causal chains are publicly neither anticipated nor recognized: deprivation and privilege appear instead as the rewards and penalties of individuals' traits and performances, or as the unfortunate but unavoidable by-product of the technical functioning of a developing urban—industrial society.

Our attention is, therefore, directed to an analysis of much wider processes. Notwithstanding the variations among CDPs in the detailed issues faced and the specific strategies adopted, their reports suggest the foundations of a common diagnosis comprising perhaps three principal elements. It may be helpful to illustrate each of these strands by reference to one of the original projects, that in Coventry, which also claimed our attention in the previous chapter. Judging by the final reports that have appeared from other projects, there is little ground for major anxiety that the Coventry analysis will prove to have been markedly atypical. The Liverpool project, admittedly, differs in the inferences it draws for action, as we shall see in previous chapters, but in its historical diagnosis of deprivation it is broadly consonant with what follows:

(*i*) Many of the individual project reports have emphasised the fatefulness of investment and employment decisions by private industrial concerns whose organization and policy-making are at a national—or even an international—level. Such decisions affect both the extent and the kind of employment and income opportunities—that is, the overall demand for labour and relative demand for different skills (National CDP, 1977, esp. Chs 1, 3). Several of the CDPs have examined the responsiveness of these decisions to regional policies; their findings suggest that such policies have only minimal impact in the face of market forces, and that they are insufficiently sensitive to small-scale variations in local needs.

In Coventry, dominated by the car industry, the post-war boom in domestic car production has passed its peak; further concentration of the industry nationally may put at risk the city's traditionally buoyant demand for labour. This is likely to hit the unskilled in particular, who over the past half-century have increased markedly in relation to skilled manual workers. It is these workers and their dependants who have come to form a major part of the population of Hillfields, the target area of the CDP, with its stock of cheaper and older housing. The neighbourhood, the CDP team argue, has come to serve as a 'reserve tank of labour' for the motor vehicle and associated industries in the city, with many of its employable residents readily available for unskilled work in times of boom but easily made redundant in times of slump. Its deprivation must, therefore, be seen as having as one of its major sources the changing fortunes—and the national and international reorganization—of the motor industry (Coventry CDP, 1975a, paras 7.0-7.27; 1975b. Paper 6).

This defines, therefore, a basic disjunction between the interests of industrial enterprise—in this case most notably the motor industry—and those of the city and, more particularly, the residents of such areas as Hillfields. An immediate corollary is a similar disjunction between residents' interests and the goals of local authority policy-makers, in so far as those goals, as we saw in previous chapters, are heavily moulded by industrial and commercial interests. Instead, the CDP analysis distinguishes those sections of the city population who enjoy the benefits and bear the costs of industrial prosperity and expansion. It also exposes the costs, in terms of infrastructure and social services, imposed by industrial development on the local authority, and the dependence of local authority services' adequacy upon the demographic changes that investment and employment decisions by such nationally and internationally oriented industrial corporations induce (Coventry CDP, 1975b, Paper 7, paras 7.2-7.4).

(*ii*) A recurring theme in the reports has been the unanticipated tendencies of certain types of key decision in the public sector—both nationally and locally—to perpetuate and multiply this deprivation. Local·authority decisions over land use, redevelopment and rehousing in these neighbourhoods are portrayed as typically promoting planning blight and exacerbating a competition over scarce inner-city land in which residents are least capable of securing their interests (cf. pp. 120-1, 123-5 above). Central and local government decisions over rents and rates have been the other principal area of public sector activity diagnosed as multiplying deprivation. Recent shifts in the burden of rates from industrial to domestic property have hit CDP residents particularly hard (National CDP, 1974, para. 5.11; cf. para. 5.30), as has the shift to 'fair rents' as a result of the 1972 Housing Finance Act.

Thus in the Coventry CDP, the fatefulness of public sector policies for the generation of deprivation is highlighted by the finding that if anything distinguished Hillfields from the rest of Coventry it was 'the lengthy assault of stop-go redevelopment'. We looked at these redevelopment programmes for Hillfields as a case study in the formulation and application of policy; here, in contrast, our interest is in their largely unanticipated consequences for residents.) 'Piecemeal and sporadic' action 'has set in motion a vicious spiral of planning blight, eroding certainty in the area and contributing to its physical, social and economic decline'. Industry and commerce have extended their share of Hillfields' valuable inner-city land, as also have public services oriented to the concerns of the wider city, e.g. the ring road. Likewise, the Hillfields experience is that shifts in rating and rents policies can unintentionally and at a stroke take more out of disadvantaged areas and...cities than the whole of the extra money put in through' the Urban Programme and similar forms of positive discrimination (Coventry CDP, 1975a, paras 5.4, 7.38, 7.40, 2.4, 7.33).

(*iii*) Alongside these economic and political processes of deprivation, there is a source more strictly 'social' in the sense of involving the social identities of individuals and neighbourhoods, for the deprived areas and their residents are typically the objects of stereotyping and stigmatisation by members of the wider society. This serves not only to underpin negative official definitions of such neighbourhoods and to discourage diagnosis in terms of wider societal processes, but also to promote changes in the social composition and amenities of such neighbourhoods that have the effect of a self-fulfilling prophecy (National CDP,

1974, para. 3.15). Hillfields in Coventry again offers a particularly clear illustration. Its persisting dilapidation has been conventionally attributed to the supposed internal pathology of the neighbourhood. Among official decision-makers, such labelling has hitherto served to reduce acceptance of official responsibility for the neighbourhood's physical environment and to legitimate minimal attention to residents' expressed preferences; it has ensured disproportionate attention from the police and the media; it has also accelerated the decline in property values (Benington, 1972, paras 3.12, 3.9).

Typical, then, of the conclusions offered by the CDPS in their analysis of deprivation is that of the Coventry team: 'as the root causes... operate largely outside democratic control, they cannot be dealt with by tinkering with technical procedures; they demand new kinds of political intervention which reach beyond existing jurisdiction, to claim greater local public control over the situation' (1975a, Concluding Propositions, para. 3.1). Whether as efforts in action—research the CDPs have promoted attempts at such enhanced control will be one of our concerns in the next chapter. These investigations therefore undermine any assumption—such as that common among liberals—that explanations of the generation and persistence of deprivation can be separated from more general accounts of inequality. First, the disadvantages prevalent in these deprived areas are different not in kind, but at most only in degree, from those of residents in other areas. The use of social indicators of area deprivation to guide programmes of positive discrimination has therefore only limited rational justification. Such justification requires that policy-makers recognize the diversity of areas in which various forms of need may be particularly high; such programmes must be situated within a universalist infrastructure, in recognition of the social and geographical universality of need (Hatch and Sherrott, 1973). Such indicators cannot, therefore, be taken as validly measuring the pathological traits of disadvantaged areas, as political liberals are wont to assume.

Still less can multiple need be taken as reliably indicated by low incomes, as market liberals would commonly avow (cf. pp. 163-4 above). Jordan points to similarities between the needs of the poor and of those with higher incomes. Social deviance and breakdown of social networks, taken by many recent writers including Seebohm as indicating 'social needs' (cf. p. 106 above), are high not only in areas of high unemployment and declining industry and population, but also in more prosperous immigration and reception areas, where populations are highly mobile (see, for example, Jordan, 1974, pp. 4, 12). The causes and symptoms of social deprivation may differ, then, as between those conventionally labelled 'the poor' and the wider population; but in kind and even, perhaps, in degree, no such difference prevails, although there *are* likely to be differences in the resources they can call on to cope with such deprivation—and hence in the long-term cumulative consequences of the latter. (Cf. pp. 159-60 above on the class-related consequences of illness.)

Programmes of positive discrimination towards educationally deprived areas have been the other major national action—research innovation in recent anti-poverty measures (cf. p. 131 above). As with the CDPs, their initial remit betrays official commitment to a broadly liberal diagnosis of deprivation. Positive discrimination was meant, not merely to raise the quality of schools in such areas to the national average, but 'quite deliberately to make them better. The justification is that the homes and neighbourhoods from which many of their children come provide little support and stimulus for learning. The schools must provide a compensating environment' (quoted in Halsey, 1972a, p. 31). It is in the local institutions of home and community that the most deep-seated sources of educational under-achievement are assumed to lie.

The Halsey Report, however, as a result of the national action—research experiment, argues a very different diagnosis, which blends with that elaborated in our discussion of the CDPs. Educational under-achievement springs from the irrelevance of the curriculum to pupils' prospective adult destinations—particularly occupationally; from the apparent hopelessness of aspiring to any individual or collective future that is other than multiply disadvantaged; and from the mutual incomprehension and negative stereotyping of educators and parents—resulting in dissociation and incongruence between pupils' learning experiences at home and at school (Halsey, 1972a, pp. 11-12, 189-98, Chs 9-12). Effective measures for countering educational deprivation must, therefore, not only offer formal qualifications but also equip with the skills and competences relevant to likely adult destinations. Second, they must provide milieux that engender 'constructive discontent'—with collective criticism of the political decisions and non-decisions that govern those allocative processes of which this multiple deprivation is the fruit. Third, they must involve not compensatory but complementary and community education—with a partnership between teachers and parents who, while hitherto uncomprehending, are far from unconcerned about their children's education. (Halsey, 1972a, pp. 77-18; cf. p. 163 above). In short, effective measures for countering educational deprivation must be predicated upon a diagnosis that acknowledges its rootedness in the prevailing relationships between education and the occupational, political and community milieux (cf. pp. 132-3 above). Again, it will be in previous chapters that we investigate the directions of group formation and action that have accompanied such educational action—research.

Not, however, that this diagnosis has been uncritically accepted by the social scientific community. Indeed, officially sponsored research into the causes of deprivation has in some cases seemed reluctant even to acknowledge the CDP experiment and its findings. Some of the DHSS Cycle of Deprivation studies, for example, initiated by the Conservative government in 1972, scarcely join battle with the CDP diagnosis. We are thereby alerted to the inadequacies of any naive positivistic view of cumulative advance in the findings of social science, and to the sensitivity to the prevailing political climate of the assumptions employed in social scientific research, especially given the contemporary importance of governmental sponsorship.

Theoretical Implications

If, however, the diagnoses of the CDPs are accepted, including their findings on the effectiveness of the main branches of social policy in alleviating deprivation, then significant implications follow for our evaluation of competing perspectives on social policy. We have already observed that the CDP and EPA programmes seem initially to have embraced a broadly *liberal* diagnosis of deprivation. The critique we have traced of this official remit therefore extends to liberal theories also. For example, these action—research projects have come to focus attention upon differential power and advantage as determinants of deprivation and to deny any 'automatic' benign trend.

Evaluation of the Social Democratic and neo-Marxist approaches—both being critiques of liberalism—in the light of the foregoing is rather more difficult. The Coventry CDP studies seem in important senses to vindicate the *neo-Marxist* case; indeed, the team there explicitly embrace such a stance. They seem to demonstrate, for example, that there is a fundamental identity of interests between the deprived and the working class, rooted in their common powerlessness vis-a-vis the means of production in a world of multinational corporations. Likewise, the Coventry studies in particular seem to demonstrate that the various factors contributing to deprivation are significantly moulded by industrial and commercial interests, and that it is therefore individuals' class situation that is the pre-eminent determinant of deprivation.

Yet our discussion suggests that in at least three respects the neo-Marxist approach is vulnerable. First, the deprivation of the CDP areas is typically reinforced and exacerbated by negative stereotyping by the wider society—stereotyping that is unjustified in terms of the social conditions actually obtaining, but that serves to legitimate irresponsible local authority policies and to promote blight and social decline. That is, social and political processes operate *selectively—and* at least partly independently of economic processes—with regard to certain areas, but not others, occupied by individuals in particularly weak class situations. Second, in the Coventry studies an overlap of interests is revealed between the residents of the CDP area and those of the wider city, given the trends in the multinationally organized motor industry, trends that have only accelerated since the team reported in March 1975. There are grounds for anticipating and building an alliance between the lumpenproletariat of such areas as Hillfields and the broad mass of the working class. Yet this constellation of interests seems to be contingent upon these particular employment and investment prospects; whether similar constellations will exist elsewhere must surely remain a matter for further empirical investigation. Third, the Coventry analysts look to 'new kinds of political intervention...to claim greater local public control' over the sources of deprivation in general and over industrial and commercial decision-making in particular. They leave open, however, whether this requires socialisation of the means of production as a necessary condition for such reduction in the power of private property. In our discussion of policy development in the city, moreover, we argued the perennial fragility of the alliance between those exercising public and private power, and questioned thereby the cohesion and invulnerability of any capitalist 'ruling class'. To accept the CDP critique of liberal views does not, therefore, require that a distinctively Marxist position be embraced. It does, however, call for an analysis of deprivation (and of the associated patterns of interests) in terms of diverse forms of power exercised in political, community and production milieux—in line with the Social Democrats.

Nevertheless, *Social Democrats* such as Titmuss have often left such an exercise only superficially explored. They have instead been content to portray social needs as the precipitate not of such a continuing struggle but rather of technologically deterministic urban—industrial change (Sinfield, 1978, p. 134). They can tend in consequence to see statutory efforts to meet such needs as a legitimate responsibility of the state, compensating for costs imposed by society in general rather than by specific advantaged groups. The social rights they espouse are then—as the neo-Marxists would claim is more generally true—at most the collective reparation for depradations wrought by irresponsible minorities. The conditions under which this pattern of social responsibilities is accepted or challenged by citizens at large will be one of our concerns in the next chapter.

Second, the Social Democrats have at most suggested some of the constellations of interest that may develop between the deprived and members of the wider society; they have been slow to acknowledge, with Weber, the task of responsible political leadership that articulation of such common interests involves. We have, however, pointed to the variety of such possible constellations: the Child Poverty Action Group has tended to redefine the 'new corporate interest' in terms of a family lobby rather than a poverty lobby; the National Consumer Council is promoting a consumer lobby as the most promising vehicle for dealing with deprivation or 'consumer detriment' (Williams, 1977); finally, as we have seen in the present section, some writers espouse trade unions of organized workers as potentially the most willing and effective allies of the poor. Among these alternatives, competing political leaders cannot but make responsible but fateful choices, in terms of their potential for engaging effective action for social reform.

Summing UP

The two empirical investigations in which we have engaged may seem somewhat unconnected. There are, however, important continuities and complementary conclusions. To start with, in both sections we found it necessary to explore how differences in power and advantage readily become generalised, with virtuous and vicious circles of privilege and deprivation at the extremes. We traced the economic, social and political powerlessness of CDP neighbourhoods and the cumulative deprivation this permits. We argued that the consequences of illness are commonly worse for the lower social classes and tend, when chronic, to promote downward mobility. At the same time, however, we have seen how the advantaged are most able to restrict the visibility of their privileges and of the processes whereby the costs of those privileges are imposed on others less powerful. As Sinfield has argued, 'inequality in the visibility of benefits is an important and integral part of the social division of welfare'.

In both of the preceding sections we have, moreover, seen how, notwithstanding the formal elimination of the cash nexus from the relationship between client and welfare professional in universalistic services, differences in power and resources continue to influence outcomes. Thus differences in knowledge of—and attitudes towards—health care and services seem important in explaining the significantly worse treatment received by the lower social classes and by such weak groups as the chronic sick and aged. The 'social distance' between medical professionals and lower-class patients also seems influential here.

Likewise, in section III we saw that the educators in multiply deprived areas—in contrast to those elsewhere—have commonly disregarded as a resource of value the learning that their pupils undergo in home and neighbourhood, and have permitted the purposes and procedures of the educational process to be mysterious and incomprehensible to parents and pupils alike. That is, the exercise of professional power seems to have been significantly influenced by the resources that their clients are variously able to bring to bear, but in ways that none of our competing macro-theories emphasise. The enunciation of common social rights to be met by universalist services may then be a necessary but, *pace* the Social Democrats, is not a sufficient condition for the appropriation of these rights.

We have also explored the patterns of interest identity and conflict that the contemporary social division of welfare involves. In both sections we considered, for example, the impact of 'broad-grain' policies on different groups in the population. Preventive health measures may, we saw, benefit different social classes differentially, precluding any presumption that they are unambiguously in the common interest. In Coventry, public utilities may have benefited suburban commuters and the industry on which the city's prosperity until the 1960s was based; their benefits for Hillfields have been much less obvious. More generally, we sought in section II to trace the lines of common and conflicting interest among the users of a universalist service; while in section III we considered the conflicts and harmonies of interest among the neighbourhoods of the deprived, the mass of the local working class and the regional population at large. Yet in none of these cases have we found the liberal or neo-Marxist portrayals of interests adequate—and even the Social Democratic account has proved too superficial. To all of these issues we return in the previous chapters, examining the typical directions of action and group formation in relation to these patterns of interest.

To conclude, we argued that attempts to implement the social right to medical care have tended to expose to political scrutiny those wider societal processes that vitiate its universal appropriation—not merely fiscal and occupational welfare benefits, but also the content of the work and residential activities of different social groups, with their unevenly distributed consequences for morbidity and other social needs. Likewise, the CDPS have pointed to an analysis of deprivation, not in terms of individual pathology or the technical demands of an urban—industrial society, but rather as the precipitate of socially unaccountable power. Thus the reproduction of the social division of welfare is revealed as in part dependent upon essentially political decisions, and therefore upon directions of political leadership. Furthermore, the very recognition of inequalities is in part a political process. For example, differential group outcomes and class gradients in health care may inform measures of positive discrimination; but they are not immediately visible to the advantaged or the disadvantaged. Finally, the pattern of interests flowing from the division of welfare is not, as we have just seen, self-evident, but rather requires articulation within a political arena if it is to issue in action. It is through a process of selection by competing political leaders that we must expect these inequalities to become relevant to social action and social change. Not that such action will necessarily express self-interest alone. Rather, we shall need to investigate the conditions under which political leadership can and does mobilise support for social policies from those whose self-interest is unaffected—or even adversely affected—by them.

8

Social Welfare Models

Beveridge and Keynes both believed that the reform of capitalism offered the best prospect for enhancing welfare and that collectivist social policies could make a vitally important contribution to that reform. At the time there were those who opposed this thesis and argued in defence of the *status quo.* There were others who saw the replacement of capitalism by socialism as the only way of creating a more just and humanitarian society.

There was a rift in socialist opinion between those who thought that social policies could serve as an important instrument in effecting this transition and those who maintained that radical political changes would have to precede social policy reforms. By 1945 all three major political parties were committed in varying degrees to manifestos embodying Keynesian and Beveridgean prescriptions for change, but the election of that year put the Labor Party into office, and thereafter collectivism and socialism seemed for a time to be synonymous. Within the discipline of social policy and administration this tendency to associate collectivism with socialism has become stronger and now represents, in normative terms, the conventional wisdom of the subject. Of the various major writers on British social policies only Marshall, and possibly Donnison, seem to have accepted with a measure of equanimity the values of the mixed capitalist economy, which have survived largely intact in our society throughout the post-war years.

Titmuss frequently reminded us of the need to make these choices and of the implications of the dilemmas of choice at every level of social policy debate. In our view, however, he oversimplified the general issue by treating it as a choice between no more than *two* alternatives — the values of the economic market and those of the social market. He, thus, defined the problem in such a way as either to exclude the middle way of the mixed economy from serious consideration or to place it firmly within the context of the economic market alternative. In so doing he effectively severed the discipline from its most vigorous normative roots, which in turn had been nourished by the most productive welfare tradition of all.

Titmuss by defining the problem in this way, was inviting those who were attracted neither by capitalism nor by socialism to choose what would be for them the lesser of two evils, when there was no reason why they should choose either. It should also be noted that Titmuss equated the values of the social market with socialism and that he did not include Marxism in this side of his dichotomy. Consequently both the tradition of collectivism which had contributed so much to the creation of welfare systems under capitalism and the tradition of Marxism which had provided the most forceful and sustained critique of welfare-capitalism were effectively left out of the debate as possible choices. Titmuss left out Marxism because he thought that it was a morally repugnant doctrine. Repugnant or otherwise, it remains an important political option in the world today.

Any theory of social policy must be firmly grounded in the institutional and psychological realities of its time. Analytical models based upon oversimplified distinctions between egoism and altruism fail to take into account the ambivalent nature of perceived interest and of felt obligation stemming from a variety of institutional loyalties which may be based upon family, community, nation or class. Three major normative assumptions may be said to underlie the various theories which seek to explain and evaluate the relationship between social order, social change and social welfare. These can be broadly described as classical economic theory, Marxism and its socialist derivatives, and the traditions of mercantile collectivism.

Classical economic theory is based upon the premise that there is no basic incompatibility between the competing interests and loyalties which characterise a free society. Marxist theory asserts not only that these interests and loyalties are incompatible but that only through the intensification of such conflict and the heightening of class conflict in particular is change possible and real freedom attainable. The ultimate objective of change is the abolition of the forms of property and the division of labor out of which sectional interests and inequalities arise. China, Russia, all the nations of the east European bloc, and many of those in the Third World are committed to the eventual creation of societies based on the teachings of Marx. In addition to socialising the means of production they have already built up complex systems of collectivist social services. It is not so easy to identify a comparable group of societies which are actively committed to a significant enlargement of the scope of the free market and private enterprise.

Wilensky describes how in all the richer nations of today collectivist sentiment and economic individualism coexist, so that 'pro-welfare-state doctrines are perhaps as widely popular as the ideology of success'. Friedman bitterly laments the growth of total government spending in the USA from about 10 per cent of national income in the years before 1929 to about 40 per cent today. In the United Kingdom the level has gone still higher, and the same trend in levels of government spending has been observed in the other major Western nations. This general trend towards collectivism has in the main only tenuous connections with socialism and in some cases none at all.

While Marxists argue that these massive collectivist interventions in industry and welfare are designed merely to preserve capitalism, many liberal economists complain that they are certain to destroy it.

It can be argued that collectivism on this scale does not have to be consistent with either capitalism or socialism and that its influence has already been sufficiently pervasive to create a new social system which will subsequently develop without regard for either of these doctrines. What this new version of collectivism lacks is a coherent body of theory, a set of explicit normative assumptions, and an articulate and committed political movement which will continuously assert and remind us of its distinctive properties. These properties do, however, enjoy a historical pedigree antedating both capitalism and socialism, as they represent a modern revival of the much modified mercantilist doctrines challenged by the rise of classical political economy, although the continuing and distinctive influence of mercantilist doctrines can be traced not so much through protective social policies as through protectionist economic policies.

Given that it is collectivist, this revived neo-mercantilist tradition stands in ideological opposition to the individualistic values of classical political economy. Insofar as it is not socialist in the terms of Marxist theory and may indeed appear in societies which are anti-socialist, it stands equally in opposition to Marxist collectivism. This is not to advance another version of the 'convergence thesis'. The possibility still exists that some, if not all, of the present socialist societies will move towards a state of communism which accords with Marxist theory. The history of capitalist societies so far suggests a general trend towards governmental regulation of the free market, but we cannot rule out the possibility of a reversal of that trend.

Contemporary Marxists reject the assertion that the

extent of governmental intervention can go so far in a capitalist society that society will cease to be capitalist to any significant degree. Their argument is that, so long as the means of production remain even nominally in private ownership and so long as the forces of production are organized and rewarded on the basis of economic market values, the society will remain essentially capitalist. A welfare capitalist society is still a society in which the members of a ruling class — the owners of the means of production — further their own interests at the expense of the workers through the agencies of the state. At the same time, as we have noted, contemporary liberal economists would attribute most of the deficiencies which they observe in such a society to its gradual abandonment of capitalist virtues. Thus we are left with two interpretations, one of which asserts that however much state intervention occurs in a capitalist society, it remains capitalist in every important respect. The other interpretation measures the mixed economy against an ideal of perfect competition and finds it substantially wanting in every important respect.

Our own position is based on the view that both classical economic theory and its ideal state of capitalism and Marxist theory and its ideal state of communism offer attractive prescriptions for the maximisation of human welfare which, when they are put into practice, also become instruments of oppression and diswelfare. The same criticism can be levelled at the third model of welfare — a form of mercantile collectivism in which the state comes to serve so many coalitions of interest that for all practical purposes it ceases to be the instrument of any single ruling class. Nonetheless we recognize that circumstances can arise in which it will become such an instrument, and the nature of such outcomes is more difficult to predict than it would be in the case of overtly free-market or socialistically controlled societies. The reason for such a high degree of uncertainty is obvious — mixed economies occupy the middle ground with regard to the balance between freedom and control and the choice between the totalitarian styles of either the left or the right wings of political theory and practice.

We commit a fundamental error, however, if we judge all the alternative and possible forms of social organization by reference to the two paradigms of capitalism and communism, since this makes us voluntary prisoners of two historical modes of thought, both of which embody highly deterministic theories of social development. Capitalism does not necessarily collapse or suffer irreparable damage if the free play of market forces is modified. Neither does it inevitably give way to socialism when the time and circumstances are ripe. It is perfectly reasonable to argue that capitalism will develop in ways which we are not able to anticipate or predict; it has done so in the past.

Furthermore, the factor of nationality and national culture is regularly underestimated by theorists of social change. It would be rash to predict the eventual outcome of the impact of Western ideas on the new nations of the Third World. The indigenous culture of a nation is a catalyst which transmutes alien philosophies like capitalism and socialism in ways which we simply do not understand at present. How many metamorphoses will these societies have to undergo before we can cease to use such terms to categorise them? If we admit that there is a high potential for cultural autonomy and innovative response among the countries of the Third World, why should we not allow as much of the industrialised nations of the West? We have reached a stage in social thought at which we allow Marxists — as we once allowed classical political economists and the founding fathers of the Christian church before them — to define in advance our universe of discourse, to set out the very questions of import which we are required to answer before we can ask our own questions, and to lay down for all times and all places what are in fact intelligent analyses of earlier times and places as paradigms, against which the past, the present and the future must be judged and found worthy or wanting. No doubt at the time of the Reformation it was sensible to judge Protestantism largely by reference to the canons of Roman Catholicism, or in the early stages of the Industrial Revolution to judge new modes of capitalist enterprise by reference to an unreformed and backward-looking mercantilism. But there came a time when Protestantism and capitalism had to be understood not only by reference to their antecedents but in terms of what they had become in their own right. Equally we cannot rule out the possibility that in their historical development societies rediscover and take on modified forms of much earlier traditions of thought and organization. The recent revival of the notion of community, for example, owes much to the earliest traditions of thought about social organization. Similarly the precepts of mercantilism survived with remarkable tenacity even in the hey-day of *laissez-faire* Victorian England.

This third approach therefore rejects the possibility of either a natural harmonisation of welfare interests through the free play of economic market forces or the inevitability of a conflict, with the eventual reconciliation of these interests being effected by the replacement of capitalism by socialism. It is possible to argue that the welfare ideals of this tradition can best be realized in a society that is neither capitalist nor socialist in any ideal sense.

Social administration has tended to develop a set of concepts and theories of the middle ground which are collectivist in value orientation and critical of capitalism, but lacking in any explicit political theory which might convincingly explain either how what is deemed to be a defective economic system can be changed or what alternative social order might take its place. In this sense the subject mirrors the contradictions and ambivalences of the societies in which it has grown to maturity as a discipline and in which collectivist social policies have been used to modify the free play of market forces. The perceptive student might conclude that these reformist theories of the middle ground suffer from the analytical weaknesses which arise from normative uncertainty — and from a failure to make logical connections between political means and ends. In contrast the theories both of classical political economy and of Marx may be said to suffer from the weaknesses that arise from over-certainty regarding the connection between these means and ends.

It was never likely that social policy and administration would provide a significant theoretical and normative vindication of the values and aims of the free market. Its doing so now would amount to a singularly impressive demonstration of professional altruism. Nonetheless an important individualist approach to the study of social welfare has persisted, largely outside the mainstream of normative thought within the discipline itself, like the sociological critiques from the welfare state which drew their inspirational theory from Marx.

What follows now is an attempt to relate more clearly the potential and actual contributions of thinking in social policy and administration to our concern with the collectivist renaissance in recent British history and its affinities with the institutional framework of obligation, entitlement and exchange. In our historical approach we have focused on a subject which has been largely neglected in social policy studies — the relationships between free trade, protection and reform — partly because the poor law has received very extensive attention, and partly because the subject has allowed me to concentrate on certain developments in economic policy and thought which prepared the ground for the positive assertion of collectivist philosophies from the 1870s onwards.

The welfare theories of the individualist tradition can be traced from Smith and Ricardo, through Spencer, Sumner and Dicey, to Hayek, Powell and Friedman. It is harder to find agreement about what constitutes the Marxist tradition in the West, if we limit ourselves to those who gave special attention to social policy. George's and Wilding's choice of Laski, Strachey and Miliband as its exemplars in the British context is open to question, but it is hard to find better alternatives. Between these polar extremes of classical economic individualism and Marxist collectivism George and Wilding also recognize another collectivist tradition, but their interpretation of this tradition differs from our own.

They do their best to identify its main elements by distinguishing between the 'reluctant collectivists' represented by Keynes, Beveridge and Galbraith and the 'Fabian socialists' represented by Tawney, Crosland and Titmuss. In seeking to explain their classification George and Wilding distinguish between those who 'saw the extension of public ownership not as an end in itself but as vitally necessary to the general achievement of socialist objectives' and those who believed that 'public ownership is to be used pragmatically and selectively for the achievement of specific objectives'. The traditions of 'Fabian socialism' and Marxist collectivism are further differentiated from that of reluctant collectivism by their rejection of acquisitive individualism as a commendable human motive, and their rejection of capitalism on the grounds that the free market system inevitably leads to an undemocratic distribution of power, an unjust and unequal distribution of wealth and an inefficient use of resources. Furthermore 'The free market system has not abolished, will not, and cannot abolish poverty, let alone inequality.'

In our view it is misleading to attribute a quality of reluctance to the collectivism of Keynes and Beveridge on the grounds that they were not enthusiastic nationalisers.

Keynes and Beveridge were enthusiastic collectivists with regard to social policy because they were both anti-socialist. Similarly the way in which George and Wilding define acquisitive individualism does not do sufficient justice to Keynes's and Beveridge's views about economic morality. Keynes and Beveridge believed that the profit motive and competitive self-interest, like most other human sentiments, swiftly become unlovable when taken to excess. In their different ways, however, they also believed that, unless the spirit of entrepreneurship was allowed to flourish in a free society, there would never be a general in- crease in prosperity sufficient to abolish poverty.

George's and Wilding's choice of Laski, Strachey and Miliband as examples also restricts their scope for exploring a further distinction of vital importance within the Marxist tradition. They note that Laski, Strachey and Miliband opposed 'the use of violence to achieve their ends' and believed that a peaceful transition to socialism was possible. These convictions set them apart from the central tradition of Marxist thought exemplified particularly in the writings of Marx, Engels and Lenin, who accepted violence as a regrettable but necessary means to the political end of achieving socialism and eventually a communist society. So far history offers no example of a party which is committed to these ends achieving and retaining power by non-violent parliamentary means.

This difference among Marxists over the choice of means seems to be of greater political importance than any declared identity of ends. The weight of historical evidence suggests that revolutionary Marxists are correct in their choice of means, even if they choose violence only as a last resort. George and Wilding would have brought out this fundamental distinction more clearly if they had given the Webbs a central role in their analysis. The Webbs had far greater illustrative significance in the development of collectivist thought than Laski, Strachey or Miliband because, more than any other authority, they helped to give intellectual coherence to the Fabian doctrine of gradual collectivist reform. Having done so, they renounced Fabianism, when in their last years they were converted to Soviet communism and accepted the necessity of violence at least in countries other than their own.

When the choice of means is between violence and non-violence, this carries such profound implications for the ends of political action that it seems to me to represent a distinction of fundamental importance within the tradition of Marxist collectivism. The advance of collectivism under conditions of parliamentary democracy owes much to coalitions of interest among a variety of ideological groupings. But collectivism has ideological affinities with non-socialist as well as socialist political movements. Collectivism may involve no more than commitment to a significant degree of state intervention in the maintenance and enhancement of welfare. It can have ideological connections with either the Left or the Right. The errors lie in equating collectivism only with socialism and in assuming that collectivism without socialism always implies a 'reluctant' commitment to state intervention. Although socialism is inevitably associated with collectivist welfare policies, the converse does not follow. In the history of Western Europe, North America and industrialising nations in other continents we can observe many versions of collectivism, ranging from communist societies, through various types of mixed economy and corporate state, to outright fascism.

Keynes and Beveridge provided the intellectual and philosophical framework within which our post-war collectivist social policies developed. They set out the theoretical and normative case for Britain to follow a middle way between the free market and the command economy. In large part post-war developments in British economic and social policy have followed the direction of their prescriptions until very recently. In 'Social Policy and Social Justice' we discussed some of the reasons why the post-Beveridge era of social security is coming to an end, with particular reference to Beveridge's 'fundamentally inegalitarian view of family life' and his insistence on the necessary association between citizenship and the insurance principle. At the same time we regretted the decline of the 'spirit of community' and the erosion of the 'common moral framework' at a national level which were characteristics of British society so deeply valued by Beveridge and Keynes.

It is, however, a central part of our thesis that the collectivist tradition represented by these qualities still has an important role within the discipline of social policy and administration. Mine is an approach which sees no fundamental incompatibility between the enhancement of social welfare and the values of the mixed economy and a pluralist social order. Indeed the subject and the richness of its potential contribution to the policy sciences would be diminished if this tradition were not to prosper in the future.

At the present time the tradition is intellectually closest to the pluralist theories elaborated by political scientists like Braybrooke, Lindblom and Dahl, with their emphasis on disjointed incrementalism as a technique of social reform, on the role of the state as one among several creations of power and influence in society, on the virtues of diversity and the delegation of authority and the reconciliation of conflicts within a broadly consensual political framework.

Donnison recognizes the contribution of pluralist theory to our understanding of the role of interest groups in the ordering of social priorities and to the actual workings of the political process. He identifies it with a particular view of the good society which abjures Utopian planning and is administered on a basis of piecemeal engineering directed towards gradual improvement. He also criticizes the lack of a historical dimension in pluralist analysis and its indifference to the ideological aspects of social life. In this sense pluralism lacks the synoptic vision of Keynes and Beveridge, although it may still help to elucidate the types of change and the problems of decision-taking which are most likely to occur in a mixed economy.

Our understanding of the functioning and the distinctive nature of the mixed economy, which is neither capitalist nor socialist, owes much to pluralist theories. It is true that these theories lack historical perspective and that, as Halebsky has recently argued, they tend to underestimate the extent to which the least powerful interest groups are neglected in democratic processes and in the resistance of the private industrial sector to collective interests. In a lengthy preface to the new edition of *Politics, Economics and Welfare* Dahl and Lindblom respond to such criticisms of their approach to pluralist theory. They admit that in neither the USA nor Britain have the problems of poverty and racial inequality yielded significantly to piecemeal reform, and that in pluralist societies powerful minority groups can delay for long periods changes which are in the common interest. They also recognize that collectivist policies of social reform have little hope of success while income in- equalities buttress political inequalities.

At the same time Lindblom and Dahl argue that, despite these valid criticisms by social scientists in the West, social pluralism is winning more support from authorities in Eastern Europe and in the communist parties of Western Europe. If pluralist societies tolerate too much organized autonomy, socialist societies suffer in other ways from too little. The temptation in the West is to adopt more highly centralised systems of political control, but, they add, those who move towards that goal are likely to meet equally disillusioned Marxists travelling cautiously in the opposite direction. Thus Lindblom and Dahl remain committed to incremental rates of change and limited structural reforms. In the Soviet Union and China they identify the concentration of power in the state as a major obstacle to change. In the USA they admit that the free market is a cause of social inequalities, but they also claim that it is a major source of innovation. In recognizing the need to revise their original formulation of pluralist theory Lindblom and Dahl restate the case for a middle way between the Utopian paradigms of the free market and the command economy of the highly centralised state. In their analysis they come very close to a mercantile collectivist position which lays greater emphasis on social unity than social conflict, and on change within existing social structures rather than change through the overthrow of those structures.

We have emphasized the need for social administrators to give more attention to the theoretical and philosophical issues involved in an understanding of the relationship between social policy and social change and the relationship between social policy and different conceptions of the good society. Nonetheless one of the enduring strengths of the discipline has been the involvement of so many of its practitioners in specific problems of policy and administration and developments in particular service fields. Again it is this concern which accounts for the growing importance of political science theories in recent social policy analysis. We have already referred to Hall's, Land's, Parker's and Webb's study, *Change, Choice and Conflict in .Social Policy,* which makes extensive use of such theories. The basic framework of analysis is taken from Easton's systems analysis model, but the authors go on explore the use of class theories and pluralism in their analysis of political processes. They formulate their hypothesis in such a way as to take account of both these approaches: 'that the making of day-to-day policy on social issues in Britain does operate within a distinctly pluralist *process,* but that the *limits* of policy-making are set by elites which for many purposes are indistinguishable from what Miliband calls a ruling class'. This emphasis on limitations refers to the authors' characterisation of 'the policy process as *bounded pluralism*', although they add that the class model does not necessarily explain 'the nature of the boundaries within which the process operates'.

We have referred again to this study because its authors show that it is useful to apply more than one theoretical approach to the same social policy problem. In exploring the links between policy changes and change at a broader societal level they clearly find class theory more useful than systems and pluralist theories. They also illustrate the extent to which normative theories can be employed with impartiality, especially within a discipline which is able to draw on a number of such theories. Furthermore the variety and range of the case studies in *Change, Choice and Conflict* remind us that a large part of social policy is conducted at a level of enquiry at which conflicts over basic values need not arise, although, as Kogan suggests, it is not always easy to distinguish between the issues of policy principle and those of administrative process.

Although social policy and administration is frequently criticized for being too widely derivative in its borrowings from the other social sciences, we think there is a case to be made that it has not been sufficiently eclectic. The pluralist theories which we have discussed owe more to political science than they do to sociology, but their actual and potential contribution to social policy studies tends to be underrated by sociologists of welfare. The same could be said of the contribution of history, philosophy and economics. Sociologists of welfare often talk as if sociology ought to have a special relationship with social policy and administration, and several consequences follow from this assumption. First, it licenses sociologists to berate from time to time their dull, pragmatic relations for being a-theoretical. Secondly, it allows them to assume that their discipline has a near-monopoly of theories which are relevant to social policy studies. Thirdly, it encourages sociologists to believe that the majority of social administrators are — or ought to become — sociologists. In fact the majority of social administrators are not sociologists either by training or choice, and a small but increasing minority could point out that they entered on their careers as social administrators and not sociologists. This is not to deny that sociology has something of value to offer to social administration — as one among several contributory disciplines.

Such eclecticism can be defended on two grounds. First, it preserves the discipline from catching any of the ideological infections which may be afflicting the related social sciences, and sociology in this respect has a singularly bad health record. Secondly, eclecticism can provide a more comprehensive basis for the development of theories and concepts which are indigenous to social policy and administration as a subject. Given the variety of disciplinary interests which already coexist under the name of social policy and administration, it is neither likely nor desirable that any one of them will make a dramatic theoretical contribution which will swiftly and unanimously be understood and adopted within the subject. Social administrators are jointly engaged in a difficult interdisciplinary exercise. Learning from the range of relevant disciplines is a slow and piecemeal process. Nonetheless, so long as a balanced universe of discourse is maintained, there is likely to be a gradual development of theory indigenous to the subject, some of which will no doubt have its origins in sociology. We can already observe in the works of Titmuss, Donnison and Marshall (who is a sociologist) contributions which are social policy and administration in an eponymous sense.

We believe that there are other potential contributions from sociology which have not yet been exploited in social policy studies. Among these we would pick out the work of Elton Mayo and his school which has been drawn to our attention by John Smith in his recent reappraisal and commentary. The problems which Mayo studied in industrial life, namely, those stemming from the need to develop the skills and status of citizenship in the work situation, are the same as those which Marshall emphasizes in the context of social policy and political life. Similarly, as Smith observes, Mayo's interest in the practical possibilities of delegation and decentralisation in decision-taking has obvious relevance to current debates about the same issues in social administration.

At the same time there are clear signs of a developing and productive relationship between social policy and administration and legal studies which will deepen our understanding of the links between public opinion and law and between changes in law and changes in social policy. The contribution of O.R. McGregor from his earlier study of divorce to his recent work on the Finer Committee reminds us that in studying the legal aspects of social welfare we may often acquire a clearer understanding of the inconsistencies which characterize our divided treatment of citizens on the one hand as members of families and on the other hand as workers. McGregor observes, for example, that 'The inescapable conclusion from many recent studies of women's experience in trying to reconcile the claims of marriage, motherhood and work is the existence of a firmly rooted double standard of occupational morality. As a society, we pay lip-service to equality for women whilst practising discrimination.' Similarly the pioneering work of Kathleen Bell and her colleagues on national insurance tribunals has brought out other inconsistencies and anomalies in our treatment of citizens, once they become welfare appellants, in what is a relatively new but increasingly important context of adjudication.

A discipline which is well grounded and also involved in issues both of a general theoretical and normative nature and of a more immediate and practical kind is not likely to be overwhelmed by ideologies which prescribe total and chiliastic solutions for our social ills. It will abjure the extremes of moral sentiment, recognizing that any ideal Kingdom of the Saints, religious or secular, would be a discomfiting place to live in. As a genuinely humane discipline social policy and administration would work towards the making of a welfare society in which the terms of exchange and the understandings of obligation and entitlement were decently conditional, neither vulgarly egoistical nor impossibly altruistic.

Each of the major traditions of thought to which we have referred expresses the conviction that it alone offers the best prescription for the enhancement of social welfare and the creation of a better society. What we have tried to do is to rehabilitate one of these traditions within the discipline of social administration because we think that it has fallen into neglect, if not disrepute, and that this has happened in large part because the terms of the debate have been progressively narrowed. In our view the range of normative choice within a discipline ought to be set out as generously as possible. With a variety of theoretical resources at their disposal, the practitioners of the discipline should find scope for co-operation and compromise as well as conflict.

Risk, Retrenchment and Reform

We have tried to demonstrate that three major theoretical traditions have contributed to our understanding of the role of social policy in enhancing the welfare of industrial societies. Both classical economic theory and Marxist theory have their intellectual origins in the Industrial Revolution and the rise of capitalism. Classical economic theory was the intellectual vindication of these momentous events. In outlining an alternative to capitalism Marx became its most formidable and influential critic, and his social theory inspired a range of revolutionary and reformist socialist prescriptions for the transformation of capitalism. The origination of mercantilist doctrine coincided with the rise of the modern nation state which preceded the Industrial Revolution and the rise to influence of the other two doctrines. Throughout the nineteenth century mercantilist doctrine continued to exercise a greater influence on the course of economic policies in continental Europe than was the case in either Britain or the USA. More recently, as we have suggested, Keynes rehabilitated significant elements of mercantilist economic theory, albeit in greatly modified forms. These and other aspects of the doctrine have played a large part in the growth of collectivist social policies and the development of theories of the welfare state. This revival has been sufficiently radical and sufficiently extensive to bring about significant changes in the structure and values of most of the advanced capitalist societies of the West. It has provided the normative and instrumental rationale for the emergence of the modern welfare state, as we know it.

Nonetheless, despite the record of its real achievement, the third way — the pluralist commitment to the mixed economy — with its emphasis on social protection and mitigating reforms, evokes among social administrators at best a defensive apology rather than a positive commitment. By contrast neither the classical economic nor the Marxist paradigm of welfare has so far been adopted in its ideal form, nor has either one proved to be particularly effective in a modified form. This situation is all the more difficult to account for if social policy and administration is taken to be a subject characteristic of the forms of applied social science which are specifically required and nurtured by the mixed economies of mercantilist collectivism.

This state of affairs can be partly explained by the way in which the subject has developed over the past twenty years. This period has seen the adoption of a dominant normative consensus, which regards the values of the competitive economic market with such hostility that it cannot sustain coherent theories of social consensus or change which are at all sympathetic to those values. Any theory about the enhancement of social welfare must be addressed to issues of consensus and change, and it must be normative, in the sense that it will single out certain policy objectives and outcomes of change as being morally preferable to others.

One of the main problems in British social policy and administration is that too many of its practitioners feel that the social services as agencies of both consensus and change have to function in a society whose basic values are antipathetic to its own social policies. This fallacious model is preserved by the practice of treating the economic and social markets as if they were separate institutional entities. Consequently it is impossible to analyse in any consistent way the various functional and dysfunctional relationships which hold between the processes of production and distribution. Whatever else can be said of classical economic theory and Marxist theory, they do not fall into this error, both displaying a normative consistency between the means and the ends which they prescribe for the enhancement of human welfare, and it is this consistency which accounts for their conceptual unity and explanatory appeal.

In discussing the character of social policy and administration Titmuss denied that it was merely 'a messy conglomeration of the technical *ad hoc*', and he argued that 'Its primary areas of unifying interest are centred in those social institutions that foster integration and discourage alienation.' Within the terms of his personal value commitment, however, it is difficult to see how social policies could serve these ends, even in a mixed economy. From what we know of Titmuss's beliefs about the alienating qualities of the economic market, integration of this kind could only be achieved within a socialist society, one moreover in which the majority of the citizens were committed socialists. In default of this ideological transformation a Titmussian social administrator would find himself in conflict with the dominant values of the mixed economy and with the ends of the social services as defined by those values — unless those services bore a remarkably high degree of normative autonomy.

The way out of this problem has been to treat the values of the social market as if they possessed a self-evident moral superiority to those of the economic market. In discussing concepts like 'market', 'need' and 'justice' itself we have reached a point at which we use the term 'social' as if it were synonymous with 'sacred'. Even the norm of reciprocity, which is essential to the creation of wealth, stands lower in the moral hierarchy of welfare studies than the norm of unilateral gift-giving.

In his critique of 'welfare sociologists' Gouldner indicts them for having colluded in some systematic way with the 'powers- that-be' in helping to preserve the mixed economy of welfare capitalism, or, as he describes it, the 'welfare-warfare' state. It would perhaps have been more accurate to accuse some 'welfare sociologists' of pretending that social policies could be used as instruments for the peaceful transformation of capitalism into socialism and others of lacking any clear commitment to either capitalism or socialism. In both cases the outcome has been the same — the assumption of a holier-than-thou attitude towards the values and imperatives of the economic market.

Since the Second World War British social policy analysts have tended to adopt a largely critical attitude towards industry and industrial values. It is symptomatic of this generally negative cast of mind that throughout the major works of Titmuss economic forces are described in the main as exploitative forces, or as the cause of social costs for which society must offer compensation through social policies. The cause of national efficiency and the association of social policy with patriotic sentiment which Beveridge brought as an Edwardian legacy to his Report have ceased to be dominant themes in social policy studies. Yet within this tradition social policy and administration had a vitally important intellectual and practical role to perform.

With the demise of this tradition, we are left with a residue of ill-assorted philosophies of welfare which point at one and the same time towards gestures of international altruism on behalf of strangers and towards the revival of local community loyalties on behalf of our next-door neighbours. Such moral imperatives appear to be somewhat irrelevant at a time when Britain is seeking its future as an economic pauper in the very continent on whose behalf it lost an empire, little' more than twenty years after the inception within its national boundaries of a new multi-racial society based upon the peoples of that lost empire. These immigrants were brought into the country to meet short-term labor needs, and they now constitute a growing proportion of the economically and socially disadvantaged. If their social and economic circumstances are not improved, these immigrants are likely to become a danger to political stability. Yet our policies for social and economic renewal at home continue to be financially impoverished, while we maintain — in a state of post-imperial euphoria — a programme of international aid.

A concern with the immediacies of human suffering is a natural and commendable quality. Indeed it can be argued that one of the most admirable features of social administration is the reluctance of its practitioners to treat even minority groups as means to the realization of more glorious societal ends, whether they be perfect competition or perfect communism. But social administrators must have a broader concern in social welfare than the needs of poverty-stricken minorities, because these needs can only be met if the relatively privileged are willing to make some sacrifices on their behalf. Since the privileged are no more altruistic than the poor, there is no reason to assume that they will be content to make sacrifices in an unconditional and continuing sense. They will require some consideration of their own needs and some regard for their own conception of justice, which will probably have more in common with the values of the economic market than those of the social market.

A satisfactory compromise between these competing claims is most likely to be achieved in a society with some overriding sense of collective purpose and pride in its common productive endeavours. A collective purpose of this order requires accommodation rather than conflict between the claims of the social market and those of the economic market, yet the present relationship is so clearly based on an assumption of conflict that the very notion of a 'welfare right' is taken by many social administrators to be vested exclusively in the values and practices of the social market. Nonetheless every 'welfare right' implies a claim on someone else's productive obligation, and the increase in the number of academic courses in 'welfare rights' for students of social policy and social work indicates a perilous insulation of these subjects from economic realities and popular notions of justice. This one-sided idea of a welfare right fits naturally into a discipline which conceptualizes social services as a defence against an essentially predatory economic system. Carried to extremes in a society fighting for economic survival, such a philosophy of welfare will end by converting social services into predators on the economic system, thereby prejudicing still further our chances of social survival.

Until recently most of our deprived minorities have been poor, because they have been unemployable or only marginally employable. These minorities include the old, the physically and mentally ill or handicapped and children in care. They will continue to be a central and proper concern of the social services. Today we face new challenges in the form of a dramatic increase in the incidence of unemployment among the able- bodied and the growth of a large minority of coloured citizens who suffer from a variety of disadvantages, including poor educational and employment prospects.

In response to these relatively new challenges many social policy analysts will undoubtedly take a more comprehensive view of the relationships between the economic and social markets and the processes of production and distribution. Any such reappraisal is likely to lead to a deepening of ideological differences within the discipline. There will be those who interpret our present economic crisis as further evidence of the impending collapse of welfare capitalism, with some prescribing socialism as the remedy and others recommending a return to a more competitive free market.

A third school of thought will argue that the mixed economy of welfare capitalism is capable of overcoming the present crisis, just as it has survived similar episodes in the past. Indeed it will be claimed that our present state of affairs has much in common with the crisis which occasioned the collectivist renaissance of the 1940s, that is, a serious loss of productive efficiency and the return of mass unemployment. Today, however, there are no collectivists of the intellectual stature and influence of Keynes or Beveridge who share their conviction that the mixed economy of welfare capitalism is worth saving.

Social policy and administration retains its instrumental links with the mixed economy of welfare capitalism, but the positive commitment to this kind of society embodied in the contributions of Keynes and Beveridge is no longer a major influence. Yet even the middle way of cautious and prudential reform requires a measure of committed support, if it is to succeed. There is, of course, less scope for Utopian speculation in attempts to repair an existing social system which is malfunctioning than there is in attempts to replace it with a totally new system. A normative commitment of this order, if it is to recover its place in the debate about welfare, must take its stand on an explicitly anti-Utopian basis. It entails an acceptance of the imperfections of human nature and hence of all possible human societies and it offers no more than a highly conditional optimism about our future. It will have to balance the necessity of economic risk-taking against the need to reduce social and political risks to a minimum.

Classical political economy and Marxism are both doctrines which offer us dramatic welfare possibilities, but, in inviting us to play for the highest stakes, they also require us to take the greatest risks. Moreover all prescriptions for radical change lay it open to the political barbarians of our time to assume the governance of our lives. In the last analysis the idea of welfare must embody non-material as well as material components, among which the notion of freedom and the right to a measure of self-determination have to be included.

The continuing influence and popularity of the classical economic and Marxist paradigms of welfare can be partly explained by the fact that their respective protagonists are still able to claim that they have not yet been in a position to prove their theories workable. Another explanation lies in the fact that both paradigms explicitly postulate an ideal future state in which there will be an inevitable reconciliation between individual and collective welfare interests. Nonetheless in their different ways both theories do presume to determine the conditions of our freedom: in the one case we are free to fulfil ourselves only within the terms of economic market imperatives; in the other we are free only to ride on the locomotive of history.

The third possibility offers an equally conditional view of freedom, but it seeks the most equitable accommodation between the various liberties and constraints which determine the conditions of life in any type of society. We return here to the structural problem described by Marshall to which he says that there is 'no purely structural solution', namely, the problem of reconciling 'a man's value in the market (capitalist value), his value as a citizen (democratic value), and his value for himself (welfare value)'. Indeed there is no solution to this problem, and the third tradition does not presume to offer one; it does, however, provide through the procedures of representative government and the influence of mitigating social reforms some protection against the danger that any one of these moral imperatives might achieve sufficient predominance to threaten the relative authority of the others.

This approach to the problem of distributive justice rests on the assumption that the idea of welfare is sustained by a number of moral imperatives and that a relative preponderance of any one of these will rapidly produce a situation of diminishing returns. It is part of a philosophy of welfare which, far from heralding the 'end of ideologies', recognizes their prevalence but itself offers policies of incremental and prudential change as a sensible way of keeping a tight ship and avoiding storms on an increasingly hazardous political sea. The purpose of the voyage is not to discover new continents but to keep the ship afloat and steer clear of the various eldorados along the shore, where the life is rumoured to be less arduous than the life on board — rumours belied only by the warnings of fugitives from those alien shores, clamouring to be taken along, Of course the voyage is worthwhile only if the crew come to love their ship and discover the joys of good seamanship; without that common bond they might as well scuttle and be damned.

Though social policy and administration retains its instrumental affinities with the tradition of mercantile collectivism, it has lost that sense of national destiny and common purpose which inspired Keynes and Beveridge. Indeed our love for Britain seems to be conditional on its becoming a society that is radically different from what it is and what it has been. Yet, if a popular loss of confidence in a nation's economic future customarily precedes a revival or an intensification of mercantilist sentiment, it would be reasonable to look for signs of such change at the present time. The signs are undoubtedly there, but in disheartening forms. On the far Left we are exhorted to retreat into the mentality and practices of a socialist siege economy, protected by high import quotas and rudely divorced from the European Economic Community. On the far Right we are offered a different version of the siege economy, explicitly xenophobic and viciously discriminatory not only towards the outside world but towards a minority of our own citizens. It would be a sad thing if the sentiment of patriotism were to become by default the prerogative of two sets of extremists, either of which would speedily transform the basic culture and traditions of British society.

In the end we have to choose between competing philosophies of welfare. In this chapter we have emphasized one of these philosophies partly because we believe that it has more- than enough contemporary relevance to merit recovery from its present state of neglect, and partly because the range of choice ought to be as wide and as open as possible. Although the cautiously prudential mood of this philosophy has much in common with the political and economic uncertainties of the present time, it will not have an instant and obvious appeal for idealists. Its objectives, like its expectations, are modest.

In contrast classical economic theory and Marxist theory can be seen as the inspiration of assertive and expansionist political doctrines. They are assertive in their confidence regarding a better future for humanity in terms of both individual and collective welfare. They are expansionist in their respective claims to international relevance. As macrotheories they can be fully tested only in an international context. In this respect both theories generate a mood of intellectual imperialism and optimistic expectation, and both equally imply commitment to a high degree of economic and political risk.

The tradition of mercantile collectivism can best be described as a reactive set of political doctrines. It possesses neither the theoretical coherence nor the consistency of classical political economy or Marxism. Given the various political ends to which mercantilist forms of collectivism may be directed, it is impossible to speak of it as a singular tradition. We can put forward the hypothesis that the doctrines of mercantile collectivism are most likely to gain ascendancy at times when political confidence in the present and the future has been badly shaken. These are doctrines which react to events, in contrast to doctrines which, forearmed with systematic theories, presume both to anticipate and to make the future. Mercantile collectivism is expansionist only in the sense that its doctrines gain in popularity insofar as they follow the adversities of political and economic life from one nation to another. As reactive doctrines the forms of mercantile collectivism might well be adopted by nations whose confidence either in the free market or in socialism has been undermined by sudden disaster or gradual decline. Alternatively a nation in the early stages of industrialisation might simply move from one form of pre-capitalist mercantilism to another, which is more suited to the exigencies of industrial life, as happened in the case of Hohenzollern Germany.

Mercantile collectivism gives rise to national rather than international doctrines. Doctrines of this sort are the intellectual heirs of fear rather than hope, of uncertainty about the present rather than confidence in the future, and of a disposition to avoid rather than to take risks and to accept collective responsibility for risks which cannot be avoided.

The literature of social administration abounds with examples of this prudential philosophy, but it is most concisely and elegantly expressed by Titmuss, when he rejects the 'argument for allowing the social costs or diswelfares of the economic system to lie where they fall', on the grounds that in modern societies it is 'increasingly difficult to identify the causal agent or agencies' of those 'diswelfares'. He concludes that 'Non-discriminating universalist services are in part the consequence of unidentifiable causality. This view of individual responsibility and the right to collective safeguards against risk can be compared with the views of Captain Shotover in *Heartbreak House,* when he caustically explains to his son-in-law, Hector, 'we did not let the fear of death govern our life; and our reward was, we had our life. You are going to let the fear of poverty govern your life: and your reward will be that you will eat, but you will not live.' A more authentic expression of the philosophy of the free market was of course made by Chief Inspector Davy, when he advised the Royal Commission on the Poor Laws in 1906 that 'The unemployed man must stand by his accidents' and 'suffer for the good of the body politic.'

This disposition to sacrifice the welfare of single individuals in the interests of broader principles and long-term objectives has its parallel in Lenin's views on the costs and risks involved in the building of socialism. He writes that during the transition from capitalism to communism political suppression by 'the state' will still be necessary. Nonetheless he goes on to say, 'The suppression of the minority of exploiters by the majority of the wage slaves *of yesterday* is comparatively so easy, simple and natural a task that it will entail far less bloodshed than the suppression of the risings of slaves, serfs or wage laborers, and it will cost mankind far Less.'

Perhaps we should stop judging the mixed economies of the West simply on the basis of their divergence from the ideals embodied in the theories of classical political economy or Marxism. Neither of these systems of thought is a body of revealed truth in a sense which gives it a right to define all other systems as heresies or deviations. In most other countries of the West the history of social and economic development has tended to follow or to revert to policies which have their origins in the mercantilist doctrines of the seventeenth and eighteenth centuries. Social policies now assume an important role in that development, because governments now possess the wealth, the will and the administrative expertise to regulate economic life in ways which were not open to them in the past. Social policy and administration is at best an irrelevance and at worst a threat to the political and economic ideals of both classical economic theory and Marxist theory. Some of its practitioners at least should bear witness to their affinities with the third tradition, which alone allows that they may have something useful to say about social welfare and justice.

It is tempting for those of us who live amongst the recurring crises and contradictions of Western parliamentary democracy to equate the middle way of the mixed economy with a seemingly endless *via dolorosa*. Yet the comparative history of social policies does not appear to offer any less arduous form of pilgrims' progress to a better world.

REFERENCES

Alvin W. Gouldner, *The Coming Crisis of Western Sociology*, Heinemann Educational Books, London, 1971

Elton Mayo, *The Social Problems of an Industrial Civilisation*, with a new Foreword by J. H. Smith, Routledge & Kegan Paul, London, 1975.

Harold L. Wilensky, *The Welfare State and Equality: Structural and Ideological Roots of Public Expenditures*, University of California Press, Berkeley, 1975, p. 37.

Kathleen Bell, Peter Collison, Stephen Turner and Susan Webber, 'National Insurance Local Tribunals: A Research Study', Parts I and II respectively in *Journal of Social Policy*, 3, 4, 1974.

Maurice Kogan, 'Social Policy and Public Organizational Values', *Journal of Social Policy*, 3, 2, 1974.

O.R. McGregor, 'Equality, Sexual Values and Permissive Legislation', *Journal of Social Policy*, 1, 1, 1972.

Pinker, 'Social Policy and Social Justice, *Journal of Social Policy*, 197418.

R. Miliband, *The State in Capitalist Society*, Weidenfeld & Nicolson, London, 1969.

Sandor Halebsky, *Mass Society and Political Conflict*, Cambridge University Press, 1976.

Vic George and Paul Wilding, *Ideology and Social Welfare*, Routledge & Kegan Paul, London, 1976.

Appendix

STUDY QUESTIONS

1. Identify as many social welfare services as you can in the community in which you live or go to school. You can try looking in the telephone book; what are you going to look under? Many communities also have special directories of social-welfare agencies; where do you think you could check to see if your community has one? After you have put together your list, study it and try to figure out how many kinds of needs are dealt with by these agencies: Can you also determine how many of the agencies are supported through public funds, and how many are supported through private funds (fees and contributions)?
2. From the list you put together in the preceding exercise, select an agency that interests you. Visit it and record your impressions. What kind of professionals work there, and who goes there for service? What does the agency look like? Do you consider it attractive? Modern? Welcoming? Does it seem well run? How do you think you would feel if you needed to use its services? Do you think others would be likely to feel as you do?
3. Try writing down your personal value system. How much freedom and responsibility do you think each individual should have? What rights and responsibility do you think each individual should have? What rights and responsibility do you think society has? Try to project the kind of social-welfare system that would result if it were created on the basis of your values.
4. What kinds of needs have you encountered in your own life— health needs, financial needs, counseling needs, and so on? How were your needs met? Were any not

met? How did you find out about resources available to help you meet your needs? Were you satisfied with the help you got?

5. All of us have needs. Sometimes they are painful needs that we consider very serious, as when we get sick or hurt or lose our jobs. Other times they are fairly routine, like trying to get a bus schedule or getting our car repaired properly and economically. How does it feel to be in need? How comfortable are you in asking for help? Does your degree of comfort vary according to the type of need? Why do you think this is so?

Select Bibliography

A.W. Coats, "The Classical Economists, Industrialisation and Poverty," in Institute of Economic Affairs, *The Long Debate on Poverty,* IEA Readings 9, London, 1972.

Adam Smith, *The Wealth of Nations,* Vols. I and II, Everyman Edition, Dent Dutton, 1937.

Alvin W. Gouldner, *The Coming Crisis of Western Sociology,* Heinemann Educational Books, London, 1971

Armand Lauffer, *Working in Social Work,* Newsbury Park: SAGE Publication, 1987.

Beulah R. Compton, *Introduction to Social Welfare and Social Work* (Illinois: The Dorsey Press 1980).

C.A. Bodelsen, *Studies in Mid-Victorian Imperialism,* Glydendalske Boghandel-Nordisk Forlag-KJQ Benhaven, Kristiana, London and Berlin, MDCCCCXXIV.

Carl Johannes Fuchs, *The Trade Policy of Great Britain and Her Colonies Since 1860,* Macmillan, 1905.

Charles Wilson, *England's Apprenticeship, 1603-1763,* Longmans, 1965.

D.R. Sachdeva, *Social Welfare Administration in India.* Allahabad: Kitab Mahal, 1993.

David Ricardo, *The Principles of Political Economy,* Everyman Edition, Dent Dutton, 1929.

David Thomson, "The United Kingdom and Its World-Wide Interests,' in J.P. Bury (ed.) *The New Cambridge Modern History,* Vol. X, *The Zenith of European Power, 1830-1870,* Cambridge University Press, London, 1967.

Elizabeth, Wickendon, *Social Welfare in Changing World,* U.S. Washington DC: Dept. of Health Education, and Welfare, Welfare Administration, US Govt. Printing Office, 1965.

Elton Mayo, *The Social Problems of an Industrial Civilisation,* Routledge & Kegan Paul, London, 1975.

Eric Roll, *A History of Economic Thought,* Faber and Faber, 1973.

Gertrude Williams, *The Coming of the Welfare State,* London: George Allen and Unwin Ltd. 1967.

Hajira Kumar, *Social Work: An Experience and Experiment in India,* New Delhi: Gitanjali Publication, 1994.

Harold L. Wilensky, *The Welfare State and Equality: Structural and Ideological Roots of Public Expenditures,* University of California Press, Berkeley, 1975.

Hinsley, Introduction to *Material Progress and World-World Problems.*

J.W. Burrow, *Evolution and Society: A Study in Victorian Social Theory,* Cambridge University Press,, 1979.

Jacob Viner, 'Power versus Plenty as Objectives of Foreign Policy in the Seventeenth and Eighteenth Centuries,' in D.C. Coleman (ed.), *Revisions in Mercantilism,* Methuen, 1969.

John Hicks, *A Theory of Economic History,* Clarendon Press, Oxford, 1969.

Joseph A. Schumpeter, *History of Economic Analysis,* Allen and Unwin, 1963, pp. 251-2.

Karl Polanyi, *The Great Transformation: The Political and Economic Origins of Our Time,* Beacon Press, Boston, 1968.

Kathleen Bell, Peter Collison, Stephen Turner and Susan Webber, 'National Insurance Local Tribunals: A Research Study', Parts I and II, *Journal of Social Policy,* 3, 4, 1974.

Kilson G. Clark, *The Making of Victorian England* (London: Neshuen 1965).

M.R. James, *Social Problems and Policy during the Puritan Revolution, 1640-1660,* George Routledge and Sons, 1930.

Maurice Kogan, 'Social Policy and Public Organizational Values', *Journal of Social Policy,* 3, 2, 1974.

O.R. McGregor, 'Equality, Sexual Values and Permissive Legislation', *Journal of Social Policy,* 1, 1, 1972.

Oliver MacDonagh, *A Pattern of Government Growth 1800-1860,* MacGibbon and Kee, London, 1961.

Paul Holmos, *Introduction of Welfare: Concept and History,* Great Britain: The Open University Press Wallow Hall Hilton Keynes, 1978.

Paul Holmos, *Introduction to Welfare: Concept and History* p. 127.

Pinker, 'Social Policy and Social Justice', *Journal of Social Policy,* 1974 18.

R. Miliband, *The State in Capitalist Society,* Weidenfeld & Nicolson, London, 1969.

Sandor Halebsky, *Mass Society and Political Conflict,* Cambridge University Press, 1976.

Vic George and Paul Wilding, *Ideology and Social Welfare,* Routledge & Kegan Paul, London, 1976.

Wayne and Vasey, *Government and Social Welfare,* New York: Rinehart and Winston Inc. 1958).

Werner Coze, "The German Empire,' in Hinsley (ed.), *Material Progress and World-Wide Problems.*

Wilensky and Lebeaux, *Industrial Society and Social Welfare,* New York: Free Press, 1965.

William Ashworth, *An Economic History of England 1870-1939,* Methuen, London, 1960.

William Beveridge, *Social Insurance and Allied Services,* London, Macmillan, 1942.

Winifred Bill, *Contemporary Social Welfare,* New York: Mac Millian Publishing Company Inc., 1983.

Index

□□□